ETHICAL ISSUES IN ART THERAPY

ABOUT THE AUTHOR

Bruce L. Moon, Ph.D., ATR-BC is a professor of art therapy with extensive clinical, administrative, and teaching experience. He is a registered and board certified art therapist who holds a doctorate in creative arts with specialization in art therapy. Dr. Moon's clinical practice of art therapy, focused on the treatment of emotionally disturbed children, adolescents, and adults, has spanned over thirty years. He has lectured and led workshops at many college, universities, conferences, and symposia in the United States and Canada.

Dr. Moon is the author of *Existential Art Therapy: The Canvas Mirror, Essentials of Art Therapy Training and Practice, Introduction to Art Therapy: Faith in the Product, Art and Soul: Reflections on an Artistic Psychology, The Dynamics of Art as Therapy with Adolescents, Working with Images: The Art of Art Therapists, and Word Pictures: The Poetry and Art of Art Therapists.* He has also written a number of journal articles. Bruce's many years of experience in clinical and educational settings coupled with a rich tradition of interdisciplinary training in theology, ethics, art therapy, education, and creative arts provide this text with a thought provoking and engaging theoretical and practical approach to ethical issues in art therapy.

Second Edition

ETHICAL ISSUES IN ART THERAPY

By

BRUCE L. MOON, Ph.D., ATR-BC

Mount Mary College
Milwaukee, Wisconsin

CHARLES C THOMAS • PUBLISHER, LTD.
Springfield • Illinois • U.S.A.

Published and Distributed Throughout the World by

CHARLES C THOMAS • PUBLISHER, LTD.
2600 South First Street
Springfield, Illinois 62704

©2006 by CHARLES C THOMAS • PUBLISHER, LTD.

ISBN 0-398-07626-X (hard)
ISBN 0-398-07627-8 (paper)

Library of Congress Catalog Card Number: 2005053802

With THOMAS BOOKS *careful attention is given to all details of man-
ufacturing and design. It is the Publisher's desire to present books that are sat-
isfactory as to their physical qualities and artistic possibilities and appropriate for their particular use.* THOMAS BOOKS *will be true to those laws
of quality that assure a good name and good will.*

Printed in the United States of America
CR-R-3

Library of Congress Cataloging-in-Publication Data

Moon, Bruce L.
 Ethical issues in art therapy / Bruce L. Moon.--2nd ed.
  p. cm.
 Includes bibliographical references and index.
 ISBN 0-398-07626-X -- ISBN 0-398-07627-8 (pbk.)
 1. Art therapy. 2. Art therapy--Moral and ethical aspects. I. Title.

RC489.A7M6575 2006
615.8'5156--dc22
                                                      2005053802

FOREWORD

Art therapy is fortunate to have Bruce Moon adopting ethics as a major focus of his teaching, scholarship, and professional practice. Where so many other professions rely on specialized ethicists from outside the domain of practice, we have one of our most prominent art therapists making a serious and sustained commitment to the examination of comprehensive ethical principles.

In addition to authoring and updating this important book in the current edition, Bruce Moon served the American Art Therapy Association as Chair of the Ad Hoc Ethics Committee and worked with his predecessor, Terry Tibbetts, in coordinating a major new Association document entitled *Ethical Principles for Art Therapists* (2003). I served as AATA President during this period when Bruce, building on the work of Terry and his committee, systematically engaged people from every sector of our community in an open dialogue about what really matters in relation to the ethical practice of art therapy. As a result of these efforts, art therapy now has a set of ethical standards that educate all of us, from the most senior practitioners to aspiring students, in relation to a wide spectrum of situations and challenges that we encounter in our work with others. These principles of ethical practice truly define our profession; they guide and inspire our efforts to serve others.

I believe that the most effective and credible ethical standards are shaped by people with a comprehensive and open-minded understanding of the varied experiences and conflicts that characterize practice. All too often, we are faced with situations today where people with limited understanding of particular professional situations, or others intent on advancing a particular moral code, work to impose their perspectives onto others. The classical study of ethics reinforces the existence of universal principles of moral conduct, categorical standards which transcend relativism and individual freedom. But no matter how committed we may be to transcendent ideals and beliefs, the practice of ethics is always circumstantial and involved with the personal interpretation of situations and problems; a true interplay between guiding tenets and action in the world as demonstrated through sections of this book.

Although all professions involving work with other human beings share common moral underpinnings, fields such as art therapy present unique opportunities and challenges that can only be appreciated and understood by ethical guides who truly know the terrain. Bruce Moon's commitment to the ethical treatment of images in art therapy exemplifies how important it is for art therapy ethics to grow from a deep sympathy with the complete context of practice. The art therapy field has a pervasive concern for the needs of people who suffer and whose life circumstances make it difficult for them to advocate for themselves, yet we do not always show this same compassion and responsiveness to the rights of images within the context of clinical practice. In our zeal to help others and understand their expression, we often overlook the dignity and unique authenticity of images, reducing them to what we think is wrong with the person we are trying to assist.

As an artist, Bruce Moon is sensitively attuned to the autonomous life of images, their existence as living things, like the great symbols that permeate our collective cultures and histories. The images of art affect people in endlessly varied and personal ways and from art therapy practice, we know that this relationship is often characterized by a sanctity that must be protected. The safety and respect that we establish in relation to images in many ways provides an ethical framework for how we treat one another. There is thus a very direct correspondence to the more universal ethical principle of examining the value our own lives in relation to how we treat what might be perceived as "the lowliest" amongst us.

Can we deeply empathize with the expression of an image while suspending judgment and the urge to explain it according to our point of view? Can we view the process of interpretation as opening to what it has to say about itself and perhaps learn something new? How do our relations with images analogize to the way in which we treat others? Like Bruce Moon, I believe that the way in which we approach images has everything to say about how we relate to others.

Bruce Moon's approach to the images of art therapy as equal participants in the overall process, with rights and needs for proper care and attention, exemplifies how the most unique aspects of our particular domain can inform an overall approach to ethical practice that not only guides the art therapy field, but suggests to other disciplines how they might further sensitivity to overlooked aspects of professional practice. *Ethical Issues in Art Therapy* has a great deal to offer people inside and outside art therapy through its creative and sensitive expansion of the moral discourse.

In this book, Bruce Moon offers a truly fascinating and provocative spectrum of situations that closely correspond to the practice of art therapy. The issues and questions that he presents are closely tied to different sections of the AATA's *Ethical Principles for Art Therapists* and they invite serious contemplation by any person involved with art therapy, from the most experienced therapists to students, consumers, and the general public.

Although this book focuses on "ethical issues," I am struck by how it offers an excellent and comprehensive description of art therapy practice. What better lens than ethics can a person have when it comes to looking at everything we do? The application of ethical reasoning to true life situations accounts for the book's effectiveness and authority. Rather than providing a series of simplistic directives, Moon immerses the reader in the context of practice and the living experience of ethical deliberation from the different perspectives that he clearly describes. The genius of this text lies in its ability to involve the reader in the most introspective, intimate, and complex moral reflections, while simultaneously maintaining a true professional calm and even-handedness.

This emphasis on personal encounters with conditions that occur in art therapy practice reinforces my belief that ethics is too important to be approached as yet another separate "subject" to be taught in an increasingly long string of prescribed professional courses in our graduate programs. Ethical considerations lie at the essence of everything we do in all areas of art therapy training and practice, and especially in the realm of supervision, an area that Bruce Moon knows as well as any person who has ever practiced art therapy. The supervision chapter in this book is another of its distinctive features, offering new ideas to the art therapy literature. The descriptions of mentoring are particularly engaging and when Bruce speaks about this area, I find myself imagining his long and inspirational relationship with his mentor, Don Jones, who has given so much to all of us who practice art therapy.

In keeping with the pure strain of art therapy experience, readers of this book are invited to use the arts themselves as ways of knowing, problem-solving, and creative insight. We are encouraged to paint pictures, write poems, and utilize the intelligence of creative imagination to complement verbal analysis and access the wisdom that can be gained through an extended inquiry and process of communication about practice.

Ethical Issues in Art Therapy offers a living engagement with the purpose and values of art therapy with a depth that only Bruce Moon can convey. I have known him well and watched him carefully in the most challenging professional situations for three decades and I can affirm his legacy as the conscience of art therapy as manifested by the books he writes and the way he treats others, both people and images. Bruce Moon leads through example rather than prescription, through the way he shapes the conversation so that each of us can examine our experience with the goal of doing the best we can to help others.

Shaun McNiff, Ph.D., ATR, HLM
University Professor
Lesley University, Cambridge, Massachusetts

FOREWORD TO FIRST EDITION

It is a delight to write the foreword for Bruce Moon's book, *Ethical Issues in Art Therapy*. Many books on the market deal with the history, theories, and practice of art therapy, yet few have challenged or addressed the personal qualities inherent to becoming an effective, sensitive, and ethical art therapist. Throughout this book, Bruce Moon generously shares his expertise and wisdom in this area. Based on many years of practice, he offers the reader a path through the maze of issues, dilemmas, and moral questions we inevitably face each time we engage with a client, whether in a hospital, clinic, private practice, or studio. This is a timely, relevant work that will have an important place in the education and training of art therapists and as a refresher course for those already in the field.

Ethics was once a subject formally relegated to a single classroom session during a semester and relatively recently has been recognized as an intrinsic and integral element in the training of helping professionals (Corey, Corey, & Callanan, 1993). When I was training as an art therapist almost twenty years ago, the discussion of ethical and legal issues usually came up for informal discussion when someone in a class or supervision group had an ethical dilemma or moral question about the treatment of a client. I cannot remember being assigned a single reading on the subject and there were very few articles discussing the specifics of ethics of the practice of art therapy at that time. In any case, those informal discussions were a haphazard way of learning about ethics and how to make ethical decisions; it certainly was not a very effective way of learning how to think critically when an ethical dilemma arose.

After I graduated and entered the work world as an art therapist, I found myself employed in a shelter for women and children from violent homes. I occasionally think back to that time in my career life and realize how unfortunate and ill-equipped to understand and recognize the many ethical issues that confronted me on a daily basis. In the domestic violence shelter, I provided assessment and treatment for hundreds of children each year who were physically or sexually abused, and almost the same number of women who had experienced violence at the hands of a spouse or partner and were often child survivors of abuse and neglect themselves. Needless to say, there were numerous issues to consider: when and how to report child abuse, confidentiality issues, and, most of all, the disposition of children's art expressions, many of which contained vivid elements and literal stories of their experiences of abuse and neglect. Luckily, my colleagues provided excellent supervision, helping me to learn to recognize and process ethical issues as they arose and to understand how to work both ethically and legally within child abuse reporting laws. More importantly, they guided me on how to work with each person's case with an ethical eye and to develop openness to many possibilities and answers to the inevitable ethical dilemmas in this setting. So I learned about how to make ethical decisions "on the job," but it would have been much more helpful to have formal guidance in ethics while in graduate school. Luckily, in recent years, educational training programs for art therapists have come a long way and ethical discussions are interwoven within the entire fabric of graduate study. Most programs now have specific courses on ethics and professional issues specifically relevant to the practice of art therapy. However, up until now, educators have had to compile readings from art therapy journals, monographs, and books, and material from related professions to create a template for classroom learning and discussion.

Bruce Moon's latest work has filled this gap in art therapy education by bringing together this information into one practical, thought-provoking text. Readers may be surprised, however, that the underpinning of this book is not a structured template for solving ethical dilemmas; there are no cut-and-dry answers provided here. Moon instead offers a multi-dimensional way of exploring subject matter through examining models of ethical decision-making, creative and experiential work, and investigation of a variety of ethical issues. He has fashioned a book that is not only rich in didactic information and practical discussions, but is also interactive through exercises and activities that can be used to stimulate classroom learning, develop skills and competencies, and promote discussion among professional peers and colleagues. Moon interweaves the importance of experiential learning with practical material to help students and professionals investigate their own ethical beliefs and philosophies in both dynamic and creative ways.

Regardless of the setting—clinic, hospital, studio, community agency, or private practice—all helping professionals are constantly confronted with ethical decisions. Typical ethical decision-making can include issues such as record-keeping and reporting, confidentiality, duty-to-warn, dual relationships, and research with human subjects. However, as Moon underscores throughout this book, these issues take on unique meanings and contexts with the field of art therapy and we often confront ethical questions and situations which no other helping professionals face. Because we deal with images and the image-making process, art therapists naturally have to consider dimensions such as individuals' responses to the creative process, clinical relationships within a studio environment, display and disposition of art, and personal art making as a component to their continuing education.

With the advent of the digital age, we are now also forced to address new and unforeseen ethical questions in using computer technology, electronic mail, the Internet, and the impact of the growing field of "telehealth" on the practice of art therapy and the transmission of images (Malchiodi, 2000). I believe that we will see many of the same issues that Moon describes in this volume reemerge in our thinking about and understanding of the ethics of images, image-making, and therapeutic contact in this newest frontier for art therapy.

In thinking about this foreword for this important book, I recalled how in 1994 I wrote the following: "Ethics and legal issues are two confusing areas for both trainees and their supervisors. Even the most seasoned professional will be faced on occasion with a situation that stymies one's own professional knowledge base in these areas . . . it is imperative that a supervisor or instructor have an open mind to the variety of possibilities for interpretations of ethical situations, as well as a responsibility to stay current in laws and regulations governing therapeutic practice" (p. 204).

The study of ethical issues remains an area that is often confusing and overwhelming, given the complexities inherent to ethical decision-making and the impact of ever-evolving regulations, codes, and laws that affect clinical practice. This book is a great step forward in guiding art therapists through the scope and depth of the ethical issues that are part of clinical practice, whether one is a student just beginning in the field or an advanced professional. Bruce Moon has provided us with a text that outlines a philosophy of how to be sensitive and thoughtful in ethical decision-making rather than simply giving us a manual of what to do. In this day and age of changing health care, he has offered us a way to continue to explore who we are, how we think about what we do, and how we see our clients. Most of all, as Bruce has stated in his introduction and throughout this book, he has given us a way to sort out "what is right and what is good."

Cathy A. Malchiodi, ATR, LPAT, LPCC, REAT

PREFACE

This second edition of *Ethical Issues In Art Therapy* is written for art therapy students, art therapists, and expressive therapy professionals. It is intended as a textbook for art therapy courses dealing with topics such as professional ethics, and art therapy supervision, or as a supplemental text in art therapy theory and practice courses. This book may also be helpful in stimulating discussion in art therapy supervision groups. The issues I address in this book are specific to art therapists but may also apply to therapists from other disciplines that engage clients in metaverbal treatment modalities utilizing visual arts, music, drama, movement, or poetry.

The ethical dilemmas discussed are typical of those encountered by creative arts therapists throughout their careers. Readers will be engaged in a process of learning to wrestle with professional moral issues that profoundly affect the daily practice of art therapy. This process of wrestling begins, and probably will end, with questions. How does an art therapist go about considering moral questions in relation to profession work? What does it mean to be an ethical professional art therapist? How do moral, professional, ethical, and legal issues overlap? How do creative arts therapists maintain professional boundaries? Are there particular ethical problems indigenous to art therapy and other metaverbal modalities? What are the characteristics of high quality art therapy supervision? When is it appropriate to reproduce, exhibit, or publish a client's artwork? Who owns the artworks created in the art therapy session? Do the artworks themselves have rights? What impact do issues of diversity have on the practice of creative arts therapy? As artist-therapists, what responsibilities do we have to our society?

There are four primary goals of this book. First, I want to raise questions and provide information related to the ethical dilemmas art therapists face. Second, I want to present models of how to think through and resolve the difficult ethical problems art therapists face during their professional lives. Third, I intend this book to be used creatively by course instructors and art therapy supervisors as a basis for engagement with students or supervisees around ethical problems. Finally, I hope to provide artistic activities that serve as creative means to grapple with ethical dilemmas.

In some instances, I will offer examples of how a particular ethical question might be argued. However, I do not intend my views to be edicts for the behavior of others. I present my arguments only in an effort to provide examples of ethical reasoning. I hope this will encourage the reader to give form to her or his own positions. I am passionate about the art therapy profession and sometimes in writing my fervor can come off as pretentious. Please know that I have wrestled with this demon in the course of creating this book. I hope I have held him in check.

In this second edition, I often refer to the *Ethical Principles for Art Therapists* (AATA, 2003). I also refer to *Code of Professional Practice* of the Art Therapy Credentials Board (ATCB, 2005). These documents are reprinted with the permission of the American Art Therapy Association and the Art Therapy Credentials Board in the appendices to this text. The AATA (2003) document may also be obtained by contacting the National Office of the American Art Therapy Association.

American Art Therapy Association
1202 Allanson Road
Mundelein, Illinois 60060.
Phone (847) 949-6064
Fax: (847) 566-4580
        or
1 (888) 290-0878 (toll free)
E-mail: info@arttherapy.org
Web Site: http://www.arttherapy.org

While ethics documents are extremely helpful, they are ultimately inadequate to cover every circumstance. In the end, students and professionals have to wrestle with questions of moral professional behavior as they arise. Each art therapist must decide how the statements in the ethics document applies to the particular problem he or she is facing. This can be difficult, sometimes confusing, and sometimes-frightening work. I hope this book will be of help along this challenging path.

Throughout the text, I give examples of ethical dilemmas with the hope that these examples will provide opportunities for discussion and debate in the classroom or supervisory group, or provide thought for individual reflection. I envision course instructors and supervision group leaders drawing upon the depths of their own professional experiences to model how the struggle with professional morality continues throughout one's career. Within the chapters, there are dilemma-laden vignettes intended to stimulate this reflection and discussion. Most chapters include a series of questions pertaining to practical applications aimed at helping readers review the material and begin to formulate or clarify their own positions on key issues. Also included are lists of suggested artistic tasks intended to help the reader engage with the topics in a meta-cognitive, kinetic, visual, and sensory way. The illustrations in this text are examples of artistic responses to the suggested tasks created by former graduate students at Marywood University. People learn in many different styles (Gardner, 1983, 1994) and making art about these topics is one way of deepening knowledge (Allen, 1995). Experience in teaching from this text in its developmental stages leads me to recommend educators and supervision group leaders use the suggested art tasks as a way to begin class/group sessions. Approaching the difficult and anxiety provoking topics inherent in the study of professional ethics in art therapy through creative engagement serves to enrich intellectual discussions of the subjects. In order for the artistic tasks to be meaningful, they must be engaged in with seriousness and respect. Each task holds metaphoric implications for art therapists. However, not every task will be useful to all art therapists at any given time. Art therapy instructors and supervisors are encouraged to use and adapt the artistic tasks as they see fit and to create their own directives.

When students and supervisees are sharing or displaying artworks created in response to the suggested tasks, instructors and supervisors are advised to avoid making interpretations or suggestions about the individual's problems or potentials as an art therapist. As Malchiodi and Riley (1996) note, "Being able to witness the work with a sense of objectivity may be the most helpful, thus respecting the very tender place that many novice supervisees [and seasoned practitioners] are in with regard to their work with clients and their own developing identities" (p. 101). It is more beneficial, in my experience, to just encourage the artist to tell the story of the artwork.

If you are coming to this book in search of black and white answers to the innumerable ethical questions arts therapists face, you will be disappointed. The real world of professional ethics in art therapy is, more times than not, a spectrum of shades of gray. When I wrote the first edition of this book, there was no text that specifically addressed the particular ethical quandaries unique to the creative arts therapies. I did, however, refer often to Corey, Corey, and Callanan's (1998) *Issues and Ethics in the Helping Professions.* I encourage you to explore that text as well. It is a thorough look at the ethical dilemmas faced by counselors, social workers, and psychotherapists. Many of the basic principles they address can be applied to the creative arts therapies. Art therapists, however, encounter ethical issues that are unique to the discipline of art therapy. It is my hope that this text will, in some measure, fill the void.

This second edition is necessary at this time due to significant changes that were made to the AATA Ethics Document in 2003. I served as the Chair of the AATA Ethics Committee from 2001-2003 and during my tenure shepherded the revision of the document. The Ethics Document titled *Ethical Standards for Art Therapists* that was in effect from 1997-2003 was fraught with paragraphs that began, "Art Therapists Shall. . . . In fact, of the eighty paragraphs in the document, sixty-eight of them began in that manner. Of the twelve paragraphs that did not, eight included *shall*, or *must* later in the paragraph. I make no claim to be a skilled mathematician, but by my count, that's seventy-six paragraphs of imperatives; "art therapists thou shalt." So you see, the 1997 ethics document was a little like the Ten Commandments, except in that case, it was the Seventy-six Commandments.

As the members of the ethics committee began the process of revision, we were faced with a dilemma: Did we want to attempt to revise the document in such a way as to create a more comprehensive rulebook, one that would cover every conceivable ethical quandary? Or, did we want to fashion a set of statements that ethical art therapists aspire to? If we could write an exhaustive rulebook, then art therapists would not have to think about their behavior. They would just have to find the right rule to apply to a given situation. Of course, the committee realized that writing a comprehensive rulebook would be difficult, since there would need to be hundreds, maybe thousands of rules.

Another option for the ethics committee was to create an ethics document that positively described the intentions of ethical art therapists. In this mode, the statements in the ethics document would describe the aspirations of art therapists and the document would establish an affirmative attitude regarding professional conduct rather than an imperative or punitive tone.

Regardless of which of these approaches to revision we settled on, legalistic rules or aspirations, it was agreed that the document ought to be consistent in tone. One of the perceived problems with the 1997 *Ethical Standards for Art Therapists* document was that it was inconsistent. Most of its sections were clearly phrased as commandments, while others seemed almost to be suggestions.

Suffice it to say that when you take a good look at the 2003 *Ethical Principles for Art Therapists* you will find no paragraphs that begin with, "Art Therapists Shall . . . " and no "Art Therapists Must." Rather than simply construct an updated version of the seventy-six Commandments, the ethics committee chose to provide statements of aspiration. In the preamble I wrote:

> This Ethics Document is intended to provide principles to cover many situations encountered by art therapists. Its goals are to safeguard the welfare of individuals and groups with whom art therapists work and to promote the education of members, students and the public regarding ethical principles of the art therapy discipline. The development of a vigorous set of ethical principles

for art therapists' work related behavior requires a personal commitment and constant effort to act ethically; to encourage ethical behavior by students, supervisees, employees, and colleagues; and to consult with others concerning ethical problems. (p. 2)

In 2003, the membership of AATA voted to adopt the new Ethics Document thereby condemning us all to think for ourselves. To paraphrase Joseph Campbell (1968), the tyranny of "Thou Shalt," the social fiction of moral law, has been supplanted by self-discovery. Alas, we are condemned to reason . . . to struggle . . . to search for our own moral truths.

All of us, whether we are seasoned professionals, novices, or students of the field, find ourselves confronted with ethical problems in our professional lives. It is critical that we wrestle with these dilemmas before they occur, while they are happening, and after the fact in order to shape and understand our professional demeanor. Setting a tone for this self-reflection is what this text is all about.

The ethical dilemmas explored in this book are from the viewpoint of a visual arts therapist. It is my hope that poetry therapists, music therapists, dance/movement therapists, recreation therapists, occupational therapists, and drama therapists will be able to recast the problems and ways of thinking about them into their own disciplinary context. Early in my career, I was fortunate to have the opportunity to work closely with and learn from professionals from a variety of action-oriented therapy disciplines. In my clinical work, I have often utilized poetry, music, movement, and drama in conjunction with painting, drawing, and sculpting. Still, I am clearly most knowledgeable about and most at home with the visual arts and this is evident in my writing.

In N. Richard Nash's (1957) play, *The Rainmaker*, the central ethical theme emerges in a scene where the morally outraged brother of a lonely, unmarried girl threatens to kill the Rainmaker. The brother is outraged because the Rainmaker made love to his unmarried sister. The Rainmaker's intent was to restore the spinster's sense of femininity and desirability. The girl's father snatches the gun away from his son and proclaims, "Noah, you're so full of what's right you can't see what's good." Many of the ethical problems discussed in this book are about being right in the middle of such quandaries. Effort must be put into sorting out what is right and what is good. I wish us all well.

Bruce L. Moon, Ph.D., ATR
Mount Mary College
Milwaukee, Wisconsin

AUTHOR'S NOTE

The clinical vignettes in this book are, in spirit, true. In all instances, however, circumstances have been fictionalized in order to ensure the confidentiality of the persons with whom I have worked. The case illustrations are amalgamations of many specific situations. This has been done to offer realistic accounts of ethical issues faced by art therapists while protecting the privacy of individuals.

ACKNOWLEDGMENTS

I am indebted to many colleagues, teachers and mentors who shaped my approach to ethical reasoning. Among these are faculty members of The Methodist Theological School in Ohio, especially my professor of ethics, the late Dr. Ron Williams. Don Jones, A.T.R., H.L.M. helped to lay the groundwork for my understanding of moral and ethical professional behavior. I am thankful for the encouragement I received from Jerry Corey, co-author of *Issues and Ethics in the Helping Professions* (Corey, Corey, and Callanan, 1998). I wish to thank my friend, Mr. Paul Smith, Esq. for his legal research and advice. I appreciate the support of the leadership of the American Art Therapy Association. Their kindness in allowing me to refer often to the *Ethical Principles for Art Therapists* was most helpful. I am indebted to the student members of an art therapy ethics course that I taught at Marywood University, who experimented with this book while it was still in manuscript form. The critical responses and constructive suggestions given by Wendi Boettcher, Amy McBride, Marc Essinger, Holly Highfill, Annette Nemeth, Heather Picarsic, Heidi Ridgeway, Pauline Sawyer, Keli Schroeffel, Suzanne Wernette, and Rebecca Yoder were most helpful. They have all completed their art therapy educations and are now practicing in the field. I also appreciate that several of these former students, along with Lolita Nogan, John Roth, and John Meza, contributed artworks used as illustrations for the book. I wish to express my gratitude to Randy Vick, Lynn Kapitan, and Bob Schoenholtz, art therapists who read the early drafts of the first edition of this manuscript. Their feedback was very helpful and I wouldn't have wanted to write the book without their support. Finally, special thanks go to Catherine Moon for her patient, constructive critiques of the text. Cathy's painstaking assistance was instrumental to the original writing and subsequent revision of this book.

CONTENTS

ILLUSTRATIONS

ETHICAL ISSUES IN ART THERAPY

Chapter I

THREE ROADS:
MODES OF ETHICAL THINKING

Several years ago an art therapist working in a small private psychiatric hospital had the following experience. A client with whom he had worked for a few weeks came to the art studio to tell him good-bye. The client hugged the art therapist and told him that her time in the studio had been very meaningful to her. She was about to leave the building when the art therapist remembered that she had an unfinished painting in the drying rack. "Don't forget to take your painting with you," he said.

She turned to face him and replied, "Nah, I think I'll just leave that thing here."

He was surprised. The client had worked very hard on the piece and it was both expressive and technically well done. "Why would you leave it here?" he asked.

"Oh, I don't know. I don't have any paints at home, and I don't really have any place to work on it either. It'd probably just end up getting messed up. Besides, it would remind me of being in the hospital. I'd rather forget all about it. Anyway, it's just a painting." Saying no more, she turned and left the studio.

Later in the week, as the art therapist was straightening up the studio, he came across the client's painting. He pulled it from the drying rack and immediately felt a vague sense of sadness. "It's just a painting," she'd said. As he looked at the canvas, he kept thinking about the artist. Somehow, it bothered him that she had left her work behind so that she would not remember. One of his colleagues entered the room and asked, "Isn't that Audrey's piece? I thought she was discharged a couple days ago."

"She was," the art therapist said. "She stopped in to say good-bye the day she left."

"Why didn't she take her work?"

"She said it would remind her of being in the hospital."

"Oh well," his colleague sighed. "We can recycle the materials. I will gesso over it tomorrow."

"No, I think we better hold onto it for awhile," he said.

* * * * *

This brief vignette highlights some of the significant ethical dilemmas with which art therapists must wrestle. Questions could be raised related to the client initiating physical contact and the therapist's response to the hug. Questions could also be brought forward regarding the manner in which this termination event was handled. Therapists of all disciplines, of course, must grapple with these kinds of questions. But there are additional questions related specifically to art therapy itself from which other therapy disciplines are exempt. Who owns the left-behind artwork? Some would suggest that the art piece is a record of the client's treatment (Braverman, J., 1995). If this is so, should artworks be kept in a manner similar to other elements of the client's chart? Is it ethical to recycle art materials from artworks that are abandoned by the client artist? Can left-behind works be exhibited?

At a meeting of the National Coalition of Art Therapy Educators, a group of art therapists discussed this topic and I can tell you there was a wide range of opinions. One educator insisted that client artwork is the property of the client-artist. Another art therapist argued that in her clinical setting, she considers client work to be her property. "After all," she said, "I am the one who buys all the materials." One colleague argued that all artwork everywhere belongs to the creative spirit of the world. Yet another suggested that the artwork made in clinical contexts is analogous to a urine sample given in a doctor's office, ergo, it is the property of the clinic. "No one asks for urine samples to be returned," he said. Perhaps questions like these cannot be fully answered in the Ethics Document published by the American Art Therapy Association, for they have to do with how we art therapists regard the artworks of our clients. Questions such as these are difficult to codify. So, what is an ethical art therapist to do?

At many points along the way in this text, questions will be raised about how ethical decisions and opinions, especially those most relevant to the creative arts therapy professions, can be justified. In all likelihood, this will lead us to wonder what we mean when we say that some thing or behavior is right, good, or just. Questions such as these have a long and honored history. Frankenna (1983) states, "Ethics is a branch of philosophy; it is moral philosophy or philosophical thinking about morality, moral problems, and moral judgments" (p. 4). Whenever a person reflects upon questions like these, the individual has entered the realm of philosophy. The study of professional ethics is an inquiry into the morality of professional behavior and reasoning.

At the beginning of any journey, it is helpful to take a look at a map (if one exists) to plan the routes to be taken in order to get from here to there successfully. The quest of this text is to explore the landscape of ethical decision-making in relation to the professional behavior of creative arts therapists. Fletcher (1966) outlined three primary modes of ethical thinking. I refer to these as the three major roads to follow, or approaches to take, in making ethical decisions. They are

1. Deontological–legalistic; the ethical doctrine which holds that the worth of an action is determined by its conformity to some binding rule rather than by its consequences;
2. Antinomian–the opposite of legalism; an unprincipled, anarchic, lawless approach;
3. Teleological–utilitarian/situational; the evaluation of conduct in relation to the end or ends that it serves.

All three of these roads have been influential in the development of the map of Western morality. However, the legalism of deontological thinking has been by far the most commonly traveled road. It can be argued that the very existence of professional ethics codes is an expression of Western deontological reasoning. In his *Situation Ethics*, Fletcher (1966) comments, "Just as legalism triumphed among the Jews after the exile, so, in spite of Jesus' and Paul's revolt against it, it has managed to dominate Christianity constantly from very early days" (p. 17). Legalism has also dominated the development of ethical codes in the helping professions for quite some time. However, questions arise in relation to deontological reasoning as to whether a rule can truly apply to every particular case. These questions are compounded when several conflicting rules exist simultaneously.

Let us take a closer look at these three roads to decision making, focusing first on the deontological approach.

The First Road to Ethical Decision Making

Deontological Legalism

The ethical reasoning road that leads to the right is deontological legalism. Art therapists who travel this road to decision making prefer to enter into ethical problem situations with a set of preestablished rules and regulations in the form of a code of ethics. An example of this kind of document is found in the 1997 version of the AATA *Ethical Standards for Art Therapists* (see

Appendix A) and in section IV. Standards of Conduct of the *Code of Professional Practice* of the Art Therapy Credentials Board (ATCB, 2005). These rules and regulations were regarded as a secure system of signposts that pointed the way to ethical behavior. When approaching problems in this manner the letter of the law reigns supreme. In a legalistic approach, the basic principles of ethical behavior are codified in rules that are viewed as directives that should and must be followed. Professional codes of ethics that are written from a deontological perspective are essentially regarded as contracts with society based on a public policy that are intended to protect the rights of citizens against unethical conduct by practitioners. In deontological codes, solutions to specific dilemmas are preset and the primary thinking one had to do was to sort out which rule applies in a given situation.

Most of the major Western religious traditions—Judaism, Catholicism, and Protestantism—have been legalistic. Fletcher (1966) notes that these religions have had tremendous influence upon the way Western societies think about ethical and moral issues. Further, they have helped to shape the development of the American judicial system. Thus, we see why deontological thinking has often been applied to professional, ethical, decision-making processes. Many published codes of ethics are a testament to the indigenous nature of this way of thinking in our culture. This situation is a natural outgrowth of the Western legal system that is based in Judeo-Christian traditions.

Deontological legalism possesses subtle and enticing qualities for art therapists. It enables a person to take a course of action based solely on what is written in a code of ethics. It removes some of the discomfort over an ethical dilemma by allowing an art therapist to look in the Ethics Document to find what should be done in a particular situation. The legalistic art therapist does not have to struggle with, or think through, the repercussions of various behaviors and decide what should be done. She must only find the applicable rule and follow it. In spirit, deontological reasoning is consistent with modernism in the art world in that the modernists sought *the truth* in artistic endeavors (Gablik, 1984). Art therapists who reason from a deontological perspective express a certain amount of faith in the truth of the ethical standards of the profession. In a sense, deontological legalism absolves the individual of personal responsibility for it requires only adherence to rules.

While it is entirely proper for art therapists to consult the AATA *Ethical Principles for Art Therapists,* and the ATCB *Code of Professional Practice,* these are only the first steps in the process of making ethical decisions. Art therapists are obliged to give careful consideration to the ethical dilemmas they face and may need to balance reliance upon the Ethics Document with their own reasoning processes and clinical context.

The Second Road to Ethical Decision Making

Antinomianism

The ethical reasoning road that leads in the opposite direction of legalism is antinomianism. The term "antinomian" means literally "against law." When an art therapist travels this road and is confronted with an ethical decision-making situation, the antinomian approach has no use for codified principles or rules whatsoever. Antinomianists view each situation as unique and insist that every individual must rely upon the moment itself to provide its own ethical resolution. While deontologists are absorbed with the stipulations of the laws and their guidelines for behavior, antinomianists are so averse to law that their ethical decisions often seem erratic, random, and entirely unpredictable. Fletcher (1966) notes, "They follow no forecastable course from one situation to another. They are, exactly anarchic—i.e. without rule" (p. 23). Jean Paul Sartre (1944) elaborates on antinomianism in *Existentialism*, ". . . we have no excuses behind us and no justification before us" (p.27). This approach to moral decision making is anchored in the belief that every situation has only its own unique singularity.

Art therapists utilizing antinomian reasoning would embrace the view that there are no general principles by which to practice; indeed, there is no underlying fabric of existence, and, therefore, no foundation upon which to build comprehensive code of ethics and so they have little use for either the *Ethical Principles for Art Therapists* (AATA, 2003) or the *Code of Professional Practice* (ATCB). When confronted with an ethical dilemma, art therapists reasoning from this perspective would argue that they would just know what was right when they needed to know. In this, there is a radical reliance upon art therapists' intuition, or what Fletcher (1966) calls a superconscience. Thus, for antinomian art therapists, making ethical decisions is a matter of spontaneity; it is factually unprincipled, purely *ad hoc*, instinctual, and impulsive.

The Third Road to Ethical Decision Making

Teleological Contextualism

The ethical reasoning road that runs between deontological legalism and antinomian anarchy is teleological contextualism. When an art therapist who reasons from the teleological perspective encounters situations in which she must make a decision regarding an ethical problem, she carries with her the moral maxims of her professional community. She treats these maxims with

honor and regards them as guidelines meant to enlighten her about the problem at hand. At the same time, she is willing to set aside particular points of
an ethics document, or to adjust them, in a given situation if a greater good
would be served by doing so. Another way to think of this is that a teleological contextualist keeps the code of ethics in her back pocket, but tries to
think through ethical dilemmas with an eye toward bringing about the most
good.

This road to ethical decision-making has many names: occasionalism, cir-
cumstantialism, utilitarianism, and situationism. As each of these descriptors
suggests, the central notion of this ethical approach is that context modifies
content. Boszormenyi-Nagy and Krasner (1986) discuss context as, "the
dynamic and ethical interconnectedness—past, present and future-that exists
among people whose very being has significance for each other" (p. 8). In
some ways, teleological contextualism is the ethical reasoning approach that
parallels the *form follows function* maxim from the discipline of architecture.
Another way to think of this core principle is that in ethical problems, the
particular circumstances of a given situation are equal in value with the generally established rules of behavior that apply to the situation.

Near the end of a class session in an ethics course, one of my graduate students recently said to me, "I come in here expecting you to answer my questions and all you ever do is stir up more questions." As an educator, I can
think of no better compliment, but this is also the nature of the teleological
approach to ethical thinking. The attempt to discover that which will provide
for the greatest good in any given situation requires a deep commitment to
asking questions. The teleological contextual approach shakes the security of
deontological legalism and challenges the random chaos of antinomianism
by simultaneously honoring ethical principles and being sensitive to the
nuances of particular situations. In a sense, the teleological approach to
ethics is similar to the position of the jazz musician who knows all the rules
governing musical theory, notation, rhythm, and progression but, in the particular moment, bends or abandons the rules altogether for the sake of the
art.

Teleological contextual reasoning suggests that art therapists must ultimately resolve ethical dilemmas for themselves. No code can do this for
them because no rule will cover every situation. And there are sure to be circumstances in which conflicting rules apply. Yet, every situation ought to be
considered in light of the appropriate professional ethics document, applicable laws, and with regard to what will bring the greatest good. This is exactly what this text is about.

A Situation

Imagine that you are the lone art therapist employed by a Children's Service Agency in a large metropolitan area. Although you have only been working at the facility for a few months, your work has been exceptional, and many people in the agency have commented on how well your methods work with the children. Recently, your supervisor asked you to prepare a handbook of creative exercises and techniques that could be distributed to all of the social workers and case managers in the system. Your supervisor said, "After all, there is only one of you and we have so many kids in the system. The handbook would make art therapy available to every child who needs it." He also told you that the Children's Services Director of Public Relations is very interested in using such a handbook as a tool to improve the public image of the agency.

Discussion

Now, let us identify some of the potential ethical questions that are inherent in the situation. Among these are the following:

- The arts are a natural way to relate to people, especially to children and adolescents. Do art therapists have an ethical responsibility to provide (or not provide) education and specific art therapy techniques to other professional disciplines so as to improve the quality of therapeutic services that clients may receive?
- Do art therapists have an ethical responsibility to their employer to complete tasks assigned to them whether or not they approve of the task?
- Is there any danger to clients, or the art therapy profession, in providing creative arts therapy techniques to colleagues from other therapy disciplines who have no special training in the use of the arts as therapy?
- Do art therapists have an ethical responsibility to their professional community to guard the disciplinary boundaries of art therapy?
- Would it be better to create the handbook of exercises or to suggest that the institution should hire additional art therapists?

Let us now apply the three approaches to ethical decision-making to the questions raised by the situation described above.

Deontological Legalistic Approach to the Situation

Do art therapists have an ethical responsibility to their employer to complete tasks assigned to them?

From a deontological perspective, we enter into this situation with our set of pre-established rules and regulations in the form of the professional Code of Ethics, *Ethical Principles for Art Therapists* (AATA, 2003) and applicable state laws. Using deontological reasoning, the answer to the question may be "yes." This is based on two legal assumptions: (1) The art therapist has signed a contract agreeing to work for the County Children's Service. (2) The task assigned by the supervisor is not immoral or against the law. The employment contract represents an implicit agreement on the part of the art therapist that she will complete reasonable tasks that are assigned to her by the employer. From this perspective, it could be legally argued that it would be unethical for the art therapist to refuse the assignment.

Since we are utilizing deontological reasoning to attempt to answer the question above, we must refer to the basic principles of ethical behavior as expressed in the AATA Ethics Document (2003), and we must regard these as directives that should and must be followed. In item 1.0 of the RESPONSIBILITY TO CLIENTS section of The Ethics Document (2003) of the American Art Therapy Association, we find the following applicable standard: "Art therapists endeavor to advance the welfare of all clients, respect the rights of those persons seeking their assistance, and make reasonable efforts to ensure that their services are used appropriately" (p. 3).

From a deontological perspective, this standard seems to suggest that the art therapist should create the handbook since the standard says, "Art therapists endeavor to advance the welfare of all patients, . . ." Clearly, as the supervisor said, the creation of the handbook could greatly expand the reach of the art therapist and make it possible for many more clients (if not all) to benefit from art therapy services. However, it could also be argued that the use of art therapy techniques by clinicians and caregivers who are not credentialed art therapists would not advance the welfare of clients because such persons are inadequately trained and might inadvertently harm clients (Webster, 1994). Thus, it is possible to reason from a deontological position that the art therapist should refuse to author such a handbook because to do so would go against item 1.0 of the RESPONSIBILITY TO CLIENTS section of the *Ethical Principles for Art Therapists.*

Is there any danger in providing art therapy techniques to colleagues from other therapy disciplines who have no special training in the use of the arts as therapy?

This question presents a difficult dilemma for it is surely true that no art therapist wants to support dabbling in their professional discipline by people who have no training in or sensitivity to the creative arts therapies. Just as it would be unethical for an art therapist to dabble with prescribing medications, so too, it would be unethical for a psychiatrist to superficially engage in art therapy techniques in psychotherapy sessions. At the same time, it is true that art therapists do not own art-making processes, just as music therapists do not own making music, and poetry therapists do not own the process of writing poetry. However, it is a fact that each of these creative arts therapy disciplines has developed a considerable body of knowledge and those practitioners who use the creative arts, as a component of therapy, should be well versed in such knowledge. It is doubtful that mastery of the knowledge base could be gained through use of a handbook as is described in the vignette above. This may suggest that the art therapist should refuse to provide the handbook in question.

From the other side of this dilemma, point 1.0 of the RESPONSIBILITY TO CLIENTS section states, "Art therapists endeavor to advance the welfare of all clients, respect the rights of those persons seeking their assistance, and make reasonable efforts to ensure that their services are used appropriately" (p. 2). As you see, from the standpoint of deontological reasoning, there is a potential conflict in this point. On one hand, this principle seems to indicate that the art therapist might create the handbook because of the potential good that it could do for the agency's clients. On the other hand, it can be argued that the art therapist would have no ability to ensure that art therapy services would be delivered appropriately by those who utilize the handbook and thus should not author the handbook.

Later in the Ethics Document, point 5.0 in the PROFESSIONAL COMPETENCE AND INTEGRITY section states, "Art therapists maintain high standards of professional competence and integrity" (p. 7). It is certainly arguable that the art therapist in the situation above would have no real control over the competence of those who might use or misuse the handbook. Therefore, from a deontological perspectiv, this statement suggests that the art therapist should not author such a handbook. Furthering this argument is section 9, titled RESPONSIBILITY TO THE PROFESSION point 9.1, in which we find the following: "Art therapists adhere to the ethical principles of the profession when acting as members or employees of organizations" (p. 8). A deontological interpretation of this statement suggests that art therapists should not author such a handbook since they could not ensure that the caregivers who would use it would be aware of, or able to adhere to, the ethical principles of the art therapy profession. Conversely, it can be argued that therapists (caregivers) who are not members of the American Art Therapy Association are not bound by that organization's Ethics Document. Webster (1994) certainly raises many concerns regarding persons who are inadequately prepared providing art therapy services. As is evident in this discussion, deontological legalism could be used to argue both positions, for and against the creation of a handbook of art therapy techniques.

Let us move on to the next ethical question raised by the situation above. Do art therapists have a responsibility to provide education and art therapy techniques to professionals from other disciplines so as to improve the quality of therapeutic services their clients may receive?

Deontological reasoning could lead one to the conclusion that the art therapist *should* create the handbook because of the statement that art therapists endeavor to advance the welfare of all clients. However, the art therapist would have no real control over the competence of those who might use the handbook, and no ability to ensure adherence to the standards of the profession. The previously cited principles, 5.0 and 9.1, seem to suggest that the art therapist *should not* create the handbook.

As art therapists walk the deontological road, they refer to the basic principles of ethical behavior that are found in the *Ethical Principles for Art Therapists*, and regard these as directives that should and must be followed. Art therapists may experience a sense of security in approaching ethical dilemmas from a deontological perspective because this method of reasoning is less reliant on personal choice and responsibility and more dependent on the ability to find the applicable rule. Deontological art therapists can look to the *Ethical Principles for Art Therapists* for what should be done to resolve an issue. In a superficial way, deontological legalism liberates art therapists from the perils and uncertainties of having to take personal responsibility for their behavior. However, as evidenced in this discussion, selecting the appropriate rule and deciding on the proper interpretation of the rule are seldom simple tasks. As this discussion illustrates, deontological reasoning can simultaneously point a person in two different directions.

An Antinomian Approach to the Situation

Since the situation described above, involving whether or not to author a handbook of creative exercises, is unique and unprecedented according to the antinomian view, then an antinomian art therapist would rely upon the context itself to provide its own ethical resolution. In contrast to the deontological perspective, which seeks the appropriate rule or principle for behavior, the resolution of the dilemma from an antinomian perspective is based entirely on the specific situation. Antinomian art therapists follow no predictable course from one situation to another because they believe that every situation has its own unique qualities.

The following are the specific questions that have been previously identified. Do creative arts therapists have an ethical responsibility to their employer to complete tasks assigned to them? Is there any danger in providing creative arts therapy techniques to colleagues from other therapy disciplines who have no special training in the use of the arts as therapy? Do art therapists have a responsibility to provide art therapy techniques to other professional disciplines?

An antinomian art therapist could argue either for or against the notion that there is an ethical obligation to one's employer. Likewise, an antinomian art therapist could reason that there is great danger, or no danger at all, in providing creative arts therapy techniques to colleagues from other therapy disciplines who have no special training in the use of the arts as therapy.

Antinomian reasoning could lead art therapists to argue that they have a responsibility to provide art therapy education about art therapy techniques to professionals from other therapeutic disciplines for the good of those practitioners' clients. In order to reach such a conclusion, the antinomian art therapist would examine her own thoughts and feelings about the clinical context. She would make an assessment of the merits of the request, consider the immediate potential benefits to the agencies' clients, and make a decision based on her intuition.

An antinomian art therapist might also conclude that she has no obligation to provide art therapy techniques to non-art therapy colleagues. In order to reach this conclusion she would assess the specific pros and cons of the request. She would take into account her feelings and thoughts regarding the agency. She would think about the potential danger to the agencies' clients and make her decision based upon what seems most right to her at the time.

For an art therapist operating from an antinomian position, the resolution of all ethical dilemmas would ultimately depend upon her intuitive sense of the particular situation at a specific time. She would regard the principles outlined in the Ethics Document as irrelevant to the particular dilemma. Likewise, she would make no effort to consider the long-term impact of her decisions because she would assume that future circumstances would have no relationship to the current context.

A Teleological Approach to the Situation

For the art therapist who reasons from a teleological perspective, the question of whether or not to author a handbook of creative exercises presents several ethical questions that have both compelling and competing interests. She will make her decisions regarding the ethical problems with full knowledge of the ethical principles of her professional community. She will endeavor to honor the ethical aspirations of her profession, while simultaneously being willing to set aside or compromise these principles if the situation warrants it. From this perspective, the professional code of ethics is regarded as a set of desired objectives rather than imperative mandates.

Let us again turn to the ethical questions raised by the situation described above. Do art therapists have an ethical responsibility to their employer to complete tasks assigned to them?

From a teleological perspective, the art therapist would take into account the aforementioned sections of the *Ethical Principles for Art Therapists*, and any other sections that she deems appropriate. She would also be willing to interpret or compromise these principles if the particulars of the specific situation warranted such give and take. Thus, the teleological art therapist might answer the above question this way. "Yes, I have a responsibility to my employer to complete the tasks assigned to me so long as they are in the best interest of the clients that I am treating. If I am asked to do something which, in my judgment, would ultimately bring harm to my clients, then the situation demands that I refuse the assigned task for the good of my clients." Commenting on this type of dilemma, theologian Deitrich Bonhoeffer (1961) states, "The question of good is posed and is decided in the midst of each definite, yet unconcluded, unique, transient situation in our lives . . . in other words in the midst of our historical existence" (pp.420-421).

A teleological art therapist might also answer the question above in this way, "Yes, I have a responsibility to my employer to complete the tasks assigned to me so long as they are in the best interest of my professional community. If I am asked to do something which, in my judgment, would somehow damage my discipline, then the situation demands that I refuse the assigned task for the good of my profession." In any case, it is clear that a teleological art therapist would have to weigh the merits of the employer's request. She would have to take into account the welfare of her clients, and consider what would be best for her professional community. In addition she would think about the consequences of her actions in the context of multiple relationships.

Is there any danger in providing creative arts therapy techniques to colleagues from other therapy disciplines that have no special training in the use of the arts as therapy?

In principle, a given situation can lead to several possible actions that are themselves diametrically opposed to one another. The choice between the possible alternative actions always involves a historical dimension that cannot be decided upon in advance on the basis of professional rules. An art therapist reasoning from a teleological perspective would have to weigh the pros and cons of this matter. She would be interested not only in the applicable sections of the *Ethical Principles for Art Therapists* and the *Code of Professional Practice* but also equally interested in knowing as much as she could about the qualifications of the caregivers to whom the handbook would be distributed. She would review art therapy literature pertaining to the question (Mills et al., 1992, 1993; Webster, 1994). She would wonder if she would be given opportunities to educate her colleagues through in-service presentations and/or workshops. She would be curious as to how the handbook would be perceived by the caseworkers. She would explore her ethical concerns and questions with regard to the larger context of the Children's Service Agency. She would examine her relationships with colleagues and clients. She would explore the potential impact that the handbook might have on the many children that the agency serves. She would carefully consider her responsibilities to her employer. After thinking through all of these aspects of her context, and many other questions, she would then make a decision based on her principles, the principles of the profession, and the human aspects of the situation.

Given that the arts are a natural way to relate to children, adolescents, and many other client populations, do art therapists have a responsibility to provide techniques to other professional disciplines so as to improve the quality of therapeutic services that clients may receive? A teleological art therapist, assuming her norm is to provide for the good of all clients, would perhaps favor providing a handbook of art therapy techniques to other professionals for the sake of the good that could come to so many children. She would reason that since art therapists do not own art processes, and since she believes art making is therapeutic for children, the greatest good will be served by creating the handbook. This does not mean she is blind to the potential hazards of misuse, but she reasons that these are outweighed by the potential good.

Conversely, a teleological art therapist might also reason that providing art therapy techniques to inadequately trained clinicians is not providing for the good and therefore she might refuse to do so.

To the ethical questions raised by the situation regarding the creation of a handbook of creative exercises described above, deontological art therapists would say, "Search the *Ethical Principles for Art Therapists*, find the appropriate and relevant sections, and follow the rules." (As noted above, however, deontological reasoning may lead one to conflicting interpretations of the applicable principles.) It is nearly impossible to predict how antinomian art therapists might answer the questions. They would scrutinize the situation, explore their thoughts and feelings about the clinical context, assess the merits of the request, consider the immediate potential benefit to clients, and make a decision based on intuition. The teleologists, if their norm were to do what is good for their clients, would examine the *Ethical Principles for Art Therapists*. They would then articulate their view of the dilemma, explore the situation, and examine their thoughts. They would consider all the persons and relationships to whom they are responsible, examine multiple aspects of their particular context, and make a decision.

Three Roads to Ethical Decision Making

Deontological Legalism	Teleological Contextualism	Antinomianism
What do the rules say? What section of the Code of Ethics applies?	What principles apply? What will bring the greatest good for the greatest number? To whom am I responsible? What will be the consequences of my actions?	Every situation is unique. I will know what is right to do when the time comes.

Discussion Questions

1. Are there other ethical dilemmas raised in the situation described above? What are they?
2. Do you think that art therapists have a responsibility to share art therapy techniques with members of other helping professions? Why, why not?
3. If your employer asked you to do something that you thought might be unethical, how would you respond?
4. On what ethical system of thought–deontological, antinomianism, or teleological–would you base your response?
5. What ethical problems can you identify related to the use of art therapy techniques by non-art therapists?
6. Does the AATA Ethics Document have any relevant section regarding the dilemmas you have identified in response to question 5?
7. If art therapists refuse to share art therapy techniques with other disciplines, does this limit the number of clients who have access to the therapeutic benefits of the arts? Can this be harmful to the clients?
8. An art therapist creates a handbook of art therapy techniques. A clinician reads the handbook and decides to use one of the art therapy tasks with a client. If the client is harmed due to the clinician's misapplication of the art therapy technique, is the art therapist (author of the handbook) responsible?
9. If an art therapist refused to complete a task assigned by an employer that the art therapist deemed unethical and was fired as a result, has the arts therapist inadvertently brought harm to all of the clients who will not receive art therapy services of any kind as a result?
10. If an art therapist at an agency created a handbook of art therapy exercises and a non-art therapy staff member of the agency misused the handbook, is the art therapist responsible?

Suggested Artistic Tasks

The following artistic tasks are intended to help you engage with the material covered in this chapter in meta-cognitive, visual, kinetic, and sensory ways. Ideally, the tasks will be completed in the context of an art therapy class or in an art therapy supervision group. The class environment or supervisory group will offer a venue for lively discussions of the artistic processes, products, and ethical issues. These discussions will deepen and enhance the learning experience. Individual readers may also want to complete some of the exercises in order to integrate the learning experience more fully. It is clear that people learn and retain information in many different ways. Art making in response to the issues raised in this text is an important way to grapple with the subjects.

1. Three Roads—Using the visual art materials of your choice, create symbolic images of the three forms (deontological, antinomian, teleological) of ethical reasoning. Share the images with peers.

2. Resolution Collage—Reflecting on the situation described above, related to whether or not to author a handbook of creative exercises, create a collage symbolizing the characters in the situation (art therapist, supervisor, director of public relations, and clients) doing something together.

3. Conflict Image—Reflecting on the situation described above, create an image symbolizing the character in the situation with which you identify the least (art therapist, supervisor, director of public relations, clients). Include in the image how you think this person feels about the situation.

4. Role-play—In a supervision group or classroom situation, assign the roles (art therapist, supervisor, director of public relations, client) to members of the group. Set the scene as an interaction among these characters that takes place a few days after the supervisor has assigned the task of creating the handbook. Prior to enacting the role-play, ask each participant to do a drawing of the character symbolizing how that character feels about the situation.

5. Poetry—In a supervision group or classroom situation, ask members to think about one of the characters from the situation. Ask each person to write a poem from the perspective of his or her character. Share the poems and discuss the ideas and feelings they generate.

6. Art therapists must determine what is ethical and what is unethical for them. Think about how you make ethical decisions. Are you a deontologist, antinomianist, or teleologist? Imagine yourself walking down a path and finding an obstacle blocking your way. How do you get around it? Create an art piece depicting the situation. Share your art-

work with peers and discuss how this relates to your tendencies in handling ethical obstacles.

7. Read through the *Ethical Principles for Art Therapists* of the American Art Therapy Association. Design a cover-image for the document that portrays your emotional reaction to it.

8. Three Faces of Ethical Reasoning—Using the art materials of your choice, create personifications (faces) of the three forms (deontological, antinomian, teleological) of ethical reasoning. Share the images with peers.

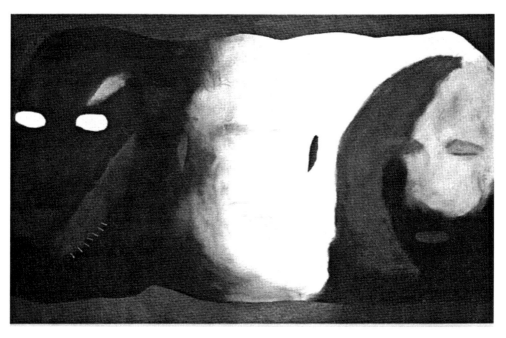

Figure 1. Three Faces of Ethical Reasoning—12" X 38" Oil Stik
Rebecca Yoder

Chapter II

RESPONSIBILITY TO CLIENTS

In order for art therapists to practice in an ethical manner, we must be aware of our responsibilities toward our clients. In the simplest of terms, this means art therapists endeavor to do no harm, promote the welfare of all clients, respect the rights of clients, and make every effort to see to it that our professional services are used properly. The *Ethical Principles for Art Therapists* state that, "Art therapists do not discriminate against or refuse professional service to anyone on the basis of age, gender identity, race, ethnicity, culture, religion, sexual orientation, disability, socioeconomic status, or any basis proscribed by law" (Section 1.1, p. 3).

At the beginning of art therapy relationships, preferably in the initial session, it is important that we discuss and clarify our clients' rights. Some clients are not aware that they have rights. By virtue of the fact that they are seeking art therapy, they may feel quite defenseless and frantic in the early stages of therapy, and, hence, they may be willing to blindly accept whatever terms the art therapist sets for the relationship. However, it is important to inform and educate clients about their rights. Wheeler and Bertram (1994) provide a twenty-item checklist for informed consent for treatment. Not all of the items listed by Wheeler and Bertram (1994) are directly relevant to art therapy; however, their list can be helpful in sensitizing art therapists to issues of informed consent. In my clinical practice, I have identified twelve areas about which I believe art therapy clients and clients have the right to be informed.

INFORMED CONSENT

At the beginning of the client-therapist relationship, art therapists ought to explain the rights that clients have to the client. They should also discuss the roles of both client and therapist and outline the expectations and limitations of the art therapy process. When the client is a minor, consent to treatment should be obtained from the parent or legal guardian of the minor client, except where otherwise provided by state law. However, the art therapist is still obliged to explain the client's rights to the minor in an age appropriate manner. Art therapists should be careful to preserve the confidentiality of the minor client and refrain from any disclosure of information to the parent or guardian that might adversely affect the treatment of the client.

It is important to note that some art therapists employ *Informed Consent Forms*, while others prefer to talk with their clients about their rights. In either case, it is important to document in your files or in the facility's record that the topics (see below) associated with informed consent have been addressed in some way with each client.

Art therapy clients have the right to be informed about:

- the art therapy process—including the theoretical approach of the art therapist
- the art therapist's expectations of the client
- limitations of the art therapy process
- what the client may expect from the art therapist (safety, predictability, and relationship—discussed at length later in this chapter)
- any risks that may be associated with the art therapy process
- confidentiality and the release of information
- limits of confidentiality—situations where confidentiality cannot be maintained
- financial arrangements—including fees and charges, and insurance reimbursement issues
- content of and access to their files
- credentials of the art therapist—including academic degrees, registration, national board certification, and state licenses the art therapist holds
- termination of therapy
- supervisory relationships the art therapist may utilize

The manner in which clients' rights are presented and discussed may vary depending upon the particular setting in which an art therapist is practicing. For example, an art therapist working with adult clients in private practice might routinely schedule time to discuss these areas during the first therapy session. In contrast, an art therapist working in an inpatient psychiatric facility may be less formal in the presentation of clients' rights because most hospitals have specific policies regarding staff members who are assigned to discuss clients' rights. In those settings, a social worker or a member of the admissions staff is often designated to inform a client about his or her rights and to obtain the client's signature on an informed consent form. Art therapists who work with minors must inform a client's parents or legal guardians of the client's rights in one way, but then should discuss these with the child in ways that are developmentally appropriate to the client. Art therapists working in public schools, community arts centers, or other nonmedical contexts may have to present clients' rights in ways that are appropriate for the setting. The personal style of an art therapist, the expectations of the clinical or professional context, and the characteristics of the client population invariably shape the information art therapists provide to clients.

It is important that art therapists develop procedures regarding informed consent in order to (a) educate the client/artist, (b) foster the therapeutic alliance, and (c) provide some measure of protection for the art therapist. As noted earlier, many clients may not know that they have rights. Educating clients about their rights provides them with information that is by its very nature empowering. Therapeutic work is ultimately aimed toward helping clients live more satisfying lives. Often, clients come to art therapy feeling disenfranchised and powerless. The process of informing clients of their rights can be of significant therapeutic benefit in and of itself. By informing clients of their rights early in the therapeutic process, art therapists set a tone for their work that is respectful and appreciative of clients' autonomy. This, in a sense, honors clients and can be an early building block of therapeutic alliances. Informing clients of their rights can also help protect art therapists. Regrettably, we live in a litigious culture in which members of helping professions have become targets of malpractice lawsuits. Malpractice claims are not only brought against irresponsible practitioners. Bennett and his collaborators (1990) emphasize the importance of anticipating potential problems and guarding against behaviors that might be considered unethical. One way to do so is to document that the client has been fully informed of his or her rights and has consented to art therapy treatment. Regardless of the professional context and the form an art therapists' communication takes, it is essential to cover the twelve areas noted above.

The following are examples of *Informed Consent* forms. The first form provides a checklist of items for discussion related to informed consent. The second is a more generic form. Each of these forms has their good points and limitations. They are included here only as examples for the sake of thought and discussion (see pages 22 and 23). Now let us turn to the twelve areas of informed consent listed and explore each in greater detail.

The Art Therapy Process

When an art therapist is beginning a new therapeutic relationship with a client who knows nothing about art therapy, it can be a daunting task to

ART THERAPY
INFORMED CONSENT FORM
(Sample 1)

I _____(client name)_____ do hereby acknowledge that __(art therapist's name)__ on___(date)___ informed me of the following:

Check all appropriate areas:

The nature of the art therapy process	_____
The art therapist's expectations of me	_____
Limitations of the art therapy process	_____
What I may expect from the art therapist (safety, predictability, and relationship)	_____
Risks that may be associated with the art therapy process	_____
Confidentiality and the release of information	_____
Limits of confidentiality	_____
Financial arrangements—fees and charges	_____
Content of and access to files	_____
Art therapist's credentials	_____
Right to terminate the therapeutic relationship	_____
Supervisory relationships the art therapist may utilize	_____

I hereby agree to participate in art therapy treatment and acknowledge that I have been informed regarding my rights in relation to the areas noted above. I hereby grant permission for the release of information relating to my psychological and physical history and status to ____(art therapist's name)____. This information is to include test results, diagnostic evaluations, and any information specifically relating to perceptual and visual problems.

I grant permission to _____(art therapist's name)_____ to contact my physician or therapist for consultation purposes before and during my participation in art therapy. I have been assured that strict adherence to professionalism and confidentiality will be observed.

Signed_____

Legal Guardian_____

Date_____

(Insert Art Therapist's Name)

Registered Art Therapist
(Sample 2)

EFFECTIVE DATE _____ CLIENT'S NAME _____

CONSENT TO ART THERAPY TREATMENT

I hereby give my consent to receive art therapy treatment by (insert art therapist's name), art therapist. This consent is valid until rescinded in writing by me.

I understand that records of therapy sessions will be kept, that these records are confidential, and that (insert name) needs my written consent to release information of either a verbal or written nature. Release without consent is permitted for court appointed attorneys for commitment proceedings, suspected child abuse, and state correction institutions and county prisons if I am referred to these facilities for treatment. In addition, release without consent is permitted if there is reason to believe that withholding such information poses a serious threat of harm to you or to others. This consent is valid until rescinded in writing by me.

I also understand that (insert art therapist's name) may discuss aspects of our therapy sessions with her supervisor and that said supervisor is held accountable to the same ethic of client confidentiality as outlined above.

_____
Signature of witness

_____
Signature of client

-or-

_____
Signature of parent or guardian if
client is a minor or dependent

FINANCIAL AGREEMENT

I agree to pay _____ per session for art therapy services provided by (insert art therapist's name). I understand that fees are due at the time of service. I also understand that I am expected to pay for scheduled sessions unless I cancel an appointment at least 24 hours in advance or unless illness or an emergency situation precludes me from keeping a scheduled appointment.

_____
Signature of client / parent / guardian

explain precisely how art therapy works. Discussing how to present the art therapy process in relation to informed consent is made even more complicated by the reality that there are many approaches to art therapy practice. I cannot prescribe what should be said. I will, however, offer a sample of the sort of things I have said to clients, not only in relation to this topic, but also in relation to the other ten areas associated with informed consent. These sample conversations are meant only to give a feel for how informed consent issues can be addressed at the outset of the relationship. You will have to develop your own style in regards to this issue. The following is a re-creation of a typical dialogue in an art therapy session from my private practice.

Bruce: Do you know anything about art therapy?

Client: No. It sounds a little strange to me.

Bruce: Well, you know, I believe that people express themselves all different kinds of ways. Some people are really good at talking about the things that are going on inside themselves. Some people don't like to do that at all. Some write poetry and some dance.

Client: I'm not much of a talker.

Bruce: That's fine. You see, I think that some of the most important things that happen in our lives can't be put into words. So, our time together is going to be about expressing things with images.

Client: I can't draw.

Bruce: It doesn't matter. I will help you with that. What does matter is that you are willing to trust me a little, and to try things.

Client: Like what?

Bruce: Like painting, or working with clay . . . and maybe even drawing.

Client: So I'll make something and you'll watch me and then tell me what it means?

Bruce: No, that's not it at all. I won't tell you what your images mean. I will be really interested in them though, and I will work with you to help you figure out what they might mean.

Client: Sounds easy . . . maybe even fun.

Bruce: I need to be honest with you. It won't always be easy, and sometimes it will be anything but fun. Being in therapy can be hard work, and you should know that it might bring up feelings that will be hard to deal with.

Client: So, what is the point of all this?

Bruce: The main thing is to help you express yourself. You see, I know that people don't usually have problems because they express feelings. But they often do have problems when they keep everything bottled up inside or when they express their feelings in ways that are hurtful to themselves or others. From what you've told me, it seems like you are a person who has a hard time letting things out and so a lot of stuff builds up. That leads to problems.

* * * * *

Again, it is important that art therapists develop their own style of informing clients about the art therapy process. Although this can be a formidable task, it is very important that clients have at least a basic understanding of how art therapy works and what they can expect to occur during a session.

Figure 2. It's About Connections–24" x 28" Craypas
Annette Nemeth

What Will Be Expected of the Client?

Art therapy clients should have a basic understanding of what will be expected of them when they participate in the art therapy process. This may include fairly straightforward things such as the expectations that the client will:

- Be on time to therapy art sessions,
- Wear clothing that is appropriate for artistic work,
- Perhaps be asked to provide some art materials,
- Notify the art therapist if he or she is going to have to miss a scheduled appointment,
- Be responsible regarding the financial obligations associated with art therapy.

It may also include information about the nature of art therapy itself, and the depth of relationship that can occur as the process unfolds. Listen:

Client: So what is this art therapy all about?

Art Therapist: Art therapy uses art processes and products as a way to deal with problems people face and to help them develop their potential to live healthy, satisfying lives. For some people, it offers a way to express feelings and communicate that is an alternative to talking.

Client: But I can't draw.

Art Therapist: Believe me, I have heard "I can't draw" so many times during my career. It is my sense that this comes from fear. You will really have to trust me about this. I wear many hats in my role as an art therapist. I'm a teacher, helper, coach, and guide. I promise that I will help you give form to the images that come from inside you. I will not interpret your art for you, but I will help you discover your own meanings through the art making.

Limitations of the Art Therapy Process

As art therapists, we cannot promise our clients that participation in art therapy will provide the life changes they may desire. There are no guarantees that clients who engage in art therapy will be happier, less anxious, have a better marriage, improve their relationship with their parents, etc. The ultimate success or failure of art therapy is always dependent upon the response of the client. New clients must understand that there is no magic involved in art therapy.

Art therapy is one of many methods of treatment. Many clients benefit from traditional verbal psychotherapy and counseling, while others make better use of treatment approaches that do not rely solely on talking, like those of music therapy, recreation therapy, poetry therapy, drama therapy, and art therapy. For some people, involving in art therapy can be a profound experience that is life changing. For other people, art therapy may be ineffective. Clients have a right to know the limits of art therapy.

What the Client Can Expect from the Art Therapist

Art therapy clients should have a basic awareness of what to expect from the art therapist. This may include expectations that the art therapist will:

- be on time to therapy art sessions,
- maintain a safe and predictable environment in which to work,
- provide basic art materials for the client's use,
- notify the client if he or she needs to reschedule an appointment, and
- maintain the confidentiality of the client except in extreme circumstances (as described earlier in this chapter).

In addition to the above, art therapists may wish to convey to clients their deep belief in the power and goodness of art making. Sometimes it is helpful to express faith in a client's ability to use his or her creativity in a positive way. Some art therapists offer their expertise as artists and as therapists. It is also important to tell clients that every effort will be made to provide a consistent, safe, and supportive environment so that they will have an opportunity to make good use of the time they have in the art therapy studio.

In my clinical practice, I often tell new clients that I will depend on and trust their expertise in matters pertaining to who they are and what they need. I share with them that I view art therapy as a journey where we each offer what we know in order to make the therapy productive.

Risks that May Be Associated with the Art Therapy Process

Art therapy clients should be forewarned about any potential risks that may be involved in the process of art therapy. Generally, these potential risks fall into one of two categories, emotional risks and physical risks.

Clients should be made aware that there are some emotional risks connected to the process of stimulating and working with images. Art therapy often stirs up feelings and thoughts that may have been neglected within the client for a period of time. This can sometimes lead to people feel worse before they feel better. Clients have a right to know that art therapy can be emotionally difficult, painful, and frightening at times. Since the outcomes of therapy are largely dependent on the response and investment of clients, it is advisable to emphasize the role of the client's responsibility. It can also be helpful for art therapists to forecast the potential emotional risks and difficulties associated with art therapy so that the client will not be unduly daunted when these occur.

Art therapy clients ought to be forewarned of any potential physical risks related to specific art media, tools, and/or processes. Art therapists need to be aware of any hazards in their work environment and should alert clients of these risks. Some people may be allergic to specific materials, and others may be especially sensitive to particular odors. Clients should be educated about what clothing is appropriate to wear to art therapy sessions and they ought to be informed there might be occasions when clothing could be damaged by certain media. Art therapists who work with a particular media that may have elements of risk associated with them should explain the risks to the client before engaging in these approaches or with such media.

Confidentiality and the Release of Information

Art therapy clients should be informed about issues of confidentiality, privileged communication, and privacy. These concepts, confidentiality and its limitations, privileged communications, and privacy, will be discussed at greater length later in this chapter. As art therapists discuss confidentiality with their clients, they may want to stipulate how issues of confidentiality will be dealt with in the art therapist–client relationship. It is advisable to discuss circumstances in which the release of information may be necessary and to familiarize clients with the forms associated with this. It is essential that clients understand their rights to confidentiality and the limitations of these rights.

The Limits of Confidentiality

Although confidentiality is considered a cornerstone of therapeutic relationships, there are situations under which it cannot be maintained. Unfortunately, the specific circumstances that call for a breach of confidence are not clearly defined, and art therapists often must use their own judgement. "When assuring their clients that what they reveal will ordinarily be kept confidential, therapists should point out that they have obligations to others besides their clients (Corey, Corey, & Callanan, 1998, p. 161). The *Ethical Principless for Art Therapists* (AATA, 2003) asserts that art therapists may reveal certain information when there is reason to believe that the client or others are in imminent danger. Ahia and Martin (1993) assert that it is permissible to breach confidentiality under the following circumstances:

- when a client poses a danger to self or others,
- when a client discloses an intention to commit a crime,
- when the counselor [art therapist] suspects abuse or neglect of a child, an elderly person, a resident of an institution, or a disabled adult, and
- when a court orders a counselor [art therapist] to make records available.

It is vital for art therapists to explain to clients the circumstances and situations where confidentiality cannot be maintained. Usually this means situations in which the art therapist is concerned about the potential harm that may come to a client as a result of one of the four areas Ahia and Martin (1993) identify.

Access to Files

Art therapists have different views about sharing their clinical files with a client. Some art therapists would prefer that their clinical notes be private, while others regard a client's file as open for review by the client at any time. Art therapists' views regarding client access to files are also influenced by their approach to documentation itself. Some art therapists keep copious progress notes, while others maintain only brief treatment summaries. And although it is not advisable, some art therapists choose not to keep therapy records at all.

Regardless of an art therapist's philosophy of documentation, clients have a legal right to examine and procure copies of progress notes, assessment write-ups, and other records kept by art therapists in the interest of their clients' welfare. For this reason, it is important that art therapists keep accurate accounts of the therapy process. It is desirable to write clinical progress notes and art therapy assessment narratives in language that is descriptive but not judgmental. The subject of documentation will be discussed in greater length in Chapter IV of this text.

The decade of the 1990s has seen a tremendous surge in the consumer-rights movement and from that perspective, it is imperative that consumer/clients have ready access to their files. It is prudent for art therapists to write their observations with the assumption that the client may read the file at some point in the future.

Financial Arrangements

Art therapists are required to inform clients about the particular fees and charges for which the client will be responsible. Both the art therapist and the client should mutually agree upon a definite schedule of payment.

When the client's therapy is going to be covered by insurance or third-party reimbursement, the art therapist should delineate her/his responsibilities associated with billing the payer. The art therapist should also explore issues of copayment and arrive at an understanding with the client of how payment will be arranged. Finally, the client should be informed of the art therapist's policies regarding any charges that will be associated with missed or cancelled sessions.

Credentials of the Art Therapist

The master's degree is the degree of entry into the profession of art therapy. Art therapy clients have a right to know about the educational and clinical background of the art therapist. An open discussion of the art therapist's qualifications, and a readiness to answer any questions clients may have about the art therapy process can help lower impractical and unrealistic expectations clients may have about art therapy. In the present-day consumer-oriented atmosphere, clients have the right to know what they are buying when they enter into art therapy. A clear description of the art therapist's credentials and areas of expertise may also serve to reduce the chance of malpractice accusations.

Art therapists ought to make available to clients evidence of their academic degrees, ATR (registration with the American Art Therapy Association), BC (Art Therapy Credentials Board certification), and any state licenses or other relevant specialty credentials the art therapist holds. Art therapists may also inform clients of particular clinical experiences they have had. They may make clients aware of areas of special expertise, and continuing education experiences they engage in. Some art therapists do this by displaying diplomas, licenses, and certificates in their offices, while others give new clients a "fact sheet" that details their credentials.

Termination of Therapy

The termination of therapy is a crucial phenomenon in therapeutic relationships (Moon, 1998). Ideally, it is an important phase in the therapeutic process for the client and art therapist alike because it represents transition and change in both parties' lives.

Clients have a right to anticipate that their therapy will conclude when they have met their goals or gained maximum benefit. In addition, clients should be informed that they have the right to terminate, or end their involvement in therapy, at any time.

Many art therapists work in institutions or agencies that have clear parameters on the number of therapeutic sessions a client can expect. In such circumstances, the client should be made aware from the outset what the limits would be. Art therapists ought to periodically remind clients about the number of allowed sessions. In other, less restricted settings, some art therapists routinely talk with their clients about the approximate length of the therapeutic journey while others assert that the process of art therapy is too complicated, and each individual client too unique, to accurately predict the length of treatment.

Termination of therapy is considered to be a critical phase of most therapeutic relationships and it should be carefully explained to clients. Kramer (1990) asserts that termination represents both a point of ending (of the therapeutic relationship) and a new beginning for the client. When I worked at an inpatient treatment facility for adolescents, the psychiatric team regarded the termination phase of therapy as a crucial phase which tested the success of the entire therapeutic process.

The termination phase of the art therapy process is a period of internalization and consolidation of the gains made during the treatment process. It is a readying to leave the artistic journey, to take a different path that inevitably separates the client from the art therapist. This is to say the client learns that he can take the relationship with him in the form of memories and experiences he has shared with the art therapist. Ideally, the client has a sense that he or she can recreate the experience of the relationship with the art therapist by creating new quality relationships in other, nontreatment settings.

During the termination, the arts provide the client with a means to express the sense of loss that is experienced as the relationship with the art therapist comes to an end. These feelings are often too difficult for the client to put into words, but are usually profoundly expressed in images. In addition, the artifacts of the journey: the sculptures, paintings, and drawings serve as tangible objects that clients take with them from the experience. These are the observable external representations of invisible internal experiences.

Moustakas (1995) describes the final phase of therapy in this way: "The aim is to bring together the *what* of the person's experience and the *how* in such a way that its nature and meanings are embraced" (p. 211). Termination work demands that the client and the art therapist put much effort into understanding the essence of what their time together has meant. This is not a simple process of summing-up, but rather a creative and intuitive construction of the core meanings of their journey together.

It is helpful for art therapists to maintain an attitude of support, neutrality and acceptance of the inevitable end of the relationship during the termination phase. Many people who are in therapy have not had successful termination experiences in the past. It is more likely that clients will have experienced pathological versions of the process of saying good-bye. The person may be inexperienced in dealing with healthy endings. The last major piece of work between the art therapist and the client is the crafting of a healthy process of letting go.

Regardless of the specific clinical context and the art therapist's theoretical orientation with regards to the appropriate length of therapy, clients have a right to know that therapy will end. This is true whether the termination is the outcome of having met their goals, or the consequence of artificial limits set by an insurance company, or the result of their exercising their right to terminate the relationship.

Supervisory Relationships

Art therapy students are required to regularly discuss their work in practicum and internship settings with their supervisors and peers, and it is good practice for seasoned art therapists to also receive consultation and supervision of their work. Art therapy students and practitioners should inform their clients about this supervision. Additionally, art therapists are obliged to obtain written consent from clients in order to share the clients' artwork in supervisory sessions. Clients have the right to know, when applicable, that the art therapist is receiving supervision and that their relationships with the art therapist may be subject to discussion in supervision sessions. It is important to assure clients that art therapy supervisors are bound by standards to protect the confidentiality of art therapists' clients. Art therapists receiving supervision ought to provide the name and credentials of the supervisor to the client. Corey, Corey, and Callanan (1998) comment, "Even though it is ethical for counselors to discuss their cases with other counselors, it's wise to routinely let clients know about this policy" (p. 121). It has been my experience that it is helpful for art therapy students and practitioners to explain to clients that supervision discussions usually focus on what the art therapist under supervision is doing and feeling rather than on the client.

ETHICAL AND LEGAL ISSUES FOR ART THERAPISTS RELATED TO CONFIDENTIALITY

There is perhaps no more important and justified expectation of clients than the expectation that the content of art therapy sessions be held in confidence. Confidentiality is essentially a commitment on the part of the art therapist to maintain the privacy of the client. Confidentiality is a cornerstone of the therapeutic alliance between the client and the art therapist. Nelson (1998) refers to confidentiality as a "sacred trust" (p. 357). This implies there is a special, private nature to therapy relationships that deserves reverential care. There are, however, limits to confidentiality. Art therapists cannot guarantee clients rights to confidentiality in all situations. There are circumstances in which it is necessary to reveal the content of the client's artwork and/or discussions from therapy sessions.

Section 2 of the American Art Therapy Association *Ethical Principles for Art Therapists* addresses confidentiality in the following manner:

CONFIDENTIALITY

Art therapists protect confidential information obtained from clients in through artwork and/or in conversation while clients are in treatment and post-treatment.

2.1 Art therapists treat clients in an environment that protects privacy and confidentiality.

2.2 Art therapists inform clients of the limitations of confidentiality.

2.3 Art therapists do not disclose confidential information for the purposes of consultation and supervision without client's explicit written consent unless there is reason to believe that the client or others are in immediate, severe danger to health or life. Any such disclosure must be consistent with laws that pertain to welfare of the client, family, and the general public.

2.4 In the event that an art therapist believes it is in the interest of the client to disclose confidential information, he/she seeks and obtains written consent from the client or client's guardian(s) when possible before making any disclosures, unless there is reason to believe that the client or others are in immediate, severe danger to health or life.

2.5 Art therapists disclose confidential information when mandated by law in a civil, criminal, or disciplinary action arising from such art therapy services. In these cases client confidences may be disclosed only as reasonably necessary in the course of that action.

2.6 Art therapists maintain client treatment records for a reasonable amount of time consistent with state regulations and sound clinical practice, but not less than seven years from completion of treatment or termination of the therapeutic relationship. Records are stored or disposed of in ways that maintain confidentiality.

According to Corey, Corey, and Callanan (1998), mental health practitioners [art therapists] have both ethical and legal responsibilities to protect innocent people who might be injured by a dangerous client. They also have responsibility to assess and intervene effectively with clients who are likely to attempt to take their own lives (pp. 164-165).

Court Cases Related to Confidentiality.

Significant court cases support the idea therapists have an obligation to protect clients and others that might be affected or harmed by a client's

Figure 3. Duty to Warn–Mixed Media
Heather Picarsic

actions. I include the following discussion of the court's ruling in the *Emerich* case and a brief summary of the landmark *Tarasoff* decision and the *Jaffee v. Redmond* case in an effort to demonstrate the complexity of the ethical and legal issues involved in confidentiality and duty to warn.

The Emerich Case

A recent court case in Pennsylvania concerning this area is *Emerich, v. Philadelphia Center for Human Development, Inc. et al.*, 720 A.2d 1032 (Pa. 1998).

In the *Emerich* case, the Pennsylvania Supreme Court was faced with three issues of law: (1) whether a mental health professional has a duty to warn a third party of a client's threat to harm the third party; (2) if there is a duty to warn, what is the scope the duty; and (3) whether under the facts of this case the trial court was correct in its judgment.

The *Emerich* case involved the tragic murder of Ms. Theresa Hausler, by her former boyfriend, Mr. Gad Joseph. At the time of the murder, Mr. Joseph was being treated for mental illness and drug problems. Ronald Emerich, the

Administrator of the Estate of Ms. Hausler, brought wrongful death and survivor claims against the Philadelphia Center for Human Development, Inc., Albert Einstein Medical Center, and Harvey Friedrich, ACSW, et al. These are the facts of the case.

Ms. Hausler and Mr. Joseph were boyfriend and girlfriend living together in Philadelphia. For a substantial period of time, they both received mental health treatment from a counselor at the Philadelphia Center for Human Development. Mr. Joseph was diagnosed as suffering from posttraumatic stress disorder, drug and alcohol problems, and explosive schizoaffective personality disorder. He also had a history of physically and verbally abusing Ms. Hausler and his former wife. In addition, Mr. Joseph's history revealed other violent tendencies. He had often threatened to murder Ms. Hausler and he suffered from homicidal ideation.

Several weeks prior to June 27th, 1991, Ms. Hausler ended her relationship with Mr. Joseph, moved out of their residence, and relocated to Reading, Pennsylvania. Angered by her decision to terminate their relationship, Mr. Joseph indicated he wanted to harm her during several therapy sessions at the Center. On June 27, at approximately 9:25 a.m. Mr. Joseph telephoned his counselor, and advised him he was going to kill Ms. Hausler. The counselor immediately scheduled a therapy session with Mr. Joseph at 11:00 that morning. During this session, Mr. Joseph indicated to the counselor his irritation with Ms. Hausler was worsening. He told the counselor she was planning to return to the apartment later that day to get her clothing, and this was causing him great stress. He indicated he was going to kill her if he found her removing clothing from the residence. The counselor recommended Mr. Joseph should voluntarily seek admission to an inpatient treatment facility, but he refused. As the session neared its end Mr. Joseph stated he was now in control and would not hurt Ms. Hausler. At 12:00 p.m., the therapy session ended and Mr. Joseph was permitted to leave the Center based solely upon his assurances he would not harm Ms. Hausler.

At 12:15 p.m., the counselor received a call from Ms. Hausler informing him she was in Philadelphia en route to retrieve her clothing from the apartment. She asked as to Mr. Joseph's whereabouts. The counselor instructed her not to go to the apartment and to return to Reading. Ms. Hausler ignored the counselor's instructions and went to the residence where she was fatally shot by Joseph at about 12:30 p.m.

Ms. Hausler's family sued, claiming all of the defendants negligently failed to properly warn Ms. Hausler and others, including her family, friends, and the police, that Mr. Joseph presented a clear and present danger of harm to her. The trial court found in favor of the defendants, arguing a duty of a mental health professional to warn a third party had not yet been adopted in Pennsylvania, and even if such a legal duty existed, the counselor's personal warning was sufficient.

The Superior Court affirmed the decision of the Trial Court and reiterated mental health care providers currently have no duty to warn a third party of a client's violent propensities. Even if such a duty existed, the Superior Court said, Ms. Hausler was killed when she ignored the health professional's warning not to go to the apartment of her boyfriend.

The Pennsylvania Supreme Court held a mental health care professional, under certain limited circumstances, owes a duty to a third party to warn of threats of harm against that third party. However, the court said the circumstances in which a duty to warn a third party arises are extremely limited. The court found in Pennsylvania, when a client has communicated to a professional a specific and immediate threat of serious bodily injury against a readily identifiable third party then the professional bears a duty to warning the third party against such danger. The court qualified this finding by holding the duty to warn is in effect only when the professional determines, or should determine under the standards of the mental health profession, his client presents a serious danger of violence to the third party.

The court noted the case of *Tarasoff v. Regents of University of California*, 17 Cal. 3d 425, 131 Cal.Rptr. 14, 551 P.2d 334 (1976) and a vast majority of other states that have concluded the relationship between a mental health care professional and his client constitutes a special relationship which imposes upon the professional an affirmative duty to protect the third party against harm.

In the *Emerich* case, the court determined the counselor had made a reasonable effort to warn Ms. Hausler, and therefore the court ruled in favor of the counselor and other defendants.

The Tarasoff Case

The *Tarasoff* case involved a woman, Tatiana Tarasoff, and her murderer, Prosenjit Poddar. In 1969, Mr. Poddar was receiving counseling from a psychologist at the student health service on the Berkeley campus of the University of California. In the course of his counseling sessions, Mr. Poddar told his psychologist of his intention to kill Tatiana Tarasoff. The psychologist made the assessment Mr. Poddar was indeed dangerous and should be committed to a psychiatric hospital for observation and further evaluation. The psychologist also informed the campus security police of the death threat and of his assessment that Mr. Poddar was dangerous. Campus police detained Mr. Poddar but later released him when he promised to keep away from Ms. Tarasoff. The psychologist also wrote a letter requesting the assistance of the campus police. Subsequently, the psychologist's supervisor ordered the letter and the therapist's treatment notes be destroyed. Ms. Tarasoff was never made aware of Mr. Poddar's threat.

Mr. Poddar ultimately killed Ms. Tarasoff. The murder led Ms. Tarasoff's parents to sue the Board of Regents and employees of the university for failure to notify the intended victim of the threat. Eventually, the California Supreme Court ruled failure to warn the potential victim was professionally irresponsible. In that case the court ruled therapists must breach confidentiality where the well-being of others is involved.

The Jaffee v. Redmond *Case*

In contrast to the *Tarasoff* decision, the Supreme Court of the United States ruled in the *Jaffee v. Redmond* case that licensed psychotherapist–client relationships and communications are privileged under federal law.

In this case, a police officer shot and killed a suspect in the course of making an arrest. The victim's family sued, alleging the victim's constitutional rights had been violated. During the court proceedings, the police officer's social worker was ordered to turn in the clinical notes she had made during counseling sessions that took place after the shooting. The social worker refused to turn over the notes, declaring the record of her conversations with the officer was protected against involuntary disclosure by psychotherapist-client privilege.

Although the federal court ruled in favor of the victim's family, the Court of Appeals for the Seventh Circuit reversed their decision, and eventually, the Supreme Court upheld the appellate court's decision. The court's decision regarding the issues in this case is significant for art therapists because it extends federal privilege beyond the bounds of psychologists and psychiatrists to licensed social workers. This may, at some later point in time, be interpreted to include art therapists and other mental health practitioners.

INFORMING CLIENTS ABOUT CONFIDENTIALITY
AND ITS LIMITATIONS

It is important to inform art therapy clients about the nature and limitations of confidentiality. For some art therapy students and seasoned art therapists, this can be an uncomfortable task. It can be awkward because all art therapists want their clients to trust them. Discussing the confidential nature of the art therapy relationship can be one way to begin to foster a sense of safety and specialness. Conversely, discussing the limits of confidentiality may seem to threaten the sense of security. Despite the discomfort discussion of confidentiality and its limits may cause, it is important to cover all aspects of the nature of confidential therapy relationships.

Problems can arise in clinical situations if all facets of confidentiality are not discussed with clients.

An Example

I once supervised an art therapy student who was working in an inpatient psychiatric hospital. She opened an art therapy group session by telling the clients in the group, "Everything you say and do in this room will stay within these walls." During the course of the session, one of the clients in the group drew a portrait of him holding a gun to his head. As he talked about the drawing, he said he had recently purchased a weapon and that as soon as he was discharged from the hospital, he intended to commit suicide. The art therapy student responded professionally to the client's images and his verbal revelations during the session. Later in the day, she made a thorough report about the drawing and the verbal interchange in the psychiatric team meeting. As a result, the client was placed on suicide precautions and his participation in an off-ward trip into the community was canceled.

The next day, when the client saw the art therapy student walking down the hallway, he angrily confronted her. He raised his voice, "I thought you said everything we did in that art group was supposed to be like a secret? You lied! And I am going to tell everyone else in the group that you cannot be trusted!" Needless to say, this was very embarrassing for the student, and it caused a major disruption in her therapeutic work with that group of clients.

During our supervisory session I helped the student to think about what she had said to the group. I asked, "Is what you told them, about everything being confidential, really the truth?"

"Well, for the most part it is," she answered.

"Let me ask again," I said. "Is everything you said about confidentiality true?"

"In some ways it is. I mean . . . but, it's not that simple," she replied.

I asked, "What if one of the clients had drawn a picture of herself doing something harmful to someone else? Would you have told anyone about it? Would you have said anything about that in the team meeting?"

"Yes, I'd have to," she blurted.

I went on, "Then your suicidal client was right. Not everything the clients say or do can stay within the session?"

"I suppose, if you want to be technical about it."

"Well," I said, "this is such an important issue, I think it is worth being technical about. I know you were trying to reassure the clients that the art therapy room is a safe place where they can be free to express themselves, but I think it is terribly important to also be honest about this issue. Do you agree that the client had every right to be angry with you based on how you started the group?"

She thought for a moment. "I see what you mean. So how can I say it better the next time? I really do want them to feel safe."

I suggested that she consider saying something like this: "It is really important that everyone in the group feel safe enough to draw and say whatever they need to. I want to assure you that, for the most part, what happens in here stays in here. But you need to know that I am a part of the psychiatric team, and I do report on things that happen in this group in the team meetings, especially when I am concerned about someone's safety."

She replied, "But that does not sound like me. It's not the way I talk."

I said, "The exact wording isn't all that important, but you want to make sure that your clients understand both the importance of and the limitations of confidentiality."

Art therapists are ethically bound to protect the confidences of their clients. Information obtained in art therapy sessions cannot be disclosed except when the client has authorized the art therapist to do so, or when the art therapist is compelled to do so by ethical responsibility or by law.

As art therapists, our responsibilities in regards to confidentiality extend beyond the bounds of therapist–client relationships because of the presence of artworks that are created in the context of therapy. Wilson (1987) notes, "Besides those confidentiality issues art therapists share with allied professionals is the further complication that clinical material in art therapy includes not only evanescent verbal data but concrete lastingly identifiable artworks as well" (p. 77). This suggests that art therapists may be equally obligated to protect the content of their clients' verbalizations that occur, and the content of artworks that are created, during art therapy sessions. This implies that both the rights of clients and the rights of images must be addressed as one considers confidentiality issues in art therapy.

Art therapists have to wrestle with serious questions that arise in relation to the rights of clients' artworks. For example, is a client's image of herself jumping off of a cliff an indicator of suicidal ideation, a precursor to a suicidal gesture, or an expression of her wish to fly above the turmoil of her life? Is it a metaphor of her longing to take a risk in her life, or is it something else altogether? The content of clients' imagery must always be explored in the context of the art therapy relationship and assessments made regarding the symbolic and/or literal meanings presented in the work. The presence of the artwork , as a third entity in art therapy relationships, is one of many factors that sets art therapy apart from other helping professions. The third entity of the artwork serves to complicate issues of confidentiality in art therapy. The tripartite nature of art therapy relationships, consisting of the artist-client, the artist-therapist, and the art processes/products, clearly compounds the complexity of ethical decision-making. The subject of the rights of images will be addressed more fully in Chapter IV of this text.

Figure 4. Weighing Responsibilities–Craypas
Suzanne Wernette

In summary of this section, there are three primary circumstances when an art therapist must breach a client's confidence. (1) When, in an art therapist's professional judgment, a client is dangerous and is likely to do harm to another. (2) When, in an art therapist's professional judgment, a client is likely to harm him/herself. (3) Whenever an art therapist has reason to suspect child abuse or neglect. None of these circumstances are easy to assess. Corey, Corey, and Callanan (1998) state, ". . . it is extremely difficult to decide when breaching confidentiality to protect potential victims is justified. Most states permit (if not require) therapists to breach confidentiality to warn or protect victims" (p.165). As discussed earlier, the Emerich and Tarasoff cases are landmark court decisions that address therapists' privileged communications, and therapists' obligations to protect clients and protect and warn members of the community at large who might be harmed by a client's actions.

PRIVILEGED COMMUNICATION

A principle that is similar to confidentiality is the legal concept of privileged communication. "Privileged communication is a legal concept that protects against forced disclosure in legal proceedings that would break a promise of privacy" (Corey, Corey, & Callanan, p. 156). The scope of privileged communications laws varies from state to state. Most such laws include attorney-client relationships as well as doctor-patient relationships and many states' laws cover psychotherapist-client relationships. Privileged communications statutes are intended to protect the privacy of clients, not the privacy of therapists. Therefore, if a client gives up this privilege, the therapist cannot legally withhold information sought by the court. It is questionable whether or not privileged communications statutes would protect art therapists' clients. This may remain unclear until it is tested in the courts. At the time of this writing, I know of no such precedent setting cases specific to art therapy.

PRIVACY

Privacy is a concept that is related to, but distinct from, confidentiality and privileged communication. In relation to the law, privacy is a constitutional right of all people to control if, when, and how they will share information about themselves with others.

Art therapists must take care to respect the privacy of their clients. In art therapy, this is a particularly complicated matter because clients' artworks may reveal feelings and issues the client is not consciously aware of at the time the artwork is created. It is possible for art therapists to inadvertently intrude upon a client's privacy through the process of discussing the artwork.

The Health Insurance Portability and Accountability Act of 1996 (HIPPA) includes a rule related to the security and privacy of health information. Art therapists must be aware of this rule and how its standards apply to art therapy practice. The HIPAA Privacy Rule created national standards to protect individuals' medical records and other personal health information and to allow clients to have power over their health information. The rule sets limits on the use and release of health records. It establishes safeguards that providers and health plans must implement to protect the privacy of health information. In general, the Privacy Rule provides that an art therapist may not use or disclose a client's healthcare information without permission except for treatment, payment, or healthcare operations. The Privacy Rule requires art therapists to do the following:

- Notify clients about their privacy rights and how their information can be used.
- Adopt and implement privacy procedures for their practice.
- Be responsible for seeing that privacy procedures are followed.
- Maintain secure records that contain individually identifiable health information.

Art therapists should also be aware of other related HIPPA regulations that provide standards for the security of health information, national requirements for electronic healthcare transactions, and national identifiers for providers.

SITUATIONS FOR DISCUSSION

Ethical issues inevitably arise when important principles are in conflict. From time to time, art therapists find themselves having to balance the principles of confidentiality, duty to warn, privileged communication, and privacy. The following situations are often faced by art therapists and involve ethical dilemmas related to confidentiality. The reader is encouraged to think through and discuss what course of action ought to be taken in each of these circumstances.

1. You are working in a community mental health agency. The art therapy room also serves as a kitchen and lounge space. During an individual art therapy session with a very depressed woman, a group of three other clients enters the room. The woman, who has been weeping while discussing a drawing with you, becomes very embarrassed, silent, and withdrawn. She suggests the session be ended, although there is still nearly half of the allotted time left. How do you handle this predicament?

- I insist that the session continue until the time is up.
- I confront my client with the reality that she is being treated in a community setting and these things are bound to happen.
- I demand that the three clients who have intruded upon the session leave the room at once.
- I end the session and assure the client that I will discuss this situation with other staff of the agency to see if alternate arrangements or rules can be made to ensure the confidentiality of these sessions.
- I end the session and apologize to the client.

2. You are an art therapist working in a large state psychiatric hospital. A psychotic client paints a bizarre, violent, and sexually provocative image. He is quite proud of his effort and asks you if he can hang it on the wall of the studio so that his friends can see it. How do you respond to his request?

- I allow the client to hang his painting in the studio.
- I tell the client that his painting is inappropriate for public display in the studio.
- I tell the client that he can hang the painting on the wall during our sessions but it should be put away at all other times.
- I tell the client that the painting is his artwork and whatever he does with it is his business.

3. During your final practicum placement as an art therapy graduate studen, you are working at a shelter for battered women and their children. One late afternoon, a woman, Marjorie, a close friend of your mother, is admitted to the shelter for protection from her husband. The next morning, your mother calls you on the telephone and asks how Marjorie is doing. What do you do in this situation?

- I tell my mother her friend is fine.
- I tell my mother I have no idea what she is talking about.
- I change the subject immediately.
- I say I am not at liberty to discuss anything about the clients I work with at the shelter.
- I say that Marjorie is not a client at the shelter.

4. One evening, you and a group of colleagues from the private psychiatric hospital where you work are out to dinner at a restaurant. At one point, the conversation turns toward funny incidents that have occurred on the job. The talk grows louder and can easily be overheard by other patrons at the restaurant. Although no clients' names are used, you become uncomfortable with this topic of conversation. What do you do in this predicament?

• I excuse myself and go home early.
• I tell my colleagues we should change the subject.
• I tell my colleagues I do not appreciate their using clients as the subject of humor and I find their behavior unprofessional.
• I warn my colleagues that if they do not stop this behavior, I will report them to the medical director of the hospital.

5. You are an art therapist working in an inpatient treatment facility for emotionally disturbed adolescents. During an art therapy group, one of your clients made a drawing depicting sadistic acts of torture against a female. As you discussed the drawing with him, he said, "Oh, this is nothing but a fantasy." Later, you asked if the girl in the drawing is someone that he knows. He replied, "Yes, yes I know exactly who she is." When you attempted to solicit more information, the client became guarded and refused to respond to any further inquiries. What do you do in response to this situation?

• I surreptitiously ask other adolescents in the program if they know who the girl in the drawing is.
• I thoroughly document this interaction and the content of the client's drawing in his medical chart.
• I immediately report this occurrence to the treatment team leader.
• I do nothing immediately, but I watch the client for other signs of potentially threatening behavior.
• I discuss this incident with my supervisor.

MALPRACTICE LIABILITY IN ART THERAPY

Considering the issues above, art therapists may question how vulnerable they are to malpractice lawsuits. After reading this chapter in the manuscript, one of my colleagues jokingly commented, "This material makes me very nervous. Maybe I should get out of art therapy while I still can." While those feelings are certainly understandable, I hope that no one leaves the profession due to fears of malpractice liability. In this section, I will offer some suggestions regarding how art therapists can avoid malpractice litigation while continuing to practice in an ethical manner.

Corey, Corey, and Callanan (1998) define malpractice as, "the failure to render professional services or to exercise the degree of skill that is ordinarily expected of other professionals in a similar situation" (p. 139). Legally, malpractice refers to professional negligence that leads to harm or loss to the client. Generally, such negligence evolves from lack of care in discharging one's duties to the client, or from inappropriate or unwarranted deviation from usual practice. As art therapists, we must abide by the ethical code of our profession and conform to legal standards of the state in which we are practicing. Failure to practice art therapy with care and with good intentions can lead to allegations of malpractice. Art therapists are human and mistakes are inevitable, but we are expected to exercise skill and good judgment, and to utilize current knowledge that is common to other art therapists.

Art therapists are vulnerable to malpractice actions. While there are safeguards against being in a lawsuit, discussed later in this chapter, it is highly recommended that all art therapists be covered by professional liability insurance. Usually, art therapists who are working in hospitals, mental health agencies, or other institutions are covered by the facilities' group insurance plan. However, it is advisable to make sure that this is the case. For those art therapists working in private practice, it is suggested that they purchase individual professional liability insurance in order to protect themselves in the event of a malpractice action.

At the time of this writing, I am unaware of any art therapist in the United States having been successfully sued for malpractice. However, there is no guarantee that art therapists won't be sued in the future. As Wirtz (1994) observed:

> Whether art therapists are called as experts or charged with malpractice, specific tools can aid them in presenting their expertise or presenting their defense. These tools include, but are not limited to, a clear, well articulated standard of practice, knowledge of the laws within the state, and adequate record keeping. (p. 294)

Perhaps the best way for art therapists to protect themselves from a malpractice action is to limit their art therapy practice to professional contexts serving clients for whom they are well prepared. It is important to know your strengths and limitations as an art therapist and to not practice beyond your scope of expertise.

The following are suggested safeguards that may help art therapists guard against malpractice allegations.

- Regard clients and their images with the utmost respect and dignity.
- Regard clients' images and the feelings that emanate from them as "facts" that do not necessarily need to be explained. This will assure clients that you are taking their issues seriously and not judging them.
- Provide art therapy services from a clear theoretical perspective (Stromberg & Dellinger, 1993). Have a rationale for what you do in therapy sessions. Don't "fly by the seat of your pants" in the name of eclecticism.

• Clearly inform the client about the areas of informed consent discussed earlier in this chapter.
• Document that you have informed the client regarding the areas of informed consent and that he/she has consented to art therapy treatment. Have the client sign a consent-to-treatment form.
• Put as much time, planning, and care into the termination process as you do in regard to all other aspects of the art therapy process.
• Engage in continuing education activities. Keep up on current trends in art therapy and other related fields.
• Practice only in the particular areas where you are appropriately trained and competent.
• Document accurately and regularly the client's treatment plan and progress. Make note of any changes in the treatment plan.
• Maintain client files for seven years.
• Report cases of suspected child abuse as mandated by law.
• Avoid conflicts of interest that might arise due to your position of power and influence in the client's life.
• Avoid engaging in dual relationships with clients.
• Avoid engaging in personal relationships with former clients for at least two years after therapy has concluded.
• Do not engage in sexual relationships with clients.
• If you have questions regarding a clinical situation or problem, seek appropriate supervision and/or consultation.
• Obtain written consent from the client prior to seeking supervision or consultation.
• Know the local and state laws relevant to your practice.
• Purchase professional liability insurance.

CHAPTER SUMMARY

Ethical practice demands that art therapists must be aware of their responsibilities toward clients. We have to always seek to promote the welfare of clients, respect the rights of clients, and make every effort to see to it that their professional services are used properly. Art therapists should inform clients of what will be expected of them, and they must be informed themselves regarding the scope of their responsibilities. Art therapy clients have the right to know about the art therapy process and the particular approach of the art therapist who is treating them. They have a right to understand the risks and benefits of art therapy. Clients have to be informed about confidentiality and the release of information, and the limits of confidentiality.

They should be aware of their financial obligations, the contents of their files, and the credentials of the art therapist. Finally, clients must be informed of their right to terminate the therapeutic relationship at any time, and of any supervisory relationships that the art therapist may utilize.

Ethical questions that surface as we art therapists wrestle with our responsibilities to clients are many. The principles of informed consent, confidentiality, privileged communication, and privacy are complex. Sometimes these principles seem to be in conflict with one another. If it were possible to always reason from a pure deontological perspective, such questions might be resolved simply by referring to the appropriate sections of the *Ethical Principles for Art Therapists* (AATA, 2003). However, when these principles are applied in clinical and professional contexts, there are often competing interests involved that complicate matters. Art therapists' primary responsibilities are to our clients, but we also have obligations to the images that emerge in art therapy sessions, to the public, our employers, the art therapy professional community, and ourselves. Wilson (1987) comments, "Art therapists encourage original and personal work that will be experienced as unique by the patient who produces it and perhaps by others as well" (p. 77). The original, personal and unique works that emerge in the context of multiple responsibilities often give rise to ethical quandaries when there are conflicts among the various parties.

To be sure, it is essential for art therapists to be familiar with the *Ethical Principles for Art Therapists* and the *Code of Professional Practice*, but these publications, and any subsequent revisions of them, cannot predict or cover every situation. This is a shortcoming of the deontological approach to ethical decision-making. There simply are too many situations where the "rules" do not adequately apply. There may be times in your art therapy career when acting on behalf of a client's best interest leads to conflict with your employer. There may be other times when doing what is necessary to protect an innocent member of the community, you have to betray the confidence of your client. In such cases, it may be helpful to think through the ethical dilemma from a teleological approach, seeking to determine what will bring the greatest good (or the least harm) to the situation.

The following artistic tasks are intended to help you engage with the material covered in this chapter in a metacognitive, visual, kinetic, and sensory way. People learn and retain information in many different ways and making art in response to the issues raised in this text is an important way to grapple with the topics. The artistic tasks may be completed in the context of an art therapy class or as homework assignments. They may also stimulate lively discussions in supervision groups. Participation in and discussion of the artistic tasks will deepen and enhance learning experiences. Individual art therapists may also want to complete some of the exercises in order to integrate the learning experience more fully.

Suggested Artistic Tasks

1. Ask each person in a professional or student peer group to create an artistic image of a situation in which an art therapist would feel compelled to betray a client's confidence. Discuss these images in the group. Make note of commonalties among the images. Also make note of marked differences in the ideas presented.

2. With a small group of peers, role-play the beginning of an initial art therapy session. Have someone in the group take note of how the art therapist in the role-play presents issues of confidentiality and informed consent.

3. In a small group, ask members to imagine an encounter with a dangerous client. (This can be based on an actual occurrence or a fictional scenario.) Have each group member write a poem about the encounter. Share the poems with the other group members and discuss the feelings these encounter-poems stimulate. Ask members to try to predict how they would handle each situation.

4. Think about how you would feel if you became certain that one of your art therapy clients (a child) was being physically abused by her father. Create a symbolic portrait of the feelings such a situation would stir in you.

5. While looking at the image that you created in response to task 4, write out the script of the telephone call you would make to the authorities to report the abuse. Read the script out loud and listen to how it sounds. Discuss with peers how it makes you feel to read the report.

6. Form several small groups of two to four participants. Assign each small group the task of creating a performance art enactment centered on an issue or theme addressed in this chapter. Instruct each small group that the enactment may include visual images, poetry, dance/movement, and/or sound. Inform each group that the performance enactment should last approximately three to five minutes. After each group presents their enactment, solicit responses and feedback from the observers.

Chapter III

RESPONSIBILITY TO THE WORK PLACE

An important component of art therapists' obligation to their clients is the responsibility to maintain the work place or studio environment. Section 1.11 of the *Ethical Principles for Art Therapists* states:

> Art therapists strive to provide a safe, functional environment in which to offer art therapy services. This includes:
> a. proper ventilation
> b. adequate lighting
> c. access to water
> d. knowledge of hazards or toxicity of art materials and the effort needed to safeguard the health of clients
> e. storage space for artwork and secured areas for any hazardous materials;
> f. allowance for privacy and confidentiality;
> g. compliance with any other health and safety requirements according to state and federal agencies which regulate comparable businese. (AATA, 2003, p. 5)

For the purposes of this text the word "studio" will be used in its broadest sense to mean the milieu in which therapeutic art making occurs. Studios come in all shapes and sizes; some are tremendously conducive to creative work while others present significant challenges. The studio may be an ideal traditional art space, or it may be a less than ideal place. Studios may be found in places such as converted classrooms, private practice offices, or even a modified bedroom on a psychiatric unit. I know one art therapist whose studio was a remodeled storage closet. Regardless of the advantages and shortcomings of the studio's physical nature, there are three core principles of structure that are necessary in order for clients to benefit from involvement in art therapy. The three central aspects of the arts studio are
1. Safety
2. Predictability
3. A focus on art making in the service of relationship building.

Figure 5. Art Street Studio, Albuquerque, New Mexico
Amanda Herman

SAFETY

Two important dynamics in therapy are safety and anxiety. The client must believe that the art therapy milieu is a safe place in which to explore and express feelings. At the same time, the client has to have some degree of anxiety in order to be motivated to make changes in his or her life. In *The Dynamics of Art as Therapy with Adolescents* (1998), I use the metaphor of a teeter-totter to describe the tension between these two dynamics. "On one end of the teeter-totter is safety, and at the other end is anxiety. In this metaphor, the midpoint, or fulcrum, is the position of the art therapist" (p. 134).

It is my experience that most clients bring plenty of anxiety with them to therapy. Generally, art therapists do not need to worry about stirring anxiety in their clients; the client will have more than enough. The art therapist needs to attend to establishing the sense of safety that artistic therapeutic work requires.

For the client, the process of exploring and expressing thoughts and feelings is a difficult task. Most clients come to therapy as a result of personal crisis and the intensity of their feelings may push them to experience art therapy treatment as threatening. Against this backdrop, it is easy to see why safety in the art studio is the first required ingredient for successful therapy. If the client does not feel that the studio is a safe environment, then no therapeutic work will take place. No matter how skilled a therapist may be, how pleasant the physical facility may be, or how fine the arts materials may be, if the client does not feel safe, therapy will not occur. Another way to conceptualize the importance of this is that the physical space is an outward manifestation of the relationship between the art therapist and the client. If this is true, then it is our ethical responsibility to attend to the safety of the therapeutic environment.

For art therapists, it is ethically imperative that we think deeply about how we establish a sense of safety in the art therapy studio, office, or group room. According to Gussow (1971), it is the process of experiencing deeply that transforms a physical location into *a place*. "A place is a piece of the whole environment that has been claimed by feelings" (p. 27). We can do many things to create the feeling that the studio is a safe place to have deep experiences. In a profound sense, this may be one of our most important tasks.

Healing is a process of transforming self-defeating and destructive energy into curative and creative energy. One goal of art therapy is to stimulate this healing energy. Curative energy can find its way into clients' lives in many diverse ways, and it is almost impossible to predict how this energy will manifest itself for each client. After years of clinical observation, however, I know that studio spaces have the ability to work mysterious *place magic*. An important element in the creation of place magic can be the presence of imagery on the walls of the studio. The walls of the studio as a living gallery, always changing and reforming, provide a powerful unspoken metaphor of the functions of the studio environment. A client entering such a studio who is greeted by a host of images is, through the presence of these images, invited to participate in the healing activity of making art. The images on the walls need not always be comfortable. Sometimes disturbing imagery can convey the message that the studio is a safe place to unburden one's troubles. The reverse can also occur, however. Sometimes disturbing imagery can frighten clients and make the place feel unsafe. For the sake of safety, it is the art therapist's task to monitor, and modify when necessary, the ambiance of the studio.

Some art therapists describe their role as being a caretaker of the studio. McNiff (1995) believes that his primary function as an art therapist is to kindle the soul of the place, to maintain its vitality and its ability to engage people in highly individuated ways (p. 180). Important functions of art therapists working in this way have little to do with what they say but much to do with how they are in the world.

The attitude of the art therapist toward the client is extremely important. Clients are often quite sensitive to unspoken cues and energies in the milieu. They may immediately sense whether the art therapist likes working with them or not. They may know, without ever being told, whether or not you regard them as people worthy of deep respect. This sensitivity is not necessarily a result of anything that the art therapist says overtly, but instead is a response to the subtle, nonverbal ways such attitudes leak out into the environment. The success of art therapy is tied directly to the attitude of the art therapist.

The art therapist's self-presentation, meaning the use of his or her tone of voice, facial expressions, body movements, energy level, and personality, are also important aspects in the studio. Art therapists ought to exude an amount of excitement, and joy in their work, while at the same time honoring the pain, sadness, and angst that so often accompanies the client in therapy. There is not one particular ethical personality type for art therapists, but it is imperative that art therapists work to develop a sense of personal power and self-confidence if they want to be effective in their work. This means that one must work with the personality traits she has and develop a therapeutic style that conveys a therapeutic persona. This persona comes in many forms. I know art therapists who are able to fill up a room with their gentle, quiet earnestness. Others create an infectious and compassionate atmosphere through their outgoing warmth and energy.

As the caretaker of the art studio, the art therapist doing group work functions in the dual roles of protector and motivator. The art therapist establishes and nurtures an artistic community that is bound by the principle of "parallel participation." In parallel participation, the activities of individual art making are joined with the communal experience of others' creative processes. This sets up a shared energy in which client-artists affect and are affected by their own images and the artworks of their peers. The art therapist maintains the structure of the place and sets the stage for parallel participation through her enthusiasm, behavior, and artistic activity.

An important factor in establishing the richness and safety of the art therapy studio is the presence of a range of art materials and equipment. Materials play a meaningful role in the design, creation process, and final product of an art form. The media is more than a means to an end, i.e., a way to get the client to do talk therapy. The media itself can alter feelings, and the functions and uses of particular tools and materials often result in changed designs and revised plans on the part of the client and the art therapist. From this, a greater capacity for flexibility in approach emerges.

Ethically, art therapists ought to consider the effects of the materials and tools they use. Some art therapists argue that the media and materials used in art therapy need to be of good quality, or there is a covert message given

Figure 6. In the Studio—Chalk on Paper
Bruce L. Moon

to the client that the process or end product of the expressive work is not valued. This can also give a subtle message that the client is not valued. It may be better to invest in a limited number of high-quality materials and tools rather than to select a wider array of cheaper, inferior products. Other art therapists employ a range of materials that would not be considered traditional media. Some art therapists, for example, fill their studio shelves with found objects, old fabric, string, rocks, beads, and odd assortments of wood scraps. Regardless of an art therapist's philosophic approach to materials, it is ethically important to thoroughly contemplate the impact of materials on the art therapy process. Just as we would not expect a verbal therapist to use words thoughtlessly, so too, art therapists have an ethical responsibility to carefully think about the art materials they use in therapy sessions.

The art materials in the studio help to generate the nourishing force of the place. The work of art therapy relies on materials of many kinds in order to foster the richness of expression, sense of safety, and artistic contagion that many clients so desperately need. As ethical caretakers of the studio, art therapists should encourage and model meaningful involvement with art materials as a primary ground for therapeutic relationship.

Every aspect of the therapeutic environment either focuses or impedes the creation of an ambiance of safety and creative contagion. The color of the walls, the type of flooring, the size of windows, the style of furniture, the floor plan, and the organization of the space all have the potential to enhance the therapeutic milieu or detract from it.

As the caretaker of the art studio, the role of the art therapist is to protect the place by establishing baseline rules of behavior. The art studio is not a democracy, and in order for it to be a safe place, there have to be some rules or principles of behavior. An example of this is found in the writing of art therapist Randy Vick. Vick (1999) describes what he terms, "the house rule" (p. 70), that no one is allowed to hurt himself, herself, or others, either physically or verbally. Like Vick, I keep the rules in my studios as simple and clear as possible. When I visit art therapy studios where the rules are overly complicated, they inevitably interfere with the creative process.

My experience tells me it is important to keep the rules in the arts studio to a minimum and to keep them simple. I offer the following examples of rules that have worked well in my art studios:

1. Use whatever you need but don't waste materials.
2. Take care of tools, brushes, and furniture.
3. Respect the rights of others.

Few, if any, situations will arise in the therapeutic arts studio that cannot be governed by these simple rules.

PREDICTABILITY IN THE STUDIO

In order for clients to meaningfully engage in the difficult work of being in therapy, it is necessary that they experience the art studio as a safe and predictable place. In fact, the predictability of the place is a prominent component of its safety. The principle of predictability is paradoxical. Art therapists can never know what will happen artistically for an individual client, yet they are deeply committed to constructing and maintaining a consistent, predictable container (studio environment) that is capable of holding the surprises of the client's artistic efforts. The paradox is that while art therapists never know exactly what will happen artistically within the studio, they can be very clear about how they, as the keepers of the studio, will be. Art therapists can also be clear about how the studio space itself will be.

Art therapists can promote an atmosphere of predictability in a number of ways:

• Be on time
• Welcome the client into the space in the same way each day,
• Have the necessary materials and tools available and well organized,
• Be consistent in affect and attitude,
• Be consistent in responses to client behaviors,
• Develop rituals to begin and end sessions.

An example of predictability is found in how I begin art therapy studio sessions. I always welcome clients into the space in the same way. I greet the client(s) at the door and say, "Welcome to the studio!" This simple phrase, spoken in the first few moments of our encounter, sets the tone for the client's entry into the studio space. I communicate a sense of excitement about the work ahead, and I try to transmit a quality of enthusiasm and genuine pleasure that he/she is here. This is an essential, subtle way to begin to establish the creative contagion that I want the client to participate in.

It is important to have the necessary supplies and tools available and well organized before the client enters the studio. Ongoing assessment of the stock of materials, ordering of supplies as needed, and maintenance of an orderly arrangement of materials ensures that clients will have what they need to do the work.

Some art therapists find it helpful to have their own in-progress works of art as an element in the studio. They indicate that these art pieces communicate a commitment to and enthusiasm for artistic expression. One colleague says that her images fill the air and become a hard-to-resist force in the studio. Henley (1997) notes, "By working in the presence of clients, the art therapist models important art making behaviors which clients can begin to identify with and incorporate" (p. 190). I have described my own art making in the therapeutic studio as "a vehicle for ritual greetings with some clients. The client enters the studio and asks, 'What are you working on now?' This gives me an opportunity to model involvement in self-exploration and expression with the client" (Moon, 1998, p. 149).

It is also important to consciously develop rituals for the beginning and ending of studio sessions. As I mentioned earlier, my, "Welcome to the studio," provides a ritual of entry. Following this there are rituals of gathering tools, materials and artwork-in- progress. Near the end of each session I announce when it is time to prepare for leaving. The specific words an art therapist uses in these rituals are not all that important, but what is important is that they be said in a similar way each day, with the same tone of voice.

Each of these things, and many more, serve to give clients a sense that the studio environment is a safe and predictable place. The clients come to know what will be expected of them, and how the art therapist will relate to them. These elements of predictability establish the boundaries of the studio container that holds the unpredictable and often powerful contents of the creative process.

MAKING ART AND ESTABLISHING
RELATIONSHIPS IN THE STUDIO

The most important contribution art therapists have to offer the individual client, and the larger treatment community, is the process of making art. There are many therapy disciplines: psychiatry, psychology, social work, pastoral counseling, and substance abuse counseling; each of these disciplines has a contribution to make to the treatment of clients. Each discipline also has limitations that stem from the verbal nature of the approach. Art therapy has the unique advantage of being able to engage clients visually, tactilely, kinetically, and aurally. In addition, art making involves the client and therapist in tasks that utilize ideas, feelings, and physical sensations. Therapy disciplines that are verbally oriented have no access to this range of sensual possibilities.

As art therapists consider the structure of the art therapy studio, special attention ought to be given to insuring that the studio is favorable both to making art, and to developing therapeutic relationships. Equal value may be placed on the process of making art and the process of developing relationships. Relationships grow from the shared experience of client and art therapist doing things in the company of one another.

Art therapy is sometimes considered to be *only* a means to an end, the end being verbal therapy. This view underestimates the powerful therapeutic value of shared activity. Making art in the therapeutic studio is not merely a means to promote talk therapy. Making art is the foundation upon which therapeutic relationships are built. Art therapists do not form relationships with their clients solely because art therapists are skilled in verbal articulation. Art therapists build relationships because they are willing to engage in doing things with clients. The things that art therapists do, of course, are artistic activities. There is reciprocity of purpose that is of great value here. On the one hand, art making creates an arena in which relationships grow. On the other hand, relationships create an arena in which art works emerge. Neither component of the studio, the art or the relationship is of greater weight in this process. When too much focus is on the relationship, both the art and the relationship suffer. For example, sometimes art therapists can become overly invested in discussion of clients' artworks and actually get in the way of art making by talking too much. Likewise, if the process of making art takes too much attention, the relationship and the image suffer. It is possible to become so immersed in art processes that clients and art therapists can lose track of the primary focus of their work together.

Ethically, art therapists have important obligations to their clients to provide a safe and predictable art therapy milieu equally dedicated to making art and developing quality relationships.

In addition to thinking about the issues raised in this chapter, it can be helpful to engage with the issues in meta-cognitive, visual, kinetic, and sensory ways. The following artistic tasks may be completed in the context of an art therapy class or as homework assignments. They may also be used to stimulate discussion of topics in supervision groups. In order to deepen and enhance learning experiences course leaders are encouraged to both use these tasks and to create their own art directives.

Suggested Artistic Tasks

1. Create an image of the ideal art therapy studio. Share your image with peers in the class or supervision group. Explore ways that your ideal space is similar and/or different from your actual work environment.

2. Draw the floor plan of the place where you provide art therapy services. Share the plan with your peers. Are there any problems with the space? Ask for feedback and suggestions about how you might alter the plan in order to make the space more conducive to artistic expression.

3. Imagine your art therapy room has a voice. Write a poem to convey what the room might say to you, to your clients, and to your employer in regards to its mission and its ability to carry out that mission. Share the poem with peers.

4. Create a performance art enactment that expresses the essence of the therapeutic environment you work in. Consider both the problems and potentials of the space. The performance may include visual art, poetry, music, dance/movement and/or sound. Share the performance with peers and solicit reactions to the enactment.

Chapter IV

THE RIGHTS OF ARTWORKS

> I explained to my wife that this eccentric project [painting] was
> an exorcism of an unhappy past, a symbolic repairing of all the
> damage I had done to myself and others during my brief career as
> a painter. That was yet another instance, though, of putting into
> words what could not be put into words: why and how a painting
> had come to be. Vonnegut (1987, p. 263)

In the discussion of ethical principles and issues in art therapy it is important to delve into questions regarding the rights of artworks created in the context of therapy sessions. Considering the place of images and artworks in our professional ethics stimulates questions not present in the ethics of other helping professions. This is a difficult topic seldom discussed in the literature. Historically, ethical and legal issues related to images and art products have been focused primarily on questions regarding four areas: interpretation of client imagery (Cohen-Liebman, 1994; Cohen, Hammer, & Singer, 1988; Cohen, Mills, & Kijak, 1994; Franklin & Politsky, 1992; Henley, D., 1987; Levick, et al, 1990; McNiff, S., 1991, 1989; Moon, B., 1995; Ulman & Levy, 1984), exhibition of client art work (Frostig, 1997; Spaniol, S., 1994, 1990a, 1990b), art therapy record keeping (Braverman, J. 1995; Malchiodi & Riley, 1996), ownership of the finished art product (Braverman, J., 1995; Malchiodi, 1995; Moon, C., 1994).

These four areas raise complex legal and ethical questions related to artworks. Ethical questions are made even more complicated when an art therapist regards images as living, *ensouled* entities, related to, but separate and distinct from, the artist who made them (McNiff, 1992; Moon, 1997b).

AUTONOMY OF ARTWORKS

McNiff (1991) writes about the difficult issues raised by this belief in the autonomy of images. He states, "In this era of ethical vigilance little consideration has been given to the rights of images, gestures and other expressions created within the therapeutic context" (p. 277). Feminist, multicultural and ecotherapy theorists offer provocative critiques of current theoretical systems in psychotherapy and art therapy that have tended to be overly egocentric and focused on the individual. The result of such self-referential thinking in therapy is the concept that the emotional universe revolves around the individual. Therapeutic methodologies emerging from this concept encourage clients to reflect upon all experiences in relation to themselves.

The rights of art works have, by and large, been disregarded in art therapy literature. This absence may be due, at least in part, to art therapy's reliance on traditional Western theories of psychotherapy for its theoretical base. This has resulted in an unfortunate void in art therapy literature. "Consideration of the rights of images does not replace our moral responsibilities to the patient, community and profession. Recognition of the autonomous lives of artistic expressions simply adds another dimension to the social context" (McNiff, 1991, p. 278).

Self-referential therapies can be deeply enriched by creative, intentional involvement with autonomous images and art materials. The creation of artworks and the personification of images transforms how the individual client views the world and his or her place within it. Many art therapists believe art making promotes an awareness and acceptance of life that is decidedly not self-referential. Life is bigger than the individual. Images simultaneously reflect and transcend, while deepening and helping to redefine the person who made them. By making art the client is reminded that the world does not revolve around him or her.

Art therapists who are respectful of the rights of artworks often begin to consider ethical questions by asking, "what does the image want?" Questions about the appropriateness of interpretation and labeling, the exhibition of clients' work, the documentation of art therapy sessions, and the ownership of finished art products, are given a profound sense of depth when art therapists seriously consider the best interests of the artwork. Imagine an art therapist's internal dialogue regarding a painting created by a client.

First voice: Is it appropriate for me to label this painting as typical of the artwork produced by people suffering from a particular form of mental illness? The image looks a lot like ones drawn by other clients who have been diagnosed with Borderline Personality Disorder.

Second voice: How will the painting feel about being labeled in this way?

First voice: I am not sure.

Second voice: Do you like being labeled by others?

First voice: That's different.

Second voice: Do you like being labeled, or not? Don't avoid the question.

First voice: All right. I don't like it.

Second voice: It really is a powerful image isn't it?

First voice: Yes, yes it is. Perhaps I should think about organizing an exhibition of some of my clients' artworks. This would be a great piece for an exhibit.

Second voice: Do you think the painting wants to be viewed in a public forum?

First voice: How can I know?

Second voice: Ask the painting. Ask the artist who painted it. You can even ask yourself.

First voice: I'd feel foolish doing that.

Second voice: Isn't it also foolish for you to make decisions for other people?

First voice: Wait a minute. Who owns this painting anyway, the client or me?

Second voice: What would the painting say about that?

Whenever I talk with art therapy students about the rights of images and artworks I am invariably asked, "Are you being literal or figurative?"

My answer is "Yes."

They ask again. "Do you really want us to literally talk to the painting, or are you speaking metaphorically when you tell us to talk to artworks?"

My answer is "Yes."

In clinical work, clients are often encouraged to engage in processes of speaking with their images, talking out loud to their artworks. Literally conversing with an image is a disciplined way of fostering sensitivity to artistic entities. Of course, there is also a figurative aspect to the process. For art therapists, attending to the sensibilities of an artistic object, process, or event can be the foundation for developing increased sensitivity to a client's feelings. The way we treat the artwork can be likened to the way we treat other people, and vice versa. When images are regarded as living, independent, personages, we are obliged to treat them with care and respect. The discipline of being with and talking with artworks in this way expands and deepens our care and respect for the persons whom made the artworks.

Images are the meeting ground of outer and inner vision. With outer vision, clients explore the world around them; with inner vision, they explore themselves. Both worlds, external and internal, are made up of sensational experiences: tactile, olfactory, visual, auditory, and kinesthetic. These sensual experiences form images which are then used to construct dreams, embody emotions, organize sensations, and ascribe meaning to experiences.

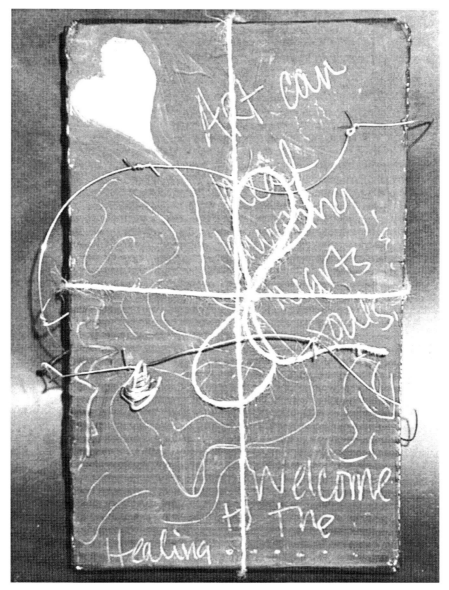

Figure 7. Welcome to the Healing–Mixed Media
Pauline Sawyer

Images give visible form to external and internal experiences that shape the person's encounter with life. Dissanayake (1992) says, "art is a normal and necessary behavior of human beings that like talking, exercising, playing, working, socializing, learning, loving and nurturing should be encouraged and developed in everyone" (p. 175). Paintings, drawings, sculptures, poems, dances, and songs are primary communications that help people move from the realm of individual occurrences into that of shared experiences.

Throughout history, people have relied on artistic images to keep them informed about the world around them, to express the essence of life as it is experienced, and to explore how humans fit into the larger scheme of things. As Dissanayake (1988) notes, "I will venture to conclude, however, that what the arts were for, an embodiment and reinforcement of socially shared significances, is what we crave and are perishing for today" (p. 200). Art making assists the process of balancing outer and inner experience and provides a mechanism for producing external images of internal reality.

Artistic processes that integrate feelings, thoughts, and sensations through creative activity form the extraordinary contributions of art to therapeutic contexts. The methodologies of art therapy have sometimes been considered subordinate to psychological theories alien to artistic and imaginal processes. To this day, it is extremely difficult for some art therapists to think of their work from any perspective other than the traditional "person-centered" position. McNiff (1991) notes, "In my training studios for professional art therapists I consistently see how simple exercises, such as speaking as a figure or gesture in a painting, meet with considerable resistance, fear and feelings of ineptitude" (p. 280). This is consistent with the inclination of some art therapists to overidentify with the ego. Such over-identification leads to a tendency to evaluate the significance of a phenomenon based on one's personal comfort with it.

The rights of artworks within the context of therapy is an aspect of ethical issues unique to art therapy. Paying attention to the imaginal other, to what the art object wants and needs, has profound implications for everything art therapists do. Questions regarding the appropriateness of interpretation, the exhibition of clients' artwork, the record keeping of art therapy, and the ownership of art products can be considered in the light of this perspective.

THE ETHICS OF INTERPRETATION

I will now examine some of the ethical questions associated with the phenomena of interpreting and labeling client artwork. The primary ethical concerns regarding interpretation and classification revolve around the potential good and possible harm these phenomena can bring to client-artists and the images they create. Henley (1997) notes, "As a trained art therapist I found myself analyzing all the time, yet it was what I did with these interpretations that defined my role as a teacher and therapist. These interpretations were used to guide and inform my interventions" (p. 65). While many art therapy educational programs have emphasized the interpretation of images, I am convinced that our nature is more about being interested and curious about imagery. This is very different than interpretation, because being interested and curious generates questions and engagement.

There are benevolent and malevolent aspects to interpretation and analysis of imagery in art therapy. Malevolent aspects of the word *interpret*, in relation to art therapy, are encapsulated in the following portions of the definition: (1) to explain the meaning of, make understandable; (2) to translate; (3) to have, or show one's own understanding of the meaning of; to construe (Webster, 1988). Each of these definitive statements implies that interpretation is a solitary and independent event whereby one person [art therapist] translates or shows the meaning of something [client imagery]. When the art therapist's interpretation of a client's artwork is an internal event (within the art therapist), there is potential for abusive labeling of both the image and the client-artist.

Many art therapists view interpretation as essential to their work (Cohen, Hammer, & Singer, 1988; Franklin & Politsky, 1992; Gannt, 1987; Levick, 1983; Wadeson, 1980). They regard the translation of their clients' metaphoric images into cognitive psychological constructs as a professional responsibility. There are two primary purposes for this kind of interpretation: (1) diagnostic clarification, and (2) interdisciplinary communication.

Diagnostic Interpretation of Images

According to Cohen, Mills, and Kijak (1994), the long-term survival of the art therapy discipline hinges upon the capacity to expertly analyze and interpret imagery for the purpose of diagnostic inquiry (pp. 105-110). Horovitz (1987) goes so far as to suggest:

> It is hoped that art therapists will continue to develop evaluative tools such as the Silver Test (ST) for inclusion in diagnostic assessments. Perhaps such contributions will convince other mental health professionals of the significance and impact of art therapy. . . . (p. 128)

The effort to connect illness with artistic products, however, may be ethically problematic because of its twofold reductionism. First, the client/person is reduced to being represented as the diagnostic label. Evidence of this form of reductionism is sometimes heard on psychiatric units when staff members make such comments as, "We can't admit one more Borderline this week!"

Such comments are expressions of staff members' feeling stretched beyond their limits. Referring to the diagnostic category, Borderline Personality Disorder, becomes a kind of shorthand communication among staff members that is dehumanizing to clients. Second, the artwork is diminished when it is regarded as a symbol of pathology, or as an indicator of disease. McNiff (1989) writes, "The intentional interpretation of art is widely misunderstood and limited in both psychology and art history. Both disciplines attach excessive emphasis on labeling and the classification of images according to a particular frame of reference" (p. 55). In psychology, the frame of reference is that of pathology or disease.

Some art therapists object to this form of interpretation and diagnostic labeling because they believe there is always more to a person than his or her illness and more to images than pathological symbolization. There are also questions raised regarding the legitimacy of such labeling. Wadeson (1980) comments, "There are many passages in the art therapy literature where statements are made about art expression characteristics of a diagnostic group or the meaning of an individual's picture without adequate supporting evidence" (p. 329). These questions and objections raise ethical issues relative to the interpretation of images in the context of art therapy.

Affixing a specific diagnostic or psychological label to an artwork, which appears to be the ultimate end of interpretive events, leads to what I describe as *imagicide* (Moon, 1990, 1995). Imagicide is the intentional killing of an image through labeling it as one thing and thus restricting it. One may wonder what might motivate an art therapist to commit imagicide. Can imagicide be attributed to an art therapist's need to be perceived by others (employers or colleagues) as an "authority" that analyzes and explains what images and artworks "really mean"? How does such a perception serve clients? Does being perceived as an authority serve art therapists?

Some art therapists work with assessment systems and formulae that are designed to aid in the interpretation of client artworks. Such interpretations are often used to help treatment teams clarify diagnostic issues. This raises questions regarding the ethics of assessment. Just as the original creation of an image may be a projective interpretation of life on the part of the client, so too any subsequent attempt to interpret the image may be projection on the part of the interpreter. What ethical questions are raised due to art therapists' capacity for projection? How can we take this into account so that we behave ethically when interpreting?

Art therapists working in mental health institutions and agencies inevitably face the problem of artistic interpretation in their practice. Linesch (1988) contrasts therapies relying heavily on interpretation with those focused on working through issues with adolescent clients. She asserts that there is some controversy to an interpretive art therapy approach. She believes that, "because of the adolescent's yet undeveloped ego and weak superego these interpretive efforts can be destructive to the youngster's fragile psychic structure" (p. 54). Her cautionary remark reminds us that interpretive approaches must be used with an awareness of their potential for harm. It is possible to harm therapeutic relationships by affixing pathological labels and negatively interpreting clients' artworks.

In a previously published text, I recounted a clinical vignette that is an example of the potentially harmful effects of labeling (Moon, 1998). A colleague who visited a psychiatric hospital to supervise one of her students doing practicum work there told the story to me. During the art therapy session, the client, a fourteen-year-old girl, drew a human figure with an exaggerated tongue protruding from the mouth. In responding to the girl's image, the art therapy student mentioned an article she had read in which the author suggested that protruding tongues may indicate sexual abuse (Drachnik, 1994). The adolescent left the room abruptly, saying that she would never return.

The ethical concerns raised in this vignette are fourfold. (1) The client's image had many potential interpretations. The possible indication of sexual abuse was only one possible interpretation. (2) The art therapy student's comment is an example of a premature interpretation of the client's art. The intervention proved to be counterproductive, disrupting the therapeutic alliance. It is likely that it would have been more productive if the student had given the girl an opportunity to expand upon the significance of her image. The art therapy student could have asked the client to do a dramatic enactment, tell a story, or write a poem about the person in the drawing. These responses would have been in accord with a definition of interpretation that includes artistic modalities as a means of exploring a client's work of art. (3) The art therapy student may have been attempting to establish herself as an authority in the eyes of her supervisor or her client. By making the "expert" interpretation without having established a solid relationship with the client (it was only their third session), the student damaged the delicate therapeutic alliance she was building with the girl. (4) The art therapy student misrepresented Drachnik's ideas.

Interdisciplinary Communication

Another purpose for interpretation of client images is to facilitate communications across disciplinary lines. Some art therapists describe their interpretive work as the translation of the metaphoric images of their clients into cognitive psychological constructs that may be understood by other members of the treatment team. These art therapists regard artistic interpretation as one of their professional duties. However, as Champernowne (1971) suggests, translation from one language (art) to another (words) "is bound to bring loss or error" (p. 142). When art therapists make interpretations that purport to tell clients what artworks mean, damage can be done to the therapeutic relationship. Something is always lost when clients' artworks are given pathological labels or when art therapists make "expert" interpretations outside the context of direct encounters with clients. Both of these forms of interpretation fall into the category of occurring within the therapist rather than in the context of the relationship between client and therapist. Limiting interpretations to internal events on the part of the therapist can be problematic, particularly in relation to those clients who are not able or willing to verbally verify or rebut the accuracy of an interpretation by an authority figure. The absence of the client's validation or refutation of an art therapist's interpretation can lead to mistreatment of both the artworks and the persons who made them. It is important to consider all forms of interpretation in art therapy in the light of the rights of the artworks.

TRIPARTITE NATURE OF ART THERAPY RELATIONSHIPS

To guard against the potentially abusive aspects of interpretation and labeling in art therapy, it is helpful to think of art therapy interactions as being comprised of three equal partners: the client, the artwork, and the art therapist. When there is dialogue among these three partners, the rights of artworks are more likely to be respected than when an art therapist acts as an authority empowered to tell the client what his or her artworks mean. In a discussion of this idea, a colleague asked, "Can a legitimate interpretation emerge from such a three-way discussion?"

"I think interpretations that omit any one of these three constituents are at best questionable, and at worst, abusive," I replied.

"But isn't it the art therapist's professional responsibility, in many clinical settings, to interpret client artworks?" my colleague asked.

"Of course," I said. "We art therapists are an interpretive group by our very nature. We all interpret, but there are benevolent and malevolent ways of going about this."

"What are you trying to say?"

"I am suggesting that we have to remember the context to which we refer. In the art therapy relationship in which the client/artist is attempting to make life changes, the client's interpretation of the artwork is the most legitimate, maybe the only legitimate one."

"But clients aren't trained to interpret their work."

"Of course, not. That is where the dialogue among the three constituents comes into play," I said.

"Are you suggesting that the art therapist's role is to facilitate this dialogue?"

"Yes, that's it exactly," I answered.

Benevolent qualities of *interpret* and *interpretation* are found in the following: *interpret*–to bring out the meaning of; *interpretation*–the expression of a person's conception of a work of art, subject, etc. through acting, playing, writing, performing, criticizing, etc. These definitive statements suggest a sense of give and take, and there is a quality of relationship and responsiveness. Art therapists working from this understanding view interpretation as an essential *process* of dialogue that emerges among therapists, clients, and the artworks made in the context of the art therapy relationship.

When the interpretation of a client's artwork is an *interpersonal process* (among the art therapist, client, and image), there is a spirit of respect and openness to multiple meanings that honors all of the parties involved. The artwork is a source of sequential interpretations. One interpretation begets another, which in turn begets another. Rubin (1986) concurs: "Of course, there are many meanings in products, in formal qualities and in content; but they are not to be found in neat formulas or simple recipes, much as we might crave easy answers" (p. 29). Artworks have a right to be seen for what they are, and this means that multiple interpretations may be equally valid. Rubin (1986) contends that "human beings, after all, are complex creatures, and so is their expressive behavior and the products that arise therefrom" (p. 29). Ethically speaking, there is no *one* way to interpret a client's image.

In a discussion of the role of responsive art making in the treatment of client, Moon (1997c) explores creative ways of responding to images through performance, poetry, and dialogue. McNiff (1992) agrees and encourages us to ask ourselves, "do we treat images with respect when interpreting them in therapy? As a person, how would you like to have another person authoritatively describe what 'you mean'? How do you feel when labeled? When explained by another" (p. 184)?

Having compassion for images and regarding them as independent entities, separate and distinct from the persons who made them, opens new possibilities for how we think and talk about what we do in art therapy. It also opens us to new ways of behaving toward our clients and their artworks. These new ways of thinking and acting foster relationships that are respectful, empathic, deeply therapeutic, and profoundly ethical.

In order to grapple with and retain the information presented in this chapter, it is helpful to make art in response to the issues. I encourage art therapists to engage with these ideas in metacognitive, visual, kinetic, and sensory ways. The following artistic tasks may be used to stimulate discussion of the topics. In class or supervision groups, course instructors and supervision group leaders also are encouraged to create their own art directives in order to deepen and enhance learning experiences.

Suggested Artistic Tasks

1. Share one of your recently completed artworks with a group of art therapy colleagues or fellow art therapy students whom you trust and with whom you feel safe. Without providing any explanation of your work, ask four or five of your peers to write an interpretation of the artwork. As you read these interpretations, reflect on how your peers' written comments affect you. Imagine that you are the art piece. How do you feel about the things that have been written about you?

2. Share one of your recently completed artworks with a group of art therapy colleagues or fellow art therapy students. Without providing an explanation of your work, ask four or five of your peers to do one of the following things: (a) write a poem in response to the artwork; (b) make a drawing in response to the artwork; (c) create a brief series of movements, or a dance, in response to the artwork; (d) write a story about the artwork; (e) compose vocal sounds—no words—in response to the artwork. As you read, observe, and/or listen to these responses, reflect on how your peers' creations affect you. Imagine you are the art piece. How do you feel about the creations that have been made in response to you?

3. Consider the qualitative differences between the written interpretations of your artwork received in task # 1, and the creative responses to your work received in task # 2. Make an art piece that symbolizes your feelings about these differences. Discuss the art piece with your peers.

EXHIBITION OF CLIENTS' IMAGES

Over the past two decades in the United States, there has been ever-mounting interest in the artwork of people who are mentally ill. Interest in the art of people with mental illness, however, has existed to some degree for a much longer time. MacGregor (1989) notes, "In the early twentieth century, several European artists had become aware of the art of the mentally ill and were influenced by it. Exhibitions of psychopathological art were held for the first time and a number of publications appeared that made the contents of private collections of outstanding examples of this unique art publicly available" (p. 4). While MacGregor's references to "pathological art" and "psychotic art" may be objectionable, his point is well taken that there has been a long-standing fascination with artworks made by people who are suffering emotional and/or mental illnesses. Hanz Prinzhorn, an art historian and psychiatrist, collected thousands of art pieces created by clients in Europe's stark, closed-off mental asylums during the first quarter of the twentieth century. Prinzhorn published *Artistry of the Mentally Ill* in 1922.

Spaniol (1990a) notes:

> In 1985, selections from Prinzhorn's collection made their first appearances in this country, touring four American museums and startling the art public with their powerful visual imagery and symbolic content. Since then, art by people with mental illness has begun to enter the mainstream of the American art world through exhibitions in established galleries. . . . (p. 70)

"Outsider art" and "folk art," terms that refer to art created by people who are self-taught (Borum, 1993, p. 24), has steadily grown in popularity during the 1990s. These artists have usually had no formal training but seem to be driven to create. Often outsider artists are people who suffer from mental illnesses. The public seems to hunger for the raw and primitive images these artists make.

Many art therapists receive repeated requests to organize exhibitions of their clients' works. There is an ethical responsibility to weigh the merits and potential benefits of such exhibitions against the rights of clients and images. Art therapists have to consider their obligations to protect clients and artworks from exploitation, sensationalism, and abuse. At the same time, there are potential emotional gains made possible for clients through the empowering aspects of publicly displaying artworks. It falls to art therapists to wrestle with these ethical dilemmas because other mental health disciplines either have little sensitivity to the issues or no serious interest in them. Art therapists have the opportunity to serve as supporters, defenders, and promoters of our clients and their images. Some images born into the world may long to be viewed by a large audience, while other images may be more private in nature. Indeed, these are often concurrently present in art created in the context of therapy.

Art therapists serve as allies to our clients and their creative endeavors. Spaniol (1990a) states, "As art therapists we must be prepared to advocate for our clients. We must learn to concentrate on their creative abilities as well as their psychiatric disabilities" (p. 78). By being advocates in this way, art therapists can remain true to the real nature of our work, which is all about having compassion and empathy for people and images.

Figure 8. At an Exhibition–Chalk on Paper
Bruce L. Moon

Section 4 of *The Ethical Principles for Art Therapists* addresses issues related to client artwork:

4.0 CLIENT ARTWORK

Art therapists regard client artwork as the property of the client-artist. In some practice settings client artwork, or representations of artworks, may be considered a part of the clinical record retained by the therapist and/or agency for a reasonable amount of time consistent with state regulations and sound clinical practice.

4.1 Client artwork may be released to the client during the course of therapy and upon its termination. The client is notified in instances where the art therapist and/or the clinical agency retain copies or photographic reproductions of the artwork as part of the clinical record.

4.2 Art therapists obtain written informed consent from the client or, where applicable, a legal guardian in order to keep client artwork, copies, slides, or photographs of artwork, for educational, research, or assessment purposes.

4.3 Art therapists do not make or permit any public use or reproduction of client art therapy sessions, including dialogue and artwork, without written consent of the client.

4.4 Art therapists obtain written informed consent from the client or, where applicable, a legal guardian before photographing clients' artwork, video taping, audio recording, or otherwise duplicating, or permitting third party observation of art therapy sessions.

4.5 Art therapists use clinical materials in teaching, writing, and public presentations if written authorization has been previously obtained from the clients. Reasonable steps are taken to protect client identity and to disguise any part of the artwork or video tape which reveals client identity.

4.6 Art therapists obtain written, informed consent from the client before displaying client art in any public place.

Clearly, the authors of the *Ethical Principles for Art Therapists* were writing from a perspective that is primarily client-centered yet respectful of the rights of artworks in this section of the document. It is apparent that these principles were intended to protect the rights of the client/artist. This section is also provides a solid framework for ethical consideration of the potential ethical problems inherent in exhibiting clients' artworks.

There is often an unequal power relationship in the client/therapist context. Given this reality, it is easy to imagine the anxiety a client might feel in response to an art therapist's request to use the client's artwork in any one of the purposes described by the ethics document, i.e., educational, research, public presentation, or exhibition. The pressure to acquiesce to the wishes of the therapist would be great. Wadeson (1980) cautions, "The mantle of confidentiality extends to art work as a visual form of privileged communication.

Therefore, if the purpose of the art sessions is a form of psychotherapy, art exhibits of the work are not appropriate" (p. 41).

In addition to Wadeson's concerns, there are significant pressures within therapeutic relationships that have to be well thought-out as art therapists consider asking their clients' permission to exhibit artworks. Some clients want approval from their art therapist and others are flattered by the request to exhibit their art. These pressures make it very difficult for art therapy clients to say no. Some clients might fear reprisal from the art therapist if they refuse. Other clients might assume the existence of a false level of interest on the part of the art therapist. Clients who are members of an art therapy group may use the art therapist's request as a sign that they are more valued by the therapist than other clients. Competition, resentment, and antipathy may develop among clients as a result of being included or excluded from the exhibition. All of these dynamic pressures must be painstakingly attended to as art therapists consider organizing exhibitions of client work.

Spaniol (1990a, 1990b) provides three guiding principles to serve as frameworks for developing procedures and protocols for exhibition of client artwork. These principles are sensitive to client populations and compassionate toward clients' images. Spaniol refers to these principles as providing: opportunity, safeguards, and empowerment. She describes providing *opportunity* as creating the occasion for the client-participants to immerse themselves in their identity as artists. When artworks are personified and looked upon as equal participants in therapeutic relationships, they must be talked with and listened to rather than simply talked about. Spaniol's three principles can be applied to artworks. From this perspective, art therapists not only provide the artist-client with opportunity to exhibit, but the artwork itself is given occasion to be viewed as well. Providing *safeguards* means building in protections for the client-artists. Most important among these is the maintenance of confidentiality and privacy. Spaniol (1994) explains that limiting disseminated information about an exhibit to statements written and signed by the artists allows clients to communicate as much, or as little, as they wish about themselves and their art while assuring the artists of confidentiality. Again, it is important that the principle of providing safeguards be applied to artworks as well as clients. The principle of *empowerment* refers to the necessity of including the artists and their artworks in decision-making about the exhibit every step of the way.

When an artwork is personified and regarded as an equal participant in a therapeutic relationship, it becomes an entity to be talked with and listened to rather than talked about. A three-way dialogue replaces the traditional two-way (therapist-client) communication pattern typical in verbal therapy. This expanded dialogue, in which consideration can be given to how the image might feel about being exhibited, is one of the essential and distinguishing qualities of art therapy. Consideration of the appropriateness or inappropriateness, and the other-ness, of the artwork can go a long way in helping art therapists assure themselves and their clients that they are behaving ethically when engaged in developing an exhibit of clients' artworks.

Art therapists may put themselves in the position of the painting or sculpture and ask questions of it. Am I being treated with respect and compassion in this exhibition? How do I feel about being hung in this place? Knowles (1996) believes it is, ". . . imperative that all of us who practice art therapy assess our personal attitudes and policies regarding the display of client's art" (p. 207). Spaniol (1994) and Frostig (1997) address the necessity of obtaining written consent in their discussions of the process of negotiating with clients regarding the use of their artworks. In addition, consideration needs to be given to obtaining the consent of the artworks themselves. How do art therapists acquire the consent of an artwork? Art therapists can ascertain the wishes of the artist and the artwork itself through active dialogue and engagement with an artwork and the client who created it. There are parallels between the treatment of images and the treatment of art therapy clients. These parallels have significant ethical ramifications.

Situations for Discussion

1. Marianne is working in a large County Children's Home. She has recently been asked by her supervisor to develop an exhibition of the artworks created in the art therapy studio. The supervisor is especially impressed with the paintings made by a young girl whose parents were recently killed in an automobile crash. The girl's paintings are skillful, painful expressions of the sadness and anger she feels about being orphaned. When Marianne raises some ethical questions regarding this request, her supervisor scoffs and tells her that the exhibit would really help with the annual fund raising campaign.

- How would you respond to such a request? Why?
- On what ethical system of thought would you base your response?
- Is there a section of the *Ethical Principles for Art Therapists* that is relevant to this dilemma?

2. John is an art therapist at a small private nursing home. The director of the facility asks him to organize an exhibition of the "crafts projects" that some of the residents have created. The director instructs John, "Whatever you do, don't put up any of those horrid paintings they make in your expressive groups. We don't want to encourage any depression here."

- How would you respond to this directive? Why?
- What section of the AATA *Ethical Principles for Art Therapists* applies to this situation?

3. The program director at a local TV station has contacted Sandy. The station would like to do a fifteen-minute "special report" on her work as an art therapist at a large state hospital for the criminally insane. The director makes it clear that he wants a "testimonial" from one of Sandy's clients to be included in the story. Sandy's supervisor is very excited about the positive aspects of this situation.

- What ethical dilemmas would this request raise for you?
- How would you resolve them?
- What kind of ethical reasoning would you use?
- What sections of the AATA Ethics Document apply to this dilemma?
- What sections of the ATCB Ethics Document apply to this dilemma?

Figure 9. Trembling Sobbing–Tempera and Craypas
Keli Schroeffel

RECORD KEEPING AND DOCUMENTATION OF
ART THERAPY SESSIONS

In 1994, at the Twenty-fifth Annual Conference of the American Art Therapy Association, held in Chicago, Illinois, a newly revised ethics document for art therapists was presented to the AATA members during a plenary session. A panel consisting of the chairperson of the AATA Ethics Committee, a member of the Board of Directors, and the AATA legal counsel provided a synopsis of the version of the *Ethical Standards for Art Therapists* (AATA, 1990) that was in-force at that time. Most of the subject matter of the panels' presentation stirred little or no controversy. However, when the presenters turned to discussing issues and questions regarding who owns the art products that clients create in the context of art therapy sessions, the ensuing debate was enthusiastic and sometimes heated.

Cathy Malchiodi, the editor of *Art Therapy: Journal of the American Art Therapy Association,* recounted the discussion in her 1995 editorial:

> Possibly one of the most confusing and controversial aspects of the practice of art therapy has been the maintenance, storage, and disposition of client art expressions. AATA ethics documents have addressed this issue in different ways. The 1990 version of the *Code of Ethics for Art Therapists*, under the section titled "Confidentiality" states: "Art therapists make provisions for maintaining confidentiality in the storage and disposal of records and art expressions. (AATA, 1990)
>
> The latest draft of what is now referred to as *Ethical Standards for Art Therapists* (AATA, 1994) is somewhat more explicit, stating: "Art therapists shall maintain patient treatment records for a reasonable amount of time consistent with state regulations and sound clinical practice, but not less than seven-years from completion of treatment or termination of the therapeutic relationship. Records are stored or disposed of in ways that maintain confidentiality" (Section 2.6). (Malchiodi, 1995, p. 2.)

The question of ownership of finished art products naturally leads to consideration of whether or not artworks created in art therapy sessions are considered part of the treatment record. If the artistic expressions of clients are a part of the treatment record, then clearly, clients could not claim their work as their property. Braverman (1995) noted, ". . . in many instances artwork constitutes a medical record" (p. 15). The position described by Braverman raised the specter of art therapists being required to keep all of their clients' actual artworks, or at least photographic reproductions or photocopies of them for seven years. Needless to say, the implications of this were troubling to many art therapists. For example, art therapists in private practice with a large caseload would be required to maintain a huge amount of storage space. Art therapists working in short-term treatment facilities, where several hundred clients per year participate in art therapy, were astounded by the potential expense and time involved in photographing the artworks of so many clients. Yet, as Braverman noted, "Issues of professional responsibility and potential professional liability often outweigh cost considerations" (p. 15). The panel presentation on ethical issues at the 1994 AATA conference generated impassioned "Letters to the Newsletter Editor" decrying the misguided nature of this position.

As I have continued to ponder these issues, I am struck by the absence of references to the *rights of artworks.* Braverman's 1995 article in the AATA Newsletter is clearly intended to provide information to art therapists that will serve to protect them from the potential civil litigation. Subsequent letters to the editor of *Art Therapy* address the protection of clients' rights (Neustadt, 1995) and the protection of the membership of AATA from the presumptive actions of the AATA Board (Cox, 1995), but overt concern for the rights of the artwork is not mentioned.

There are many issues regarding how art therapists maintain client treatment records. Some art therapists keep copious progress notes and some reconstruct verbatim conversations for the record. Some art therapists take photographic slides of significant artworks their clients make. Others assume ownership of the artworks themselves. In some clinical settings, art therapists are required to keep daily progress notes that aid in the institution's overall documentation for third-party payers and health maintenance organizations, while some agencies require only a monthly or quarterly written report of progress. There are even some practicing art therapists who do not keep written documentation of their work at all. They reason that the nature of their work is nonverbal and process oriented and any attempt to document in written form the nature of sessions with clients is an effort to translate the process into a form that is incompatible. These art therapists argue that it is unethical to keep records of the treatment process. Regardless of how art therapists choose to document their work, or how they are required to document their work by their employer, there are three essential principles that have to be considered in the record keeping.

1. Documentation and record-keeping should always be respectful of the client/artist and be intended to provide for the best possible treatment of the client.
2. Documentation ought to be accurate and serve as a form of protection for the art therapist in the event of litigation.
3. Documentation and record-keeping should always be done in such a way as to be respectful of the client's image(s).

Corey, Corey, and Callanan (1998) recommend that minimal requirements for clinical records be a report of the nature, delivery, and progress of psychological services. In an effort to streamline paperwork, many clinical facilities have developed forms for documentation that employ a series of checklists and numerical ratings of client behavior, mood, affect, and involvement. Some art therapists resist the temptation to utilize such shortcuts. These forms, they argue, promote a subtle reductionism that is dehumanizing to clients.

It is widely agreed that all therapists ought to keep some form of written record of their work. Art therapists who do not keep records justify this by suggesting they are protecting client confidentiality, or they do not agree with record-keeping on philosophical grounds, or they are just too busy to keep up with the demands of paper work. However, failure to document work as an art therapist is a serious matter because it places the art therapist outside the ethical principles of the profession. The *Ethical Principles for Art Therapists*, section 2.6 states:

> Art therapists maintain client treatment records for a reasonable amount of time consistent with state regulations and sound clinical practice, but not less than seven-years from completion of treatment or termination of the therapeutic relationship. Records are stored or disposed of in ways that maintain confidentiality. (AATA, 2003, p. 6)

Figure 10. Considering Documentation–Pastel Chalk
Suzanne Wernette

In keeping records of art therapy services, there are several factors to be taken into account. Generally, art therapy clinical progress notes should document the following items:

1. Client identifying information
2. The date and duration of the session;
3. Description of what the client did during the session;
4. Description of art materials the client used;
5. Description of images the client made;
6. Summary of things the client said;
7. Specific quotes from the session if relevant;
8. Reference to the current treatment goals;
9. Reference to actions the art therapist takes in addressing the current treatment goals;
10. Brief summary of the session.

Art therapy notes cannot be changed or modified after they have been placed into a client's record. Modifying a document in a client's record could be considered tampering. "Tampering with a clinical record after the fact can cast a shadow on the therapist's integrity in court" (Corey, Corey, & Callanan, 1998, p. 126).

Every institution or agency has its own particular style of record-keeping and its own demands in terms of content and length of clinical notes. In addition, state regulations will vary regarding legal requirements related to record-keeping. As mentioned earlier, documentation and record-keeping should always be respectful of the client/artist and be intended to provide for the best possible treatment of the client. It is important to remember the client has a right to view the contents of his/her art therapy file. Therefore, notes should be written in a way that is both truthful and respectful of the client and the client's imagery. As discussed earlier in this chapter, when clients' artworks are personified and regarded as equal participants in the psychotherapeutic relationship, they become entities that must be related to rather than simply reported on. The expanded dialogue, in which consideration is given to the ethical implications of including the artwork the client's record, is one of the essential and distinguishing characteristics of art therapy. This consideration of the other-ness of the artwork can help art therapists assure themselves and their clients that they are behaving ethically when engaged in documentation of their clients' progress in art therapy treatment.

When consideration is given to the positions of both the client and the artwork relative to clinical documentation, salient ethical issues are addressed. Art therapists can place themselves in the position of the artwork, and ask, "Am I being treated with respect and compassion in this record? How do I feel about being described in a certain way?" Art therapists need to consider the client's welfare and the welfare of artistic images when writing about the work. There is a positive parallel between the way art therapists write about images and the way they write about the people who make them. This parallel has vital ethical ramifications.

Situations for Discussion

1. Ellie is an art therapist working in private practice. She was previously employed in a state psychiatric hospital where there were so many requirements for documentation that she spent more hours per day writing progress notes than actually working with clients. This was very aggravating for her. Now Ellie has a private practice in art therapy. She only works with clients who are mildly depressed or who are having minor stress-related problems. When she opened her private practice, she vowed she would never again write progress notes.

- What do you think about Ellie's decision not to keep clinical records?
- Is it ethical for Ellie to refrain from writing clinical documentation?
- Are there any potential legal problems Ellie could face due to her stance on documentation?
- Does the kind of client Ellie sees for art therapy indicate there is no need for progress notes?
- Do Ellie's experiences in the state hospital justify her current behavior?

2. Steve is an art therapist who works in a psychiatric hospital. He spends a large amount of his time administering and documenting art therapy assessments with newly admitted clients. Steve was taken aback recently when one of the clients asked to read the assessment report he had written. Steve was very uncomfortable about this request because he feared the client would misinterpret the report. Steve advised the client against reading the report, vaguely suggesting it would not be helpful.

- What do you think about Steve's handling of this situation?
- Is it ethical for Steve to suggest the client should not read his report?
- Are there any potential legal problems Steve could face due to his behavior in this situation?
- Do you think clients should have a right to see their art therapy assessment reports?

WHO OWNS THE IMAGE AND THE ARTWORK?

Interwoven in the preceding discussions of interpretation, exhibition, and record-keeping is the underlying question, "Who owns the artworks created in the art therapy context?" As I was preparing this chapter, I solicited the comments of several colleagues. I asked Don Jones, Bob Ault, Frank Goryl, Bob Schoenholtz, Pat Allen, Cathy Moon, and Shaun McNiff to provide their responses to this pivotal question.

Don Jones, A.T.R., is an Honorary Life Member of AATA, one of the original pioneers of art therapy in America and a past-president of the association. Don was the director of the Adjunctive Therapy Department at Harding Hospital for many years and is now in semiretirement. He maintains an active art studio and consults on a number of art therapy projects in the Central Ohio region. He said:

> My first reaction-response is that the "artist-client" owns the work. Who owns my work? I do, until I give it or sell it. I would be unhappy if I was in therapy and the art therapist displayed, reproduced or showed my work outside of the clinical setting. I would only want it shown in the clinical setting in circumstances relevant to treatment team decisions.
>
> I do not like to see presentations that show patient's work in a way that seems, covertly, to brag about the therapist's skill. Unfortunately, in my early career, I was probably guilty of doing that.
>
> D. Jones (personal communication, January 26, 1999)

Bob Ault, A.T.R., is an Honorary Life Member and one of the original founders, and an early president of the American Art Therapy Association. Bob was on the staff of the Menninger Clinic for many years and is now in private practice. He directs the Ault Academy of Art and serves as a consultant to the Veteran's Administration Hospital in Topeka, Kansas. He said:

> First, let me say that the artwork always belongs to the patient. Period! Ownership of one's issues, responsibilities, weakness, transgressions, achievements, etc. are always understood to be a part of therapy. It is the patient who is struggling to change, or against change, and ownership of oneself is the key to helping someone achieve therapeutic goals. But the ownership and the handling of these issues can vary greatly according to the form of therapy and the role of the art making in the process. Therefore I don't believe there is a single answer that will cover all aspects of art therapy as it all goes back to the basic goals, strategy, and process.
>
> If I were working in an uncovering, analytic model, where the art making is used strictly as a technique to get to a deeper level of awareness, then the products are like the verbal aspects of the treatment. They are kept in secret by the

therapist, unless the patient releases them for display or whatever. It is like the patient can talk to anybody about what went on in the therapy, but the therapist cannot. So, the art products, often which are not of artistic merit, or are at best something that can be used for educational purposes, via exhibiting, are kept in the ownership of the patient. They might be kept with the therapist during the process of therapy, or can be taken whenever the patient wishes, and are all given over to the patient at the end of the therapy. Former patients have reported to me that they still look at their works done in art therapy sessions and remember conversations, or insights, or emotional experiences from years ago. Thus the art becomes a way of extending the therapy beyond the actual meeting time.

Another model of art therapy might be that in which there is more emphasis on the art process, and less on the insight orientation. Patients are taught how to paint, to assume ownership of their expressions, to develop self esteem, etc. The work still belongs to them, but I might encourage them to exhibit it, or honor it somehow. The patients I work with at the VA are actively taught how to make art, how to reflect on it, how to begin to feel better about themselves and function better. Sometimes I use the art to have them reflect on how it is similar to other issues in their lives and that is also helpful. The art works often become bridges for connections to others. So, as an art teacher, I would encourage the client in this model of art therapy to learn, to respect the image and materials and thus themselves, and to honor that and take ownership of it.

There are other issues of giving or receiving artwork by either the patient or therapist, exhibiting patient art in one's office, giving it back, etc. I hope you can consider some of those things too. It gets tricky when therapists are also exhibiting artists who sell their work, or when patients are exhibiting artists. The objects often take on a magical quality of their own. I have had patients leave treatment and return two years later and ask where their "blue painting is. I left it leaning against the wall there!" So, in their mind, the object has taken on a fantasy quality, as a constant connection, between the therapist and the patient. I always kept work in storage for some years before discarding it. This often allowed the patient to reenter over a "bridge of their making." Of course you can't keep everything and there comes a time you have to throw out things. This is then handled as the reality of the situation dictates.

B. Ault (personal communications, January 28, and February 13, 1999)

Frank Goryl, M.A., A.T.R., Frank is an art therapist who specializes in the use of clay as a therapeutic medium. He is an active artist and therapist who has worked with emotionally disturbed children and adolescents in residential treatment facilities and in private practice. He comments:

My response to the question: "Who owns the finished artwork that is created in the context of art therapy sessions?" comes from my experience of art therapy work done in a ceramics or clay studio and entails two basic perspectives.

1. From a philosophical point of view the finished artwork or "product" is of only secondary importance to the process of engagement with the art medium. To quote a story from M.C. Richard's Centering (1962): "A noble is riding through town and he passes a potter at work. He admires the pots the man is making: their grace and a kind of rude strength in them. He dismounts from his horse and speaks with the potter. 'How are you able to form these vessels so that they possess such convincing beauty?' 'Oh,' answers the potter, 'you are looking at the mere outward shape. What I am forming lies within. I am only interested in what remains after the pot has been broken'" (p.13).

2. From the practical point, storage space in the potter's studio is traditionally a limited resource, and it did not take long for me to adopt the policy in my studio of "immediate ownership." I emphasized that the client should take possession of their work immediately, not next week, so that I could write progress notes, or seven months or seven years later but with "still warm from the kiln" immediacy. I think most potters would agree that there has always been something special about opening the kiln after a firing to see what the kiln gods have deemed acceptable. No need to wait and delay that feeling of Christmas morning. "Ah !!!"

It was also common knowledge in my studio that any "abandoned" work finished or unfinished in the studio became part of the recycling beauty of claywork. Documentation via photography is the rule.

Frank Goryl (personal communication, Feb. 6, 1999)

Bob Schoenholtz, M.S., A.T.R., is in independent practice as an art therapist in the Philadelphia area. He is an adjunct member of the faculty of the Marywood University Graduate Art Therapy Program. Bob is the author of numerous papers and has presented nationally on such topics as imagery in art therapy, cybernetics, and the use of metaphor in psychotherapy. He said:

. . . an interesting question to which I have given much thought. In my early years as an art therapist working in a state mental hospital setting I treated the art productions of my patients as property of the hospital and kept an archive of them. This was a result of working within, and accepting, the medical model of therapy in full, from therapy to record keeping. There were occasions, however, when a patient would want to keep a piece and I would agree out of compassion.

As I developed my skills and perceptions about what I was doing with people in art therapy and moved away from the constrictions of the state hospital/medical model into private practice and into a modified learning model, it became absolutely clear to me that these art works were the property of the maker. This form of record-keeping became less important than respect for the relationship of the artist to the art work. Art work is done primarily to learn and grow, and much less for assessment, evaluation, and interpretation. The work became a way to know one's self, process, and product, and archiving became nearly irrelevant. At this time in my work with people in art therapy, if I need or want a record of their art work, perhaps for a presentation, I take a picture of it (with the permission of the artist, of course).

B. Schoenholtz (personal communication, January 26, 1999)

Pat Allen, Ph.D., A.T.R., is a member of the faculty of the graduate art therapy program at the School of the Art Institute of Chicago. She is the author of *Art Is a Way of Knowing* and has presented papers and workshops throughout the United States. She commented:

In my opinion, the image belongs to the creative force, the universe, the Divine, whatever you want to call it. The piece of paper, clay, or whatever form is the container of the manifestation of the image, belongs to whomever it came through. But, I think "belong" is the wrong word. I steward, give hospitality to, make a place for an image which is, in fact, energy, the traces of which are the "artwork." I don't believe in most aspects of intellectual property rights, as distinct from inventions, and I guess I think of the art as existing in the realm of spiritual and emotional property rights, something which cannot, in the truest sense, be owned.

P. Allen (personal communication, January 27, 1999)

Cathy Moon, M.A., A.T.R., is a member of the faculty of the School of the Art Institute of Chicago Graduate Art Therapy Program, and author of *Studio Art Therapy: Cultivating the Artist Identity in Art Therapy* (2002). Regarding the issue of who owns the art she said:

As an artist, and thinking about the art I make, the word own is a funny one for me. It's funny because a lot of the process I go through in making a piece of art has to do with working cooperatively with it, not like I am its master and it is my slave, not like I own it and it will do what I want.

But then, I must confess, once it is made I do think of it as mine. At least until I sell it or give it or barter it away. Even then though, the feeling I have about it is not best characterized by the word own. It is more like Shaun [McNiff] and others have characterized the artist/artwork relationship, as a parent/child relationship. I am protective of the artwork in that I don't want anyone to bring harm to it, but I like people engaging with it and bringing new life to it by the way they look at it and touch it, the things they say about it, the questions they ask about it. So when I exhibit it there is another piece in the cooperative process of the creation that takes place. I let my artwork become our artwork in a sense (by our I mean me and those others who view it).

As I'm writing I'm thinking about cultures who conceive of their art in a very different way than we do in contemporary Western culture. Like the Eskimos who liken their stone carvings to songs released into the air. I'm not at that level of lack of ownership. A concrete product that I can keep and hold and look at over time is very important to me.

I wonder how much this idea that we could own the art comes from our commercialization of artworks. Even when people don't sell their art, they are still a part of a culture that views art as a commercial product. It is like the idea that we could own land. A very silly idea, but we believe it and operate from that understanding anyway.

In relation to working with clients in therapy, I think the same way. The artwork is something that comes from the client, like an offspring. Just as I try not to intrude on other people's ideas about how to parent their children, I try not to intrude on my clients' ideas about how to parent their artworks. If they seek advice I'll give it to them. And if I see potential for harm I'll intervene. But in the absence of either of these two scenarios I just try to help them be the best parents they can be . . . to help them decide what is best for this created thing that has come from them.

The idea that I could own my clients' art seems absurd to me. It goes against how I view the whole artistic process. It also smacks of the "power over" paradigm that is our society's predominant way of viewing power and goes against the more feminist notion of empowerment or "power with." I prefer the "power with" idea.

In the best of all worlds, the power with notion would permeate art therapy sessions . . . in the way the client-therapist-art object relationships occur. In reality, clients often abandon their artwork when they leave treatment in an unplanned way. That is hard because a crucial piece of the power with way of determining what happens to the art is missing. I keep things for a long time because I am aware of this missing piece and don't know what to do with the art. In the end, I have to do the best I can because it is impossible for me to store art forever. I still don't know what the right thing to do is in these cases. I still have just as many questions as I did when I wrote *What's Left Behind* (1994). Maybe that's the way it needs to be. Keeping the questions out there so I always remember there are a thousand ways they can be answered.

Cathy Moon (personal communication, March 7, 1999)

Shaun McNiff, Ph.D., A.T.R., is an Honorary Life Member of the American Art Therapy Association. He is one of the most prolific authors in the creative arts therapies, and his theoretical contributions have helped to shape the discipline. He asserts:

I hate to reduce my response to "situation ethics" but there is no absolute ownership in my experience. If art is generated as part of a therapeutic milieu, isn't it necessary to hold onto the art to document and assess change, the lack of change, etc.? As an art-based person, I still see art made within an art therapy clinic as "clinical data" which the clinic maintains in order to assess and record outcomes. Yet, the clinic might determine that it is best for a particular person to keep the art. The question of ownership is thus strongly determined by the purpose and values of the context. A community studio might base its therapeutic philosophy on people taking pride in their expression and encourage the person to take the work home, display it, and use it as a source of ongoing creative energy. The art might be viewed as a talisman–Jung mentions the "magical effect" of an image which functions like an "idol" in casting life back to its maker.

Your statement, "artwork that is created in the context of art therapy sessions," thus frames the issue of ownership. "Context" is the key. If it is necessary for the art therapist to keep the art, this should be presented as a condition of participation.

Digital cameras and the ability to immediately and efficiently store and file art work may be a wonderful resolution, providing the ability to have it both ways. It is difficult to store and keep work over time even when there is no issue of patient ownership. Both sides of the issue of ownership may benefit from this method of keeping images. The digital image also makes itself available for so many different forms of presentation, research, etc.

> S. McNiff (personal communication, January 27, 1999)

Wadeson (1980) also addresses the issue of who owns the art. "Underlying the professional use made of the art productions is the issue of ownership. Since I consider art expression as an extension of the self, then I hold that the creator owns it . . . if a client or patient wishes to tear up a picture or smash a sculpture, since it belongs to her, it is her prerogative" (p. 42).

My colleagues' responses to the question concerning who owns the finished artworks created in the art therapy context suggest a continuum of thoughts on the matter. The responses range from confident assertions that the artist-client owns the work, to descriptions of situations where clients' artworks are considered to be the property of the institution, to stated beliefs about the image belonging to the universal creative force.

For the most part, these positions reflect a deontological approach to the ethical dilemma of image and product ownership. McNiff's comment that there is no absolute ownership reflects a teleological perspective. None of the art therapists I queried adopted an antinomian view of the problem. Art therapists must wrestle with this question individually. Each art therapist will have to decide how the code of ethics applies to the question of ownership and then balance this information against institutional policies and state laws applying to our practice. The real world of professional ethics in art therapy is, more times than not, a spectrum of shades of gray.

In her article, *What's Been Left Behind: The Place of the Art Product in Art Therapy*, Cathy Moon (1994) approaches the issue of ownership from a different perspective. She questions what is to be done with artworks left behind by clients when treatment is ended. In exploring this "leaving behind" behavior and some of its potential meanings, she also examines the larger issue of where and when the art therapy profession has left behind its core artistic identity. Ethical questions are raised in exploring this issue at both levels.

CHAPTER SUMMARY

As those of us who are art therapists wrestle with the ethical and legal issues of our profession, we need to keep in mind the three-fold nature of relationships in our work. We must be vigilant toward the rights of our clients, the rights of their images, and of our own rights and responsibilities. Historically, ethical discussions in art therapy have emphasized the rights of clients and the protection of art therapists, with little or no attention given to the rights of images and art products. This chapter has focused on ethical questions regarding interpretation, exhibition, record-keeping, and ownership. I hope this chapter has raised questions for the reader. I encourage art therapists to keep in mind the tenet that there is a direct correlation between the way we relate to images, the way we relate to the people who make images, and the way we relate to one another.

Chapter V

ART THERAPIST: ARTIST, THERAPIST, AND HUMAN BEINGS

It is important for art therapists to weave together their identities as professional therapists, artists, and human beings in the context of art therapy relationships. Art therapists ask clients to engage in art making as a means of clarifying and expressing identity. Clients are encouraged to look at artistic creations as objects that mirror back potential meanings and lead to recognizing different options in life. Sometimes creative self-exploration leads to change. Sometimes it leads to honoring the way things are and sometimes it leads to discovering new meanings in life. For the therapist who guides clients in such exploration through art, there are important questions to reflect on as well. Why do I make art? What gives me the right to think I can be of help to other people? What makes me think expressing feelings through art is so important? Do I "practice what I preach?"

It is nearly impossible to discuss art therapists as professionals without taking into account personal characteristics. An art therapist's values, beliefs, and way of being in the world affect the way she or he functions in the workplace. Some of the issues raised in this chapter are specifically related to the art therapists' professional identity. Although professional questions are examined throughout this book, this chapter focuses on subjects directly tied to the art therapist's personality and needs.

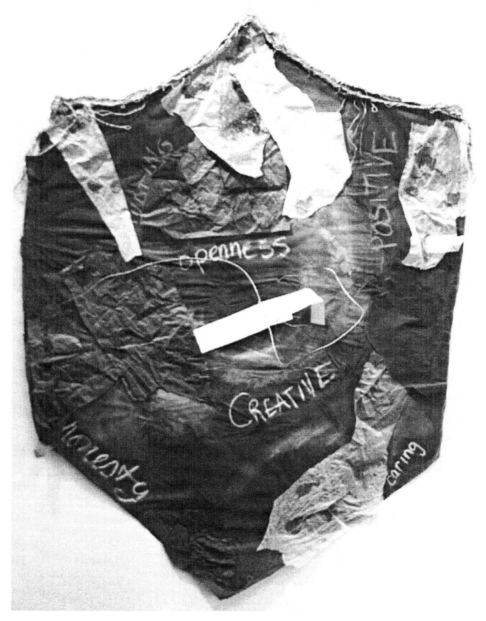

Figure 11. Art Therapists' Attributes Coat of Arms–Mixed Media
Heather Picarsic

ART THERAPY SELF-ASSESSMENT

The following self-assessment is intended to help art therapists identify attitudes and personal values related to the issues explored in this chapter. It may be helpful to complete the assessment prior to reading the rest of the chapter; then discuss your responses to each statement with peers, instructors, or supervisors.

Directions: Indicate the response that most closely identifies your beliefs and attitudes. Use the following code. 1 = strongly disagree

2 = disagree

3 = undecided

4 = agree

5 = strongly agree

1. Art therapists should be required to undergo their own personal therapy as a part of their graduate education. _____
2. Art therapists should be required to engage in personal art making in order to maintain their credentials. _____
3. Clients will not like you if you confront them. _____
4. Art therapists should undergo personality testing prior to receiving their registration._____
5. Having strong feelings about clients can be a problem for art therapists. _____
6. Having positive feelings about clients can be an indicator of interest in the client._____
7. Art therapists who attempt to meet their own needs through their work are incapable of providing quality art therapy services. _____
8. Art therapists who do not routinely engage in personal art making run a higher risk of burnout than those who are active artistically. _____
9. Art therapists who routinely engage in ongoing continuing education activities are less likely to burnout than those who do not. _____
10. Art therapists should be required to undergo periodic psychotherapy in order to maintain their registration. _____
11. Only art therapists with two years or less of clinical experience should seek supervision. _____
12. A competent art therapist should be able to work with any client. _____
13. Art therapists who are dissatisfied with their personal lives are likely to engage in unethical practices. _____
14. Art therapists who know themselves well are likely to avoid overidentifying with their clients. _____
15. Art therapists should place their professional responsibilities above their personal needs. _____

16. Art therapists should have all their emotional issues resolved before they begin practice as an art therapist. _____

17. A professional art therapist avoids getting too emotionally close to clients. _____

18. It is unethical for art therapists to satisfy personal needs through their work. _____

19. Real therapy does not occur unless clients talk about their artworks. _____

20. Feelings of frustration and doubt are signs that an art therapist is unsuitable for the profession. _____

By the time an art therapist has completed undergraduate and graduate school, a good amount of historical, theoretical, technical, and practical knowledge about how to be an art therapist has been amassed. In addition to these things which can be taught, the novice therapist also brings to the professional work unique personhood. The individual's life story, desires, longings, strengths, weaknesses, successes, frustrations, values, and fears all contribute to the humanity of professional identity.

When I was a student, my mentor often told me that the greatest tools an art therapist has are the arts and the self (Jones, 1973). He stressed the importance of knowing oneself well before attempting to be of help to another. It is possible to be very knowledgeable about art therapy assessment procedures, diagnostic categories and protocols, and psychotherapeutic techniques, and still be an unsuitable and unethical art therapist. In order to have credibility in advocating for self-discovery and self-expression in clients' lives, it is important for art therapists to authentically engage in artistic discovery and expression in their own lives. The work of being an art therapist is not solely about assessment, diagnosis, and therapy; it is about being willing to be a healthy, role model. Corey, Corey, and Callanan (1998) express this same sentiment in relation to counselors. "The willingness to live in accordance to what they teach is what makes counselors therapeutic persons" (p. 34). Problems abound, both ethical and therapeutic, when an art therapist is unwilling to provide the role modeling, or living-out, aspects of the work.

It is difficult to separate the art therapist as a professional from the art therapist as a person. Some art therapy theorists (Allen, 1995; McNiff, 1998; Moon, 1997a) suggest that art therapy is a way of being in the world, rather than simply an occupation. "What has the capacity to be deadly is given life in the form of our paintings, our drawings, our poems, our songs. They are *arted* out. This is not a job; this is not a vocation. This is life" (Moon, 1997a).

Figure 12. This Is Not Easy Work–Chalk on Paper
Bruce L. Moon

Art therapists have an obligation to be deeply aware of their personal needs and ultimate concerns. Without a solid sense of self, art therapists can unintentionally impede the self-exploration and self-expression of their clients. Corey, Corey, and Callanan (1998) posit that the focus of therapy can shift from the client's needs to the needs of the therapist when the therapist lacks self-awareness. Therefore, it is important for art therapists to be aware of their own vulnerabilities, unmet needs, and areas of conflict and to be aware of how these characteristics can infringe upon work with clients in the therapeutic studio.

While in graduate school, I occasionally wrestled with doubts about my professional future. During an academic advisement session, my adviser said, "Bruce, if you don't *have* to do this work, then for your sake and for the sake of potential future clients, don't do it." Perhaps all art therapy graduate students have doubts at times about their suitability for the profession. Sometimes these doubts are related to intellectual capacities or artistic abilities. In other instances, students question their own emotional stability. When doubts arise, I believe it is important to honestly reflect upon these questions, "Why do I make art? What am I getting out of being an art therapist? Am I cut out for this work? Do I have the necessary skills and abilities to be an art therapist?" There is no correct answer to these questions. Some art therapists have had life changing encounters with their own art making, and they want to be able to share the power of this with others. Many art therapists love the feeling that they are catalysts for others' change. Some art therapists derive a life-affirming excitement and sense of personal meaning from being with people who are struggling. Still other art therapists come to the field as a direct result of having worked through their own intense wounded-ness through art, and they long to share the process with others who are in pain.

More important than how an art therapist answers the questions posed above is the process of truly wrestling with them. Art therapists need to genuinely look into the mirror and grapple with their vulnerabilities, needs, and conflicts. Therapeutic change can be thwarted when art therapists consciously or unconsciously use relationships with clients, to address their own internal issues. Corey, Corey, and Callanan (1998, p. 35) note several factors that lead counselors into difficulties. In my years in the field I have seen evidence of these in the art therapy profession as well. They are:

1. An exaggerated need to feel powerful;
2. An exaggerated need to nurture others;
3. A strong need for approval, acceptance, admiration, respect;
4. Unresolved personal problems;
5. Unresolved personal conflicts.

When art therapists are not mindful of their own needs, they are apt to express and attempt to meet them in the context of therapy relationships with their clients. Art therapists are human beings and have personal needs, but these have to be dealt with outside their relationships with clients so they contaminate therapeutic work with clients. Art therapists must manage their own feelings or the feelings will control them.

Being an art therapist can be an intensely rewarding endeavor. One of the most potent benefits is the deep pleasure of seeing clients make significant and positive changes in their lives. Conversely, being an art therapist can also be quite painful and frustrating when clients fail to progress, or when they get worse. The successes and failures can only be enjoyed and endured when the art therapist is genuinely acting on behalf of the client rather than on his or her own account.

Art therapists may have difficulties working effectively with clients in areas where they have unresolved personal problems. Because of this, art therapists must reflect on what areas of personal unfinished business they have and how these might affect their work.

Laura's Dilemma

Laura is an art therapist who recently completed graduate school. She is working at a small partial hospital program for emotionally disturbed adolescents. Many of the clients in the program suffer from major depression and conduct disorders, and they often act out in angry, self-defeating, destructive, and negative ways. Laura came from a family where expression of anger was actively discouraged. In the art studio, Laura often finds herself surrounded by loud, angry teenagers and their aggressive imagery. She frequently feels uneasy and is sometimes frightened and intimidated by the adolescents. Sometimes she becomes very agitated and harsh with the clients. She has great difficulty setting firm limits on the adolescents' behaviors even when she is sure that it would be helpful to do so. She looks overwhelmed and stressed and has become rather sullen and withdrawn from her colleagues on the staff. During a supervision session, Laura's supervisor inquired about her withdrawal, and Laura immediately launched into a tirade about the negative behaviors of the clients in the program. The supervisor suggested that Laura may want to consider entering personal therapy in order to examine how she is being affected by her clients.

- Is there anything unethical in Laura's actions?
- What could Laura do to determine if her own personal history was impeding her ability to be therapeutic with the adolescents?
- Is the supervisor behaving ethically when he suggests that Laura consider personal therapy? Why or why not?

- Is it ethical for the supervisor to allow Laura to continue to work in a setting where she may be countertherapeutic?
- Are you aware of unmet needs, conflicts, or personal issues could impede your work as an art therapist?

THERAPY FOR ART THERAPISTS

The importance of art therapists' being self-aware cannot be overstated. Related to the issue of self-awareness are the following questions:

1. Should art therapists be required to engage in either personal art therapy or psychotherapy as a component of their educational preparation?
2. Should practicing art therapists be required to engage in personal art therapy or psychotherapy throughout their careers?

Section 1.6 of the American Art Therapy Association Ethics Document partially addresses this point, "Art therapists refrain from engaging in an activity when they know or should know that there is a substantial likelihood that their personal problems will prevent them from performing their work related activities in a competent manner" (p. 4).

This principle indirectly addresses the issue of therapy for art therapy practitioners, but it does not speak to the matter of therapy for students. As graduate students begin to practice art therapy, a host of issues arise that may support the argument for requiring personal art therapy or individual psychotherapy as a component of the educational experience. A number of educators stress that art therapy trainees need to have some experience of what it is like to be a client. They reason that because the art therapist herself is one of the most powerful tools in art therapy, it is imperative that she knows herself well. Personal art therapy can help students explore reasons why they want to become therapists, and it can help them examine their values, needs, and motivations artistically. Personal psychotherapy can also be of tremendous support to students as they enter into the world of graduate study.

Although students come to graduate level training with varied academic and personal histories, they often experience the early stages of their educational process as anxiety provoking and chaotic. Most of the educational programs that are "approved" by the American Art Therapy Association accept a blend of students who come with diverse backgrounds. Some students come directly out of undergraduate school, while others may already hold an advanced degree in a related field. Some beginning students are twenty-one years old, while others are in midlife and beyond. Some students come with extensive human service experience; others have had little or no contact with client populations of any kind. Some have had personal therapy experience, while others have not. However, one common feature is that the beginning is a chaotic experience. Experienced educators are sensitive to the disorientation that new surroundings, new demands, and new experiences can create.

While every graduate art therapy program has its own peculiarities, there are general factors that lead to students experiencing beginner's chaos (Moon, 2003). There is the practical challenge of finding one's way around the campus. Along with negotiating the geographical layout of the campus, students must also negotiate relationships with countless school officials, professors, and peers. This in itself can be overwhelming. Another aspect of the chaos is that the onset of graduate school marks the end of anticipating and planning for future education. Most students have thought long and hard about their choice of careers. Many have had to make tremendous sacrifices in order to enroll in school. Some have waited a long time between their initial decision to enter graduate school and actually beginning the process of graduate education. These circumstances cannot help but lead to some measure of anxiety as the process begins.

New students struggle with their own doubts as they embark on this new phase of their lives. They are plagued by questions such as: Is this really what I want to do? Am I good enough to be successful? What if I don't like the program after I've started it? Sometimes, old unresolved feelings and insecurities are stirred as the graduate school process starts. Finally, add to this mix the profound and deeply moving nature of the art therapy discipline itself, and we begin to get a feel for the new student's internal experience in taking the first steps of the educational journey. In *The Essentials of Art Therapy Training and Practice* (Moon, 2003), the metaphoric image of a glass snowball toy is used to describe the new graduate students' world. "Entry into training to become an arts therapist is a little like shaking the glass, creating a snow storm" (p. 32). The chaos of beginning is important, necessary, and ultimately of vast benefit. It is necessary because entry into graduate level education should be a dramatic transitional period in the student's life. An old way of being is left behind, while a new way is not yet clear. Some fear, excitement, and anxiety naturally accompany this passage experience.

Beginning graduate school and starting a new artwork are analogous. As the artist approaches a blank canvas, the possibilities are endless. Many subtle decisions are made, consciously and unconsciously. What size and shape will the canvas be? Will brushes be used, or a palette knife? Will the image be representational or nonrepresentational? Will the painting be abstracted or photographically rendered? What will the content be? What colors will be used? What forms? What shapes? What will the emotional tone of the work be? There are countless images that could emerge as the painter works. There is a chaotic sea of possibilities. Every question the artist answers and each decision she makes as the work progresses serves to bring order to the chaos so the artistic product can be realized. The gratification and connection to the work an artist experiences comes, in part, from this process of making order from chaotic potential. The involvement in art processes is an enactment of the person's potential to structure the chaos of multiple possibilities. The new graduate student is placed in the same position. The multiple possibilities can seem confusing and overwhelming. Again, the internal questions arise. Is art therapy really a valid field? Which is more important, being an artist or therapist? What client population will I do well with? Will I be good at this? What if I do something wrong and hurt someone? Why am I here?

It is important, particularly in the early stages of graduate art therapy training, to encourage students to involve themselves in the art process itself in an effort to begin to formulate answers to these questions. I remember a student coming into my office for an advisement session, closing the door and bursting into tears as she sat down. She poured out the frustration she felt toward her practicum supervisor who had made an off-handed comment about the student's theoretical approach to art therapy. The supervisor had referred to a group the student was facilitating as the "new-age-magic group." The supervisor's comment provoked the student's insecurity. I let her talk for a few minutes, then shifted the conversation towards a more detached observing-ego position. I suggested we explore possible interpretations of the supervisor's "new-age" comment. The student's frustration dissolved as she identified feelings of doubt and inadequacy regarding her self-image as a professional. At the close of the session, I suggested that she go to the studio and make art. When she arrived for the next supervisory session, she brought a painting with her. The image was a vivid self-portrait. The colors were intense, and the lines were heavily painted, as if she had used a palette knife. Artistically, she had painted out a symbolic map of her educational journey. The painting provided us with a reference point for many conversations during her years in the program. By the time she graduated, she was able to stand up for her philosophy of art therapy and at the same time see the value of her supervisor's views.

Another symbolic aspect of beginner's chaos is the parallel between embarking on the graduate school journey and a client's experience in beginning treatment. "The confusion, pain, anxiety, excitement, and fears generated in the student are a wonderful resource, for they connect the therapist-trainee with the client's experience" (Moon, 1992, p. 29). It is critical to impart to the beginning student how similar his or her fears, hopes, and anxieties are to those of a client entering treatment. This initial phase of training is a precious window into the inner experience of clients.

Many art therapy students find it helpful to involve in personal art therapy or psychotherapy as an adjunct to their learning experience. Corey, Corey, and Callanan (1998) note in relation to the issue of therapy for counselors, "Most of us have areas in our lives that aren't developed and that keep us from being as effective as we can be, both as persons and as counselors. . . . Personal therapy is one way of coming to grips with your dynamics as well as working through unresolved conflicts" (p. 39).

Some graduate art therapy programs require that students engage in personal art therapy or psychotherapy as a component of their educational experience, while other programs only recommend it. Still other programs regard personal therapy as a private matter and avoid the issue altogether. In some places, the availability of art therapists who can provide therapy to students may be limited. In such circumstances, art therapy students may want to seek out therapists from other disciplines who are receptive to art making as a means of expression and who are willing to incorporate the student's artistic expressions into the therapy sessions. It is difficult to require students to engage in personal art therapy as a component of their educational experience because this can be perceived as coercive. Art therapy students and seasoned practitioners derive much more benefit from private art therapy if they enter into it voluntarily, with a willingness to explore and share themselves.

In the best of circumstances, art therapy students and practitioners voluntarily undergo both individual and group art therapy. Individual art therapy provides the opportunity for an in-depth process of creative self-exploration and expression. It offers a venue in which art therapists can safely examine personal creative work in order to heal their own emotional wounds. Involvement in art therapy groups can offer students and practitioners the opportunity to give and receive feedback from others, receive feedback from the images they create in the context of the group, and receive the benefit of the art therapy group leaders' observations. In addition, art therapy groups offer art therapists the advantages that are inherent in collective art making.

Just as there are many reasons why art therapy students may benefit from personal art therapy, there are likewise some cautionary notes. It has long been established that it is counterproductive, or more strongly stated—unethical—for professors and supervisors to provide therapy services to their students. Section 7.2 of the *Ethical Principles for Art Therapists* states, "Art Therapists are aware of their influential position with respect to students and supervisees and they avoid exploiting the trust and dependency of such relationships. Art therapists, therefore, do not engage in a therapeutic relationship with their students or supervisees" (p. 9). There is, of course, a fine line between education and therapy. For example, a person teaching a course about group art therapy methods must facilitate the students' experience of the power of the process. This means providing the experience of art therapy group exercises in the context of a classroom situation. To some degree, there must be a simulation of the actual art therapy group process; however, the educator must keep the focus of the class/session on the learning process of the students. It is the instructor's responsibility to preserve the academic emphasis. Art therapy professors, teachers, and supervisors should not serve as therapists for their students even though quality education in the creative arts therapies frequently has an inherently therapeutic aspect.

Suggested Artistic Tasks

1. Imagine that someone has been hired to write a book about your life. Since you are an expert on the subject, you have been asked to create an image for the cover of the book and to come up with the title. Do a drawing or painting titled, "The Book of My Life."

2. Referring to "The Book of My Life" image from above, write out a table of contents for the book. Title the chapters that would highlight significant events or moments from your life. Reflect on these and ask how these events have influenced your work as an art therapist.

3. Write a poem on the topic, "I need." Read your poem aloud to a colleague or classmate. Discuss the needs you have identified and how these are, or are not, met in your relationships with friends, spouse, or significant others.

4. Reflect upon the needs you identified in the poem above. Do any of these needs get met in your work as an art therapist? If so, how? Think about how your needs influence your work.

5. Create a dance/movement performance on the topic, "I am." Perform the dance for a group of colleagues or classmates. Solicit the audience's reactions to your movements. Discuss how the things you expressed in your performance have influenced your decision to become an art therapist, and why?

6. Create three masks. One mask is to portray you as an "artist." One mask is to portray you as a "professional." One mask is to portray you as a "human being". Think about the similarities and the differences among these images of yourself.

7. Using the masks that you created in the exercise above, write a script that depicts these three different personas meeting one another. Read or enact the drama for an audience of peers. Ask for feedback about how the audience perceives the interaction between these three personas.

FEELINGS: REALISTIC AND UNREALISTIC

The work of art therapists has everything to do with feelings, both of clients and their own. The people who come to art therapists for help are often struggling with their feelings. Within the first few minutes of the art therapy relationship, the client begins to develop feelings toward the art therapist and the art therapist, likewise, has emotional reactions to the client. In addition, the processes of making images and responding to them in the session generate feelings. In psychoanalytic theory, these feelings are described as *transference* and *countertransference.* A client's transference feelings are essentially thought of as unrealistic feelings grounded in the client's past relationships and projected upon, or directed toward, the art therapist. These feelings may be either unrealistically positive or unrealistically negative. An art therapist's *countertransference* is made up of unrealistic feelings projected onto the client. This projective process is considered to be more or less universal in that it occurs in most therapy relationships. In fact, it can be argued that many relationships begin with a certain amount of mutual projection of unrealistic feelings. Certainly, this is the case in many romantic relationships. Peck (1978) describes it this way:

> Just as reality intrudes upon the two-year-old's fantasy of omnipotence so does reality intrude upon the fantastic unity of the couple who have fallen in love. Sooner or later, in response to the problems of daily living, individual will reasserts itself. . . . So both of them, in the privacy of their own hearts, begin to come to the sickening realization that they are not one with the beloved, that the beloved has and will continue to have his or her own desires, tastes, prejudices, and timing different from the other's. . . . At this point they begin either to dissolve the ties of their relationship or to initiate the work of real loving. (p. 88)

It is almost as if people often initially fall in love with images rather than real people. Somewhere along the line the illusionary image fades and what is left is a question: "Is it possible to be in love with a real person rather than an imaginary one?"

In art therapy relationships, there is a similar phenomenon. The client develops feelings for the art therapist that are illusionary, based more on the client's past experiences or what needs exist than on who the art therapist really is. Over time, the illusion fades and, if the therapy is going well, is replaced by a more reality-based relationship.

Figure 13. About Relationships–Colored Markers
Marc Essinger

In my clinical art therapy experience, I have encountered four patterns of projected feelings (*transference*) that recur time and again. They are:

1. *Art Therapist as Omniscient Wizard.* Clients generally come to therapy during periods of crisis in their lives. Such periods of crisis can be the emotional equivalent to white-water rafting (Moon, 1995). Clients may feel out of control or overwhelmed by the situations in which they find themselves. It is natural for clients to want someone in their lives to be all knowing, magical. In fact, this may be crucial for clients to believe in the early stages of the therapy. The notion that the art therapist is undaunted by the overwhelming and powerful forces, the emotional rapids, and unpredictable currents of the client's predicament serves as the foundation of trust and faith in the art therapy process. It is this projection upon the art therapist that allows the client to hope things will improve, to hope there will be some kind of magic in the art therapy process, and to hope he or she will get better.

This projective pattern, however, has its hazards. Being regarded as an omniscient wizard by a client can be gratifying and seductive. After all, many art therapists enter the profession harboring at least a trace of these same unreal feelings/images of themselves. The liability is that art therapists may enjoy this projection and promote such an unreal view. This inevitably robs clients of their own power and capacity to heal themselves and leads to an unhealthy dependence upon the magical, all-seeing art therapist.

2. *Art Therapist as Perfect Role Model.* Because clients enter therapy during periods in which they typically feel badly about themselves, it is no surprise they project upon the art therapist qualities they wish they had themselves. The art therapist is seen as an ideal parent, friend, saint, or lover. In some ways, the art making process lends itself to this projection for artistic self-expression is a "healthy" thing to do and in this sense, art therapists should serve the client as a good role model. However, when this pattern is fully played out, the client cannot imagine the art therapist ever doing anything wrong or having any blemishes. The pitfall here for the art therapist is the reality that no one is perfect; no one can ever live up to any other person's ideal. As Kopp (1972) says, the most important things that each person must learn no one else can teach us. Once we accept this disappointment, we are able to stop depending on the therapist, the guru who turns out to be just another struggling human being. When the client idealizes the art therapist, there is a concurrent process of client self-devaluation that occurs.

3. *Art Therapist as Bottomless Well.* A client occasionally attempts to place the art therapist in the position of being a never-ending supplier of emotional support. The client looks for nourishment and nurturing and behaves as if incapable of self-feeding. It is as if the art therapist is regarded as a bottomless well from which the client can continually drink. The danger here is that the art therapist may get caught up in this giving role, overextending and depleting a personal reservoir of emotional energy while at the same time impeding the client's capacity for self-care.

4. *Art Therapist as Evil Stepmother.* Clients who relate to the art therapist from this projective pattern are unrealistically guarded and defensive. They constantly test the art therapist's sincerity and trustworthiness, and they assume that the art therapist's expressed concern and caring is a sham. These clients have typically had many negative encounters with authority figures in their lives and they are convinced the art therapist is just another evil influence waiting to harm them. Such clients use their behavior and their words as defensive weapons intended to keep the art therapist at a safe distance. The art therapist who is working with this kind of transference relationship often feels demonized, devalued, deskilled, discounted, angry, and overwhelmed. In these instances, there will be no validation of the art therapist's worth coming from the client. Art therapists have to be quite secure in their own identity and purpose in order to help the client successfully work through these unrealistic feelings.

Figure 14. Pedestals–Pastel Chalk
John Roth

The inherent negative potential in the unrealistic projective patterns described above illustrates why art therapists have to be aware of their feelings, needs, and motives. If art therapists are not fully aware of their own emotional issues, they may consciously, or unconsciously, avoid significant therapeutic issues of the client. In service to avoidance, an unspoken collusion between art therapist and client may form in these instances. It must be stressed that projection (*transference*) is a naturally occurring process that cannot be avoided. In fact, projection may be regarded as essential to the formative stages of the relationship between the art therapist and the client. In order to avoid the negative effects of projections and to really understand the significance of clients' visual and verbal expression of feelings, art therapists have to be honest with themselves and open to their clients' images, words, and actions.

The following brief vignettes are offered in order to illustrate the patterns of projection described above. The reader is encouraged to think about ways of responding to each of these situations.

Jennifer

Jennifer initially enters art therapy because, as she said, "I tried a couple other therapists who just sat there and didn't say anything." She is in a difficult marriage and considering divorce, and she is in danger of losing her job because of her unpredictable emotional outbursts. During her second art therapy session, she creates an image of a wounded tiger. She describes making the image as a powerful and cathartic experience for her. She says, "I've never been able to put these feelings into words, but this image says it all." In a later session, Jennifer confides that she tells all of her friends that her art therapist is the best thing that has ever happened in her life. In a recent session, she asks for opinions about whether or not she should pursue a divorce, how she dresses, and what kind of a car she should buy. She says, "I want to spread your magic around in my life."

- If you were Jennifer's therapist, how would you respond to her comment that you are the best thing that has ever happened in her life?
- Would you express your opinions regarding her possible divorce? Appearance? Car?
- How would you react to Jennifer's comment that she wants to spread your magic around?
- What artistic tasks could be helpful in this situation?
- What would you do about Jennifer's apparent idealization of you?

Stephen

Stephen, an adolescent boy, has been in art therapy for several months. He confides to the art therapist that when he gets older, he wants to be "just like you." He says that he admires the art therapist's dedication to art and commitment to helping clients. After this revelation, the therapist notices many instances when Stephen asks for opinions on artistic matters and always implements the therapist's suggestions. He emulates the art therapist in several ways: he copies the therapist's artistic style, he wears clothes similar to the art therapist's, and he mimics some of the art therapist's speech mannerisms. He seems to idolize and treat the art therapist like a hero.

- If you were the art therapist, how would you encourage Stephen to express his feelings artistically in his own style?
- How would you respond to Stephen's idealization of you?
- What dangers might there be in his emulating you?
- What artistic tasks might be helpful to Stephen in this situation?

Andrea

An art therapy client, Andrea, becomes increasingly dependent upon her therapist. She asks to increase the frequency of her sessions from once a week to three times per week. Andrea seeks the art therapist's advice on everything, even trivial matters. She constantly requests input about her artistic expressions and bombards the therapist with endless solicitations for attention. The art therapist becomes increasingly emotionally drained after sessions with her and begins to dread appointments with her.

- If you were Andrea's therapist, how would you handle Andrea's request for more sessions per week?
- Would you set limits on her requests for your advice?
- How would you respond to her attention-seeking behavior?
- How would you handle your feelings regarding her appointments?
- What artistic tasks might be helpful in this situation?

Alec

Alec, a client diagnosed with a personality disorder, has disliked his art therapist from the first session. During an art therapy group session, she angrily said, "You only care about us because you are paid to care." When the art therapist attempts to engage with him regarding the images he makes in the group, he accuses the therapist of being cold and judgmental. Alec never misses an opportunity to devalue the therapist during group sessions, and he often makes sarcastic comments to his peers about the art therapist.

- If you were Alec's therapist, how would you respond to his overt and covert expressions of hostility?
- How would you respond to his comment that you only care because you are paid to?
- What artistic processes might be helpful to Alec in this situation?

Sorting out transference feelings that occur in art therapy relationships can be a complex process. It is helpful for art therapists to utilize artistic tasks to help clarify their thoughts and feelings. The following artistic tasks are intended to help art therapists think about the transference feelings particular clients may have about them.

Suggested Artistic Tasks

1. Review the four patterns of projected feelings (*transference*) discussed above. Create an art piece that symbolizes one of the transference patterns that occurs in your art therapy relationships.

2. Create a symbolic portrait of how you think it feels to be a client in therapy with you.

3. Create an image of your strengths and weaknesses as an art therapist.

4. Create an artistic response piece to a client you think has unrealistic feelings about you.

5. Reflect on how your clients typically see you. Write a poem that describes you through their eyes.

To this point, I have focused primarily on the feelings clients project onto the art therapist; but, as I said earlier, the work of art therapy has everything to do with feelings, both of clients and of therapists. Obviously, art therapists have emotional responses to clients as well, and sometimes these may be projections. Countertransference, that is to say, unrealistic feelings an art therapist projects upon his or her clients, can manifest itself in a host of ways. The intense emotional relationship between art therapist and client can provoke the art therapist's own unresolved emotional issues and stir up inner conflict. This is in some ways an indicator of the art therapist's identification with the client. It is extremely important that art therapists receive ongoing clinical supervision in order to identify countertransference and to sort through the projected feelings. "Ethical practice requires that counselors [art therapists] remain alert to their emotional reactions to their clients, that they attempt to understand such reactions, and that they do not meet their own needs at the expense of the clients' needs" (Corey, Corey, & Callanan, 1998, p. 49).

In my experience, I have encountered six problematic patterns of *countertransference* that art therapists seem to experience. They are:

I've Been There

"I've been there" is a form of countertransference where art therapists are reminded of their own past struggles by the circumstances of clients. This is not to suggest that art therapists' own life experiences should not inform the art therapy process. However, it is not helpful to lose objectivity and to overidentify with the client. Inexperienced art therapists may be particularly prone to this problem. In such situations, art therapists experience difficulty in distinguishing their own feelings from those of the client. They may have the impulse to reveal their own solutions for past personal problems. There is no guarantee such revelations will be helpful to clients. In fact, the imposition of art therapists' solutions to clients' problems is likely to be harmful because this can be disempowering for clients.

When I Was Your Age

This projective pattern is a variation on the *I've Been There* transference described above. This pattern is most often applied to children and adolescent clients by art therapists. In these instances, art therapists are unable to separate their own past experiences and feelings from those of their clients. An example of this occurs when an art therapist suggests solutions to an adolescent's problems, based on the art therapist's own experiences as a teenager. The danger here is twofold: not only does the art therapist disempower the client, but in addition, the adolescent often resents this approach by an adult and thus the art therapist damages the therapeutic alliance as well.

I Am What You Need

In some ways, this form of countertransference is an art therapist's reaction to a client's idealization of the art therapist. Clients who see the art therapist as a perfect role model and who long for easy and quick answers to their problems can encourage this countertransference. The opportunity to be regarded as ideal persons places art therapists in a superior, secure position of authority. As a result of being given authority, some art therapists may think that they really do have the answers for their clients. This can lead to excessive transparency and inappropriate advice-giving on the part of the art therapist. In these instances, the focus of the art therapy has moved from the client's needs and struggles to those of the art therapist.

Tell Me I Am Good Enough

Art therapists, especially inexperienced ones, sometimes have unrealistic expectations of their clients. Some want quick results in order to be reassured of their effectiveness. Just as some clients may form an unrealistic and urgent wish to please their art therapist, so too, some art therapists develop an unreasonable desire to be valued and liked by their clients. These art therapists seek reinforcement and approval from their clients in order to mask self-doubt and poor professional self-image.

Seduction/Flirtation.

The development of unrealistic sexual feelings toward a client is inherently exploitative of the vulnerability and dependence of the client. Given the intense emotional nature of art therapist-client relationships, it is normal to be attracted to certain clients. However, the potential for art therapists' sexual feelings about clients to interfere with the work of therapy is high. This is one significant reason art therapists should involve in personal therapy. It is also an important reason art therapists should seek supervision when they experience difficult feelings toward certain clients.

I Wish You Would Go Away

"I wish you would go away" is a transference pattern that is difficult for many art therapists to discuss. An explicit rejection of the client reveals unpleasant attributes of the art therapist, characteristics that we wish were not there. Often, this pattern emerges in response to very difficult clients, clients who seem too needy, too damaged, too dependent. This happens because the client challenges the art therapists' capacity to help. The art therapist senses that the client needs more than the art therapist has to offer and thus the therapist feels defeated and threatened; hence, the wish for the client to disappear before these insecurities are overtly demonstrated.

The intrinsic negative potential of the countertransference patterns described above provides an argument for the importance of art therapists' awareness of their own feelings, needs, and motives. When art therapists are unaware of their own feelings and conflicts, they can easily miss or unconsciously avoid important therapeutic issues of the client. Yet it is important to stress that art therapists' projections (countertransference) are a naturally occurring phenomena that cannot be avoided. Countertransference feelings need to be understood and worked through in personal therapy or in supervision. In order to avoid the possible negative effects of projections, art therapists have to be committed to self-awareness. To understand the importance of clients' visual and verbal expression of feelings, art therapists need to be open to exploring and reflecting upon their own images, words, and actions, in personal therapy and/or in supervision.

In addition to thinking about countertransference, it can be helpful for art therapists to engage in artistic ways of exploring such feelings.

Suggested Artistic Tasks

1. Review the six problematic patterns of *countertransference* described above. Select one of these patterns to which you feel particularly susceptible. Create an art piece to symbolize this pattern. Discuss with peers the feelings and issues the image raises for you.

2. Create an emotional portrait of how you feel when you are with one of your clients.

3. Create a portrait of a fear you feel in relation to a particular client.

4. Write a poem about your feelings for a particular client.

5. Create an artwork that sums up your reactions to the issues addressed in this section.

CARRYING THE FLAME OR BURNING OUT

It is not easy being an art therapist. The profession carries with it many stresses. Some of the sources of stress come from the nature of the work itself, some come from the environments in which art therapists work, and some come from self-imposed high expectations. It is important for would-be art therapists to know about the perils of the professional path they are choosing. Most art therapy graduate students envision their life's work as being dramatically helpful to others and deeply rewarding to themselves. Indeed, this is one edge of the professional sword. The other edge, however, less often discussed, is that being an art therapist is awfully hard work that demands a deep level of commitment to artistic expression and self-exploration. The processes of working artistically and therapeutically with clients who are suffering inevitably opens up the art therapist's own inner conflicts and feelings. The art therapist cannot help but be profoundly affected both by the client's anguish and by the reopening of the therapist's own emotional wounds.

Farber (1983) cites five client behaviors that are particularly stressful for therapists:

1. Suicidal statements,
2. Aggression and hostility,
3. Premature termination of therapy,
4. Agitated anxiety,
5. Apathy and depression.

In discussions with art therapists, the following issues have been identified as being particularly stressful in their clinical work:

- feeling devalued by professionals from other helping disciplines,
- seeing too many clients for too short a period of time,
- feeling isolated from art therapy colleagues,
- being unable to leave concerns about clients at work,
- feeling as if work issues contaminate personal relationships,
- feeling impotent as a therapist,
- having doubts about the legitimacy and validity of the art therapy profession,
- feeling unappreciated by employers.

In addition to these work-related stresses, many art therapists say that not having enough time to make art in their personal studios is also a major stress factor in their lives. This incapacity often leads to feelings of loss and/or a sense of shame that they are not enough of a "real" artist.

Members of all helping professions face situations that lead either to *carrying the flame* or *burning out* at some point in their careers. When art therapists are able to carry the flame, they provide their clients with inspiration through their dedication to making art, expressing feelings, and healthy relationships. When art therapists are burned out, they have difficulty being of help to their clients and may in fact be harmful. It is critical that art therapy students and seasoned practitioners maintain a deep commitment to their own well-being. It is essential that art therapists understand they are not the "bottomless well" discussed earlier in this chapter. Sooner or later the well runs dry when art therapists give without receiving and replenishing themselves.

There are three central aspects of a commitment to well-being. First, art therapists committed to well-being pay close attention to quality in their personal lives. It is important to meet emotional, relational, social, and spiritual needs outside of the work environment. Art therapists can get their needs met through a network of family, friends, and rewarding activities. A "red flag" should go up in art therapists' minds whenever they find they are depending too heavily upon relationships in the work place to meet these needs.

Second, art therapists committed to well-being find ways to stay active artistically. It is important for there to be artistic activity separate and distinct from artwork created in the clinical setting. Personal art making protects art therapists from the potentially overwhelming pain of vicarious traumatization. Art therapists working with people who are suffering from painful emotional and mental disturbances come into intimate contact with people who have been physically, emotionally, or sexually abused. They hear incredibly painful and horrific stories during their careers. They see countless images of brokenness, betrayal, intrusion, and rage-filled anguish. The collective weight of these images and their accompanying stories can be staggering. Seeing and hearing the effects of trauma day in and day out is traumatic in itself. Art therapists cannot avoid being moved by their clients' expressions. In fact, when therapists are no longer affected by clients' expressions of suffering, this is an indicator of burnout. Art therapists can neither shield themselves from their own feelings nor be constantly overwhelmed and traumatized by their clients if they are to be effective as therapists. One of the most effective ways for art therapists to protect themselves from vicarious traumatization is through making their own art. Making art provides a healthy, practical, and authentic mechanism for art therapists to handle the intense feelings that accompany clinical work.

Figure 15. Passing the Torch–Collage/Mixed Media
Pauline Sawyer

Third, it is important for art therapists committed to well-being to renew themselves professionally. This means staying current with new developments in the field and continuing to broaden one's information base. New research findings and an ever-expanding knowledge base in art therapy theory and practice demand ongoing education. Continuing education activity can take many forms, including professional research, disciplined reading of art therapy journals and texts, exploring the literature of related professions, attending relevant workshops and seminars, and participating in local and national art therapy conferences.

Learning never ends; new clients present new tests of an art therapist's skills and knowledge. "To assume that our skills never deteriorate or that we know everything we need to know upon graduation is naïve. If we rarely or never seek continuing education, how are we to justify this lack of initiative?" (Corey, Corey, & Callanan, 1998, p. 282).
Art therapists have an ethical responsibility to keep current with the literature in the field.

THE ARTIST–THERAPIST: ETHICAL DIMENSIONS

From the earliest days of art therapy in the United States, and throughout the history of the American Art Therapy Association, the question, "Am I an artist, or a therapist?" has rumbled around in the hearts and minds of art therapists. This question has been debated in the literature of the profession and at annual national conferences (Austin, 1976; Shoemaker & Gonick-Barris, 1976; Cohen, Ault, Jones, Levick, & Ulman, 1980; Gannt & Whitman, 1980; Feen-Calligan & Sands-Goldstein, 1996; Gorelick, 1989; Jones, 1999; Lachman-Chapin, 1983; McNiff, 1982, 1986; Robbins, 1982, 1988; Rosenburg, Ault, Free, Gilbert, Joseph, Landgarten, & McNiff, 1983; Wadeson, Landgarten, McNiff, & Levy, 1977; Wadeson, Junge, Kapitan, & Vick, 1999; Wolf, 1990).

Am I an artist or a therapist? Throughout their careers, art therapists wrestle with this primary question of professional identity. It is an essential ethical question for it gets at the very heart of the discipline. The question directly addresses where art therapy came from, and the many responses to the question define who art therapists are, both as individual practitioners and as a professional community.

Some argue that it may be ethically imperative for art therapists to hold a solid sense of self as art makers. This does not mean that art therapists have to exhibit their work, or participate in juried competitions. But it does imply that art therapists actively involve with artistic materials and use their creative abilities in the service of self-expression. For a period of time in our collective history, the artistic aspect of art therapists' disciplinary character received little attention in our literature. In an effort to establish professional status among other therapeutic disciplines, emphasis was placed instead on describing and promoting art therapy as a form of psychotherapy. Beginning in the 1990s this trend was countered by renewed interest in the artistic aspects of the collective professional persona. This has served to recenter the corporate identity of art therapy.

In relation to ethics, the artist/therapist identity question may be a matter of professional survival. This is a difficult period for all clinical disciplines in mental and physical health care. Many social workers, psychologists, counselors, and music therapists have left their fields due to the unfavorable climate surrounding health care in America. Art therapy colleagues and graduate students sometimes wonder aloud if they made the right decision when they chose the field of art therapy. Having a solid sense of self as an artist therapist helps art therapists to cope with the inevitable doubts that arise during their careers.

Many art therapists will, from time to time, have misgivings about their profession. Professional insecurities are normal in most disciplines. Some art therapists suggest that one way to inoculate against these insecurities is to establish a solid foundation in art making. They reason that making art is good for people, and the processes and the products of art therapy can provide art therapists with an emotional anchor in the midst of the tumultuous seas of professional life. Jones (1999) suggests that the times when art therapists begin to feel the dullness associated with being "burned out" are times when they have stayed away from their own studio for too long. Jones asserts that he could not be an art therapist without making art. Jones (in Feen-Calligan & Sands-Goldstein, 1996) says that his songs, poems, and paintings are as essential to his survival as eating and sleeping. This may not hold true for all art therapists, but it has been the case for many.

SUMMARY

Art therapists run the risk of having their personal emotional issues contaminate therapy with clients if they do not work at their own self-exploration and self-expression. One natural way for art therapists to do this is through ongoing artistic activity. Knowing yourself well is a crucial ingredient in the foundation upon which all therapeutic work is built. Art therapists who avoid examining their own fears, anxieties, resistances, conflicts, and needs are in danger of behaving in an unethical manner toward their clients. Harm can come to clients from an art therapist's lack of self-awareness. This is a serious ethical concern.

Art therapists have no right to ask their clients to do anything that they have not done themselves (Moon, 1995). Corey, Corey, and Callanan (1998) also support this position by stating, ". . . therapists are unable to take clients on any journey that they have not been on—ongoing self-exploration is critical" (p. 64). This is why it is so important that art therapy students and practitioners involve in both personal therapy and clinical supervision. Art therapists must go on their own artistic and emotional journey if they are to be of genuine aid to their clients.

There is a possibility for unethical conduct toward clients when therapists mishandle their own feelings. Art therapists suffering from burnout are in peril of behaving unethically. Burned-out clinicians typically lack enthusiasm and commitment to work and may go through their daily routines in a numb and mechanical fashion. It is nearly impossible to imagine a burned out art therapist being capable of providing quality care to her or his clients.

Commitment to self-exploration, self-expression, personal therapy, clinical supervision, continuing education, and ongoing artistic activity cannot guarantee that art therapists will always behave ethically. There is no simple road map to self-awareness, self-monitoring, artistic authenticity and ethical practice. However, these are the elements that will enable art therapists to face the formidable task of carrying the flame throughout their professional careers.

Becoming an art therapist involves a nearly constant refrain of questions: Who am I? What am I doing? How is this work affecting me? Developing a professional role involves honest self-assessment in regards to personal strengths and vulnerabilities. In addition to thinking about these areas of inquiry, it is important for art therapists to engage in artistic self-exploration. The following artistic tasks may be helpful to this process of inquiry.

Suggested Artistic Tasks

1. Create a drawing on the theme of why you want to be an art therapist. Think about your motivations for this kind of work. Share your drawing with a colleague or supervisor. Tell the story of how you first became interested in becoming an art therapist.

2. Create a collage image of some of the hopes and fears you have about being an art therapist. Discuss the collage and the feelings it raises with a colleague or supervisor.

3. In an art therapy class or supervision group, ask each participant to create symbolic images of the positive personal traits of each group member in relation to their work as art therapists. Share and discuss these with one another.

4. In an art therapy class or supervision group, ask each participant to create a symbolic image of his/her own personal traits that are potentially prob-

lematic in relation to their work as art therapists. Share and discuss these with one another.

5. In an art therapy class or supervision group, ask each participant to draw four concentric circles. The outermost circle is to represent superficial relating and the innermost circle is to represent intimate relating. Ask participants to fill in the circles with colors, lines, and shapes to symbolize how comfortable they are with each level of relating. Discuss these images in relation to the concept of transparency in art therapist–client relationships.

6. Create an artwork using the question, "What does it mean to heal?" as the theme of the work. You may make a painting, a sculpture, dramatic enactment, poem, dance, music, etc. Share the art piece with others. Discuss.

7. Form small groups of two to four participants. Have each small group create a performance art enactment in response to the theme, "Being an Art Therapist." Enactments may include visual images, poetry, music, dance/movement, dialogue, or sound.

Chapter VI

ART THERAPY SUPERVISION

Supervision is a fundamental aspect of training to become an art therapist. It is also an important way experienced practitioners maintain competencies required to adequately execute their professional responsibilities. "Supervision in the training and continuing education of art therapists is considered to be essential to professionalism" (Malchiodi & Riley, 1996, p. 21). No art therapist ever knows all there is to know about art therapy and no individual therapist can ever have sufficient skills and range of experience to treat every type of client. Supervision entails helping art therapists understand their clients, develop their capabilities to self-reflect, and deepen their understanding of art therapy theories and practical applications. The ultimate goal of art therapy supervision is the integration of these different areas of learning, leading to the development and enhancement of skillful, professional art therapists. This is why receiving appropriate clinical supervision is so important to both students and seasoned professionals alike.

The word *supervision* is derived from the Latin *super* (over) and *videre* (to watch, to see). Neufeldt (1988) defines supervision as the action, process, or occupation of supervising; a critical watching and directing (as of activities or a course of action)

(p. 1345). A supervisor is one who oversees, who watches over the work of another and assumes a measure of responsibility for the quality of the work. Contained within these definitions of supervision and supervisor are three implicit and distinct functions of art therapy supervision: (1) administrative, (2) educational, and (3) role modeling.

The administrative function of supervision refers to the supervisor's responsibility to monitor tasks performed by the supervisee in regards to qualitative and quantitative acceptability.

The educational function of supervision refers to the supervisor's duty to structure and promote the development of the supervisee's professional knowledge and growth through reflection upon clinical art therapy experiences. The supervisor works to establish an environment in which the super-visee is able to benefit from the wisdom, experience, and knowledge of the supervisor.

The role-modeling function of supervision refers to the responsibility of the supervisor to serve as a positive professional example for the supervisee. As role models, supervisors seek to establish a supportive and expressive supervisory milieu in order to nurture the supervisees' professional compe-tency, identity, and morale. At the same time, supervisors model art therapy professionalism and that in turn fosters self-worth in their supervisees.

MENTOR MODEL OF SUPERVISION

The administrative, educational, and role modeling functions of supervi-sory relationships are complementary. A *mentor model* of supervision is creat-ed when the administrative, educational, and role modeling functions are properly attended to. The mentor model of supervision involves the estab-lishment of a supportive and tolerant relationship in which the mentor is regarded as a significant source of support, wisdom, and expertise for the supervisee. The mentor is equally dedicated to passing on and receiving information to and from the supervisee. Paradoxically, the mentor/supervi-sor is an authority on art therapy that oversees the progress of the supervisee, while simultaneously maintaining an attitude of mutuality with the super-visee. The mentor has technical knowledge, experience, and the capacity to contain and make sense of the swirling emotional currents and cognitive quandaries of the supervisee. Supervision may be thought of as a metaphor-ic journey in which the mentor serves the supervisee as both a guide and a fellow traveler. The mission of the mentor is an attempt to free the supervisee from the supervisor. "The guru [supervisor] instructs the pilgrims [super-visees] in the tradition of breaking with tradition, in losing themselves so that they may find themselves" (Kopp, 1976, p.19).

In many ways, the mentor serves the supervisee as an observing ego. Carrigan (1993) notes, "It [supervision] is an intensive personal relationship, yet communication between the two parties must remain on a supervisory level which sometimes results in an unequal relationship that allocates most of the responsibilities and power to the supervisor, while the intern may be in danger of being disempowered" (p. 134). In the supervisory relationship, it is the supervisee's responsibility to report on experiences in the clinical context, to have feelings toward clients, and to have ideas about the course the art therapy should take. It is the mentor's responsibility to "be with" (Moustakas, 1995, pp. 84-85) the supervisee, to reflect and sort through the meanings of the supervisee's experiences.

In many ways, a mentor/supervisor's role is one of being a concerned caretaker. Boszormenyi-Nagy and Krasner (1986) discuss the therapist's role as analogous to the supervisor's role with supervisees. "The therapist-client relationship falls short of the symmetry of friendship, for example. Therapy may provide moments of genuine meeting between two people. Still, the degree of investment and the level of expectations between them are always uneven"(p. 395). Mentors display a dispassionate, objective, and yet warmly accepting attitude toward supervisees who are immersed in the multiplicity of communications they receive from their clients' images, actions, and words. Art therapy supervisees sometimes find themselves experiencing equal measures of awe, inspiration, and emotional engulfment. Sometimes art therapists feel overwhelmed by their clients' images, verbalizations, and behaviors. In such times, supervisees need the detached support and guidance of the mentor in order to sort through their reactions to clients.

Art therapists are exposed to the intense anguish, rage, loneliness, sexuality, and deep longings of their clients. Novice and seasoned art therapists alike can be overwhelmed by their encounters with such powerful forces. The mentor's observing ego provides a buffer that aids the supervisee in developing a neutral and objective view of these intense subjective experiences. In this way, the mentor creates a "holding environment" (Winnicott, 1960, pp. 140-152) for the supervisee and provides the emotional security so essential to the art therapy supervisee's professional growth.

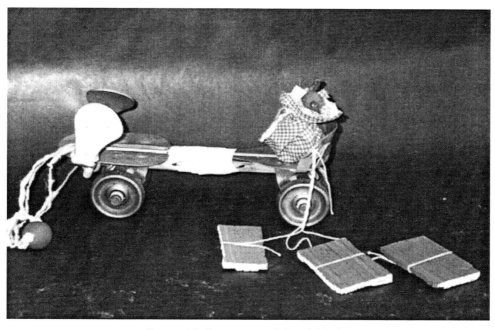

Figure 16. Supervision–Mixed Media
Pauline Sawyer

Another task of the mentor supervisor, especially in regards to novice art therapists, is to provide empathic confrontation and consolation to supervisees when clinical mistakes are made. An area often requiring empathic confrontation with novice art therapists relates to the supervisees' naive identity as a healer. While such a self-view is in some ways noble, it is nonetheless unrealistic. Therapists are not omnipotent and they cannot heal their clients. Ultimately, art therapy clients are responsible for their own healing and there is almost nothing therapists can do to make their clients get better. Art therapy clients do regress. Sometimes clients prematurely terminate therapy. Occasionally, an art therapist's client commits suicide. These events dramatically remind art therapists of just who is in charge of the therapy. Supervisees who long to regard themselves as healers must rework such an unrealistic self-view in supervision or they inevitably become the source of suffering.

> The mentor stands at the side of the road in these times, softly Assuring the heroic student that they have never healed anyone and never will heal anyone. The essential paradox is that the mentor longs to heal the pain of the patient and the pain of the intern, but knows that all he can do is encourage both to use the creative healing power of the art process. (Moon, 1992, p. 45)

RESPONSIVE ART MAKING IN SUPERVISION

One of the most important qualities of the mentor–supervisee relationship is the role modeling function of the mentor. The art therapy supervisor can provide many helpful messages and therapeutic strategies to the supervisee through unspoken demonstration, through being. In their function as role models, art therapy mentors sometimes engage in responsive art making in supervision. Responsive art making is a process that involves the art therapy mentor and supervisee in creating artworks in reaction to the images, ideas, or feelings that are the subject of supervision. This process can be helpful in supervisory relationships in three ways. First, responsive art making can help both mentor and supervisee establish empathy with one another. Second, the process of responsive art making can provide an expressive outlet for feelings often stirred up in the supervisory context. Third, responsive art making can serve as a starting place for dialogue between the mentor and the supervisee.

The mentor's artistic role modeling in the supervisory session serves the supervisee by placing emphasis on art making as the foundation upon which the supervisory relationship, and indeed the entire discipline, is built. As

Wadeson (1986) observed, "the substance of art therapy itself (art-making in relationship to another) furnishes its own means of understanding" (p. 88). Responsive art making can become the meeting place of the supervisor and the supervisee. The process of making art in reaction to one another advances and deepens the supervision by creating images of the relationship. These images become grist for the supervisory mill. By responding to supervisees through art processes, mentors demonstrate commitment to, and reliance upon, the artistic nature of the art therapy discipline. This is an invaluable gift to the supervisee.

ETHICAL ISSUES FOR ART THERAPY SUPERVISORS

Art therapy supervision, while sharing many of the characteristics of supervision in other helping professions, has some significant differences because of the artistic nature of the discipline. Among the similarities are the attention given to general treatment approaches and philosophies, client welfare, and professional ethical concerns. However, at the heart of art therapy is the art-making process. Malchiodi and Riley (1996) note there are four unique aspects of art therapy supervision deeply affected by the art element of art therapy. "These are characteristics that supervisors may need to keep in mind, recalling some of their own struggles and realizing that there may be many styles of learning among their supervisees" (Malchiodi & Riley, p. 26). These four aspects are:

1. Professional identity
2. Interpersonal skills
3. Personal philosophy
4. The heterogeneous quality of art therapy students

The artistic elements in art therapy affect each of these four areas in ways supervisors in verbal therapy modalities do not have to contend with.

Art therapists who take on the tasks of educating and supervising future art therapists ought to be aware of the heavy ethical burden they bear. Not only are they responsible to their students and supervisees, but also indirectly to all of the clients their students will interact with in the future. It is of great importance that art therapy educators and supervisors teach their students using current and scholarly information that fosters the professional growth of students and supervisees. This means that art therapy educators, supervisors, and researchers are obliged to maintain standards of scholarship and to present information in an accurate manner.

Like in any other authority relationships, the teacher–student, and supervisor–supervisee relationships involve parties of unequal power. Educators and supervisors must be sensitive to the influential roles they hold with respect to students and supervisees in order to avoid exploitation of the trust and dependency of such persons. It is inappropriate and unethical for art therapy educators or supervisors to engage in a therapeutic relationship with their students or supervisees.

Art therapy educators and supervisors are responsible for the quality of their students' and supervisees' clinical work. Therefore, it is important for art therapists to ensure that students, or supervisees provide, or present themselves as competent to provide, only those art therapy services that are within the scope of their education, training, and level of experience. It is also imperative that art therapy educators and supervisors maintain the quality of their supervisory skills and obtain consultation or supervision for their work whenever appropriate.

PROFESSIONAL IDENTITY

As noted in the prior chapter, throughout the history of art therapy, art therapists have had to wrestle with the question: Am I an artist or a therapist? This core professional identity question can be problematic for supervisees. Professional identity questions can negatively influence art therapists' work with their clients. "Thus supervision may include a focus on helping trainees produce clear definitions of the role that art plays within their work as art therapists, in addition to identifying a theoretical framework for therapeutic work with clients" (Malchiodi & Riley, 1996, p. 26).

INTERPERSONAL SKILLS

Art therapists sometimes find themselves having to explain and defend their discipline to other health professions. Because art therapy work with clients is not focused exclusively on verbal communications, art therapists need to develop interpersonal communications skills in order to translate art therapy occurrences into therapeutic concepts understandable to other disciplines. Art therapy supervisors can be especially helpful to supervisees in developing strategies for self-definition and presentation.

PERSONAL PHILOSOPHY

As the professional art therapy community developed, a philosophic debate has existed throughout the history of the discipline (Wadeson, Landgarten, McNiff, Free, & Levy, 1976). The crux of this debate is focused on a continuum of philosophic approaches to art therapy that has sometimes been described in terms of polarities: *art as therapy versus art psychotherapy.* Lusebrink (1990) writes, "At one end of the art therapy spectrum is the use of visual media with focus on the product and artistic aspects. At the other end is emphasis on process, verbal free association to the images rendered and insight"(p.10). Wadeson (1980) states, "The field [art therapy] is a broad one with much variety among the approaches of different practitioners. Some place emphasis on the art, some on the therapy. Some art therapists consider themselves psychotherapists using art expression as a therapeutic modality" (p. xi). Many art therapists integrate their art therapy clinical work with theoretical perspectives such those developed by Jung, Freud, Adler, Existentialists, Object Relations theorists, and Studio Artists. Each of these philosophic and theoretical approaches affect, and are affected by, the artistic elements of art therapy. Art therapy supervisors and supervisees may place themselves anywhere along this philosophic continuum. Clearly, the philosophic approach and theoretical perspective of supervisors profoundly impacts their supervisory style. Malchiodi and Riley (1996) suggest it is important for supervisees to find a compatible supervisor in order for the supervision to be successful (p. 26). However, there may also be some benefit in being supervised by an art therapist who embraces a theoretical model different from the supervisee.

THE HETEROGENEOUS QUALITY OF ART THERAPY STUDENTS

Art therapy supervisees come with varied backgrounds. Most have their first experience of supervision while in graduate school. Occasionally, supervisees will have had extensive human service experience; others may have had little contact with client populations outside of their practica and internships during training. Some beginning art therapists are in their early twenties, while others may be in midlife or beyond. Many art therapy students, supervisees, and supervisors enter the field from arts backgrounds in which learning has occurred in the art studio in addition to traditional academic experiences. Hence, they may expect art making will be an essential aspect of the supervision experience.

Each of the four topics in art therapy supervision: professional identity, interpersonal skills, personal philosophy, and the heterogeneous quality of art therapy supervisees are influenced by the art-making process (Malchiodi & Riley, 1996). Art therapy supervisors and supervisees are deeply affected by the art of their clients, and by their own images that emerge from these contexts. The heart and soul of art therapy and art therapy supervision involve making art and artistic expression. The role making art plays in art therapists' philosophy has a profound effect on how they practice, and in turn, how they supervise others.

RIGHTS OF THE SUPERVISEE AND THE OBLIGATIONS OF THE MENTOR/SUPERVISOR

The relationship between the art therapy supervisor and the supervisee is vital to the development of high quality art therapists. Important areas for ethical consideration in art therapy supervision are the rights of the supervisee and the obligations of the mentor/supervisor. Tyler and Tyler (1997) suggest a "bill of rights" for supervisees which include the supervisees right to:

- A supervisory session free from interruptions and distractions
- Dull awareness of the supervisors' approach to supervision
- Confidentiality with regard to supervisee's disclosure as well as that of clients, except as mandated by law
- continual access to any records maintained during the supervisory relationship
- provide feedback to supervisors concerning the helpfulness of supervision
- seek consultation from other professionals as necessary

Art therapy supervisors have a responsibility to provide the administrative, educational, and role-modeling functions of supervision in order to enable supervisees to deliver competent and ethical art therapy services. In Section 7 of the Ethics Document of the American Art Therapy Association, Responsibility to Students and Supervisees can be found the following:

Art therapists instruct their students using accurate, current, and scholarly information and will foster the professional growth of students and advisees.
7.1 Art therapists as teachers, supervisors and researchers maintain high standards of scholarship and present accurate information.

Art therapists are aware of their influential position with respect to students and supervisees, and they avoid exploiting the trust and dependency of such persons. Art therapists, therefore, shall not engage in a therapeutic relationship with their students or supervisees.

Art therapists take reasonable steps to ensure that students, employees or supervisees to perform or present themselves as competent to perform professional services beyond their education, training, and level of experience.

Art therapists who act as supervisors are responsible for maintaining the quality of their supervision skills and obtain consultation or supervision for their work as supervisors whenever appropriate.

7.5 Art therapists do not require students or supervisees to disclose personal information in course- or program-related activities, either orally or in writing, regarding sexual history, history of abuse and neglect, psychological treatment, and relationships with parents, peers, spouses, or significant others, except when (1) the program or training facility has clearly identified this requirement in its admissions and program materials or (2) the information is necessary to evaluate or obtain assistance for students whose personal problems could reasonably be judged to be preventing them from performing their training or professional related activities in a competent manner or whose personal problems could reasonably be judged to pose a threat to the student or others. (p. 9)

Art therapy supervisors are ethically and legally responsible for the actions of their supervisees. Therefore, supervisors must be aware of supervisees' caseloads and the progress of supervisees' art therapy clients.

Art therapy supervisees have a right to be informed of the objectives of the supervision process. Art therapy supervisors must inform supervisees of the objectives of supervision and how the supervisor will assess progress. Additionally, art therapy supervisors must inform supervisees of their evaluation procedures and criteria they will employ during supervision. It is important to note supervisees have legal and ethical rights to timely evaluation and feedback, both in the form of verbal communication and written documentation from supervisors.

As noted earlier in this chapter, art therapy supervisors oversee the progress of the supervisee and yet attempt to maintain an attitude of mutuality with the supervisee. Still, it is important to acknowledge the participants in supervisory relationships do not hold equal power. Art therapy supervisors hold influence over their supervisees because they function in multiple roles as overseers, evaluators, teachers, and advisors. The focus of supervision is on the professional development of the supervisee and in many ways, the supervisory relationship is like a therapy relationship. There is potential for harm to both the supervisee and the supervisee's clients if the supervisor is negligent or abusive in any aspect of his or her role.

Art therapy supervisors could be considered negligent if they did not strive to keep abreast of new research findings and this resulted in harm to a supervisee's client. Another form of negligence on the part of an art therapy supervisor could be seen in situations in which a supervisor failed to offer appropriate clinical direction to a supervisee. Art therapy supervisors could be considered abusive if they exerted undue control over their supervisees, disregarded or devalued supervisees' opinions, or in other ways mistreated supervisees. There is the possibility of damage to both the art therapy supervisee and the supervisee's clients when an art therapy supervisor is negligent or abusive in any aspect of their supervisory role.

LEGAL CONSIDERATIONS FOR ART THERAPY SUPERVISORS

There are three primary legal principles that apply to art therapy supervisory relationships: informed consent, confidentiality and its limits, and liability (Corey, Corey, & Callanan, 1998, p. 294). Art therapy supervisors must make sure their supervisees inform clients they are being supervised. Art therapy supervisees must inform their clients that they routinely meet with a supervisor to review and discuss clients' case materials (McCathy, Sugden, Koker, Lamendola, Mauer, & Renninger 1995).

Art therapy supervisors have a legal responsibility to maintain the confidentiality of client communications. There are some exceptions to this, such as when a supervisor thinks a client is dangerous to self or others. Supervisors are required to make sure supervisees inform their clients about the limits of confidentiality.

Finally, art therapy supervisors bear ultimate legal responsibility for the welfare of clients who are in the care of art therapy supervisees. Art therapy supervisors are liable for the actions of their supervisees. There are two forms of this liability, direct and vicarious. Art therapy supervisors are directly liable if they are negligent in the supervision of their supervisees, if they give incorrect advice to their supervisees, or if they give oversight to supervisees in areas they are not competent to oversee. Vicarious liability refers to responsibilities art therapy supervisors have because of inadequate or inappropriate actions of their art therapy supervisees.

Art therapy supervisors are the gatekeepers of the profession and as such, they must seek to protect the welfare of clients, supervisees, students, the public, and the profession at large.

SUPERVISION AND THE STRUGGLING ART THERAPIST

In Chapter V of this text, the artistic, professional, and human qualities of art therapy students and practitioners are discussed. Because of their human-ness, art therapists are subject to a range of factors that can have a negative impact upon their capacity to behave ethically as professionals. The list of factors includes emotional instability, alcohol and/or drug abuse, physical infirmity, and professional "burnout." These factors are sometimes the focus of art therapy supervision. Art therapy supervisees struggling with one or more of these factors are sometimes not able to perform their professional responsibilities adequately. The following are some of the characteristics associated with art therapists who are struggling with difficult personal and professional issues.

- Confused sense of professional identity
- A sense of disconnection from other art therapists and colleagues
- Emotional problems and/or instability
- Substance abuse
- Unsatisfying personal relationships
- Social isolation
- Lack of energy and enthusiasm related to one's work

There are many reasons why art therapy students and practitioners may become impaired. The multiple demands placed on graduate students, for instance, often lead to feeling overwhelmed. In an effort to keep up with the pace of graduate study, some students withdraw from other aspects of their lives which have been meaningful, such as participation in social groups or involvement in their own personal art making. Withdrawal from peers leads to a sense of isolation that can intensify feelings of being overwhelmed and inadequate.

Students from graduate art therapy programs often lament; "I haven't had time to make any art since I got into school." This is a serious problem because it can become an ingrained pattern that is undermining to the pro-fessional identity of art therapists. Jones (1999) said, "Imagine a music thera-pist who never hums or a movement therapist who never moves. It is the same for art therapists, we have to make art to survive." This is not to sug-gest that art therapists should necessarily feel compelled to make art at the same quality or production level as the professional artist, but it is important to maintain an ongoing engagement with art materials and processes.

An art therapy student once portrayed herself as a blindfolded circus entertainer juggling flaming torches and several different hats while attempting to walk across a tightrope. It is the nature of most art therapy graduate students to want to succeed academically. However, it is important that students recognize their humanness and allow time for activities other than study in order to replenish themselves. Perhaps, in the long run, a student who maintains a "B" average and also attends to personal life is more able to be a successful therapist than an "A" student who is unduly narrow in focus.

Of course, students are not the only ones under pressure. There is no magic vaccine given inoculating art therapists from the negative effects of stress when they complete graduate school and enter the professional world. Just as there are tremendous demands upon an art therapy student's time when in school, so too there are enormous expectations for art therapists in the workplace. Caseloads are often high and frequently there are many extraneous job demands placed on art therapists by employers. The pressures of contemporary healthcare create an environment in many institutions and agencies where the employees are seldom praised for good work but are often criticized for mistakes. Added to work stresses are the personal-life responsibilities of husbands, wives, children, relationships with significant others, mortgages, car payments, etc. It is easy to understand how art therapists can become over-stressed. It is also easy to see how novice art therapists begin to develop a sense of isolation in the workplace. No longer having the luxury of daily contact with art therapy peers, as they did in graduate school, the young therapist, and seasoned practitioner as well, can develop feelings of professional estrangement.

In response to the pressures of graduate school and the demands of work, one of the first activities often eliminated in an art therapist's life is personal art making. Making art takes time. Frequently students and professionals feel they do not have the time to give to studio work because other tasks must be undertaken. This is a serious problem in direct conflict with the professional identity of art therapists.

In order to help prevent the difficulties noted above, art therapy supervisors and training programs often include ongoing artistic activity as a core element in supervision and coursework and students are sometimes encouraged to seek personal therapy. It is also helpful when art therapy faculty members and art therapy supervisors provide a living example by modeling a healthy lifestyle in which their personal needs are met outside of the work context. These aspects of supervision serve supervisees by helping to establish patterns of behavior anchoring professional identity and ethical practice in art making, personal exploration, and personal enrichment experiences. It is ethically imperative that art therapy supervisors and training program faculty help students by modeling strategies for avoiding professional burnout and other forms of professional incapacity.

Art therapy supervisors can help supervisees monitor their professional behavior, especially in regard to the number of client contact hours they

Figure 17. Remembering a Client's Humanness–Colored Markers
Marc Essinger

have per week and the time and attention devoted to their own art making and other personal enrichment activities. When art therapists find themselves in a pattern of escalating client contact and diminishing personal art making and enrichment activities they may be at risk for burnout and/or other manifestations of impairment.

What can art therapy supervisors do to help supervisees promote their own well-being? Perhaps the most fundamental way to maintain energy and vigor as an art therapist and as a human being is to acknowledge the need to replenish. Art therapists are "professional caregivers" and they must realize their capacity to give out is in direct relationship to their capacity to take in. It is essential for supervisors to help art therapists to develop a plan of action in relation to personal replenishment.

An example: When a female art therapist's children were young and required intensive attention, the everyday demands of life were many. The art therapist and her spouse were both working full-time jobs. At one point during that time, the art therapist felt as if she was "running on empty." During a supervision session, she lamented that she felt she was losing touch with herself and her art making. The art therapy supervisor suggested scheduling some time each week to replenish by working in her studio. The art therapist negotiated a plan with her husband. Saturday nights, as soon as the kids went to bed, were to be her studio time. As much as she could, the art therapist committed to not letting anything get in the way of her studio time. As the schedule became routine, the art therapist experienced a positive sense of renewal in both professional and personal aspects of her life. This did not happen accidentally; it required negotiation, planning, commitment, and follow-through.

At various times throughout their careers, art therapists may naturally experience episodic discontent regarding their professional identity. They may, for brief periods, become inactive in the studio and feel a sense of isolation from other art therapists. At times, they may feel dissatisfied with personal relationships. They may experience occasional bouts of social isolation. They may even feel unenthusiastic about their work as art therapists. Such times should serve the art therapist as a "red flag," warning them trouble may be brewing. Of course, these episodic phenomena are to be expected and do not necessarily lead to impairment or unethical behavior on the part of the art therapist. However, when these phenomena are experienced together, or when any of them become chronic, the potential for difficulty is heightened. It is important for art therapists to be vigilant in relation to these characteristics, and to be honest in self-appraisal. There is the potential for unethical behavior when art therapists disregard these warning signals.

The topic of the struggling art therapist raises difficult ethical questions:

1. Can art therapists who are experiencing personal emotional turmoil be therapeutically effective with clients who are experiencing emotional pain?
2. Can burned-out art therapists do harm to their clients?
3. Can an art therapist who abuses alcohol be of help to clients?
4. What damage could an art therapist who "gives too much" do to a client?
5. Why is it important for art therapists to stay in close contact with other art therapists?
6. Is it possible for an art therapist to have an unhappy personal life and still be a good therapist?

There are no easy answers to these questions. Art therapy supervision is one place where art therapists can work to resolve these and other challenges to their personal and professional well-being. Ongoing personal artistic involvement, continuing education, personal therapy, and clinical supervision lead to art therapists who are able to stay focused on providing ethical clinical services to their clients.

CHAPTER SUMMARY

Art therapy supervisory relationships are complicated. Supervisory relationships are similar to therapy relationships; however, they clearly must stay within the confines of the administrative, educational, and role-modeling functions of supervision. The primary goals of supervision are to enhance the supervisee's professionalism, increase self-awareness, and foster the development of art therapy skills.

It is imperative that art therapy supervisors be experienced art therapists who have received special training in supervision. Art therapy supervision demands a unique set of skills beyond clinical expertise and educational understanding. Today's art therapy supervisors are charged with the weighty responsibilities of supporting, overseeing, and nurturing future generations of art therapists. At the same time, art therapy supervisors are obligated to guard the welfare of clients, supervisees, students, the public, and the profession at large.

Art therapists know that growth and learning happens during the art process. Enhancing art therapists' professionalism and expertise through supervision necessarily involves honest self-assessment. A great deal of self-understanding can occur through carefully selected artistic tasks. In addition to thinking about supervisory issues, art therapy supervisors and supervisees need to engage in artistic self-exploration.

Suggested Artistic Activities

1. Create an image of the "ideal supervisor." Identify the characteristics you would most want in a clinical supervisor. Discuss your image and the associated characteristics with peers, colleagues, and your supervisor.

2. Create an image of the "nightmare supervisor." Identify the characteristics you would most want to avoid in a clinical supervisor. Discuss your image and the associated negative characteristics with peers, colleagues, and your supervisor.

3. Draw a series of eight cartoon-boxes illustrating a positive or negative experience you've had in a supervisory relationship. Share and discuss the cartoon with your peers and supervisor.

4. Create three separate art pieces symbolizing authority figures in your life. Arrange them in relation to one another. Imagine how these authority figures would interact? Think about the similarities and differences among these authorities. Reflect upon how these images of authority have influenced you and discuss this with peers. Have your authority figures supported and empowered you? Have they thwarted or inhibited you? When you

are in positions of authority, how are you like them? How are you different from them?

5. In a class or supervision group, design a role-play situation that involves an art therapist informing a client that the therapist is under supervision. Upon learning that the art therapist is being supervised, the client becomes distrustful of the therapist's competency and concerned that he/she is not receiving adequate art therapy service. After the role-play, discuss the clinical and ethical issues this situation raises. Focus discussion on ways to deal with uncomfortable feelings generated by informed consent practices.

6. Make a list of the personal attributes you believe are most needed in an art therapist. Design a Coat of Arms with a symbol for each of the attributes listed. Share the Coat of Arms with others in a class and/or supervisory group. Make note of the similarities and differences that emerge during the discussion.

7. Create an image of a burned-out art therapist. Discuss the image with others in a class and/or supervisory group. Focus the discussion on the characteristics and circumstances that lead to burnout.

Chapter VII

MAINTAINING PROFESSIONAL BOUNDARIES

*Something to contain us or to stay our hand. Otherwise
there were no boundaries to our own being and we too must
extend our claims until we lose all definition.*
Cormac McCarthy (*The Crossing* p.153)

The focus of this chapter is on establishing and maintaining appropriate professional boundaries. In art therapy, "professional boundaries" are the limits of the therapy relationship defined and maintained by the art therapist. Establishing and maintaining appropriate boundaries in therapy relationships is a complex process. There are many internal and external forces that challenge art therapists' capacities to maintain suitable boundaries between themselves and their clients. Ethical problems can occur when art therapists do not maintain appropriate limits in their therapeutic relationships. Some of the forces that raise ethical dilemmas in relation to professional boundaries for art therapists are self-disclosure, role diffusion, dual relationships, and sexual impulses that occur in art therapy.

The ethical issues raised in this chapter cannot be entirely worked through by referring to the *Ethical Principles for Art Therapists* (AATA, 2003). Therapy relationships sometimes involve ambiguous and complicated situations where "the rules" simply cannot suffice. In many instances, art therapists have to think through and resolve for themselves the difficult ethical and clinical problems inherent in negotiating professional boundaries. A consistent theme in this discussion is the need for art therapists to be self-aware and honest in exploring the effects of their conduct on clients. Establishing clear professional boundaries requires both professional and personal sophistication and maturity, coupled with a commitment to constant evaluation of art therapists' motivations and behaviors.

Guthiel and Gabbard (as cited in Agell, Goodman, & Williams, 1995) use the term "boundary crossing" to describe professional boundary violations in psychiatry. They identify seven areas of potential concern to clinicians in regards to boundaries: role, time, place and space, money, clothing, language, and physical contact. As art therapists reflect upon issues related to professional boundaries they might consider the following:

1. ROLE. Williams (1995) notes that art therapists should be careful they are not "engaging in therapy practices or procedures that are beyond [their] scope of practice, experience, training, and education" (p. 107). Often art therapists have many roles in the context of therapeutic relationships. It is important for art therapists to reflect upon the different roles they play with their clients and to develop clear rationales for their behavior. Art therapists listen, teach, encourage, confront, challenge, counsel, and console their clients. These multiple characteristics can sometimes cause role confusion and contradiction. In thinking about these issues, art therapists should ask themselves the following questions.

- Is what I am doing appropriate for the education and training I have received as an art therapist?
- Am I straying beyond the bounds of my expertise?
- Am I providing services that are the domain of other helping professions?

2. TIME. Developing time management skills suitable to clinical situations is an important matter for art therapists. Time management can be challenging to some art therapists. Art therapists who are accustomed to devoting as much time as is needed for their own artistic process sometimes struggle with the time-limited structures of therapy. For example, in many institutional settings, there is a daily schedule of activities that clients adhere to. Art therapists working in such settings have to learn to adapt to the time frames allotted to them. Similarly, art therapists in private practice must be sensitive to their clients' time constraints. In thinking about time management issues, art therapists should ask themselves the following questions.

- Do I have clearly set time boundaries?
- Do I begin and end sessions according to plan?
- Do I allow extra time to clients who are artistically skilled or verbally articulate?
- Do I allow adequate time for art making?
- Do I allow adequate time for talking during the session?
- Is my use of time appropriate to the art therapy process?

3. PLACE AND SPACE. The importance of the physical environment in which art therapy occurs cannot be overstated. As noted in Chapter III, art

therapists work in many different sorts of places. Whatever the characteristics of the physical environment may be, art therapists are encouraged to provide clients with the best possible milieu in order to promote the therapeutic use of art. In thinking about the work space, art therapists should ask themselves the following questions.

- Is my studio, or office, set up in such a way as to facilitate or impede art making? Does the studio/office space serve to protect the confidentiality of my clients?
- Are my client files kept in a secure place?
- Does the space serve multiple functions, and have I thought through the effect this may have on the art therapy?
- Is the space flexible enough to meet the various needs of clients?

4. MONEY. It is important that art therapists think through policies regarding the costs involved in art therapy. These policies should include attention to the following areas identified in Section 10 of the *Ethical Principles for Art Therapists* (AATA, 2003):

10.0 FINANCIAL ARRANGEMENTS
Art therapists make financial arrangements with clients, third party payers and supervisees that are understandable and conform to accepted professional practices.
10.1 When art therapists pay, receive payment from, or divide fees with another professional, other than in an employer/employee relationship, the payment to each is based on the services provided (clinical, consultative, administrative, or other) and is not based on the referral itself.
10.2 Art therapists do not financially exploit their clients.
10.3 Art therapists disclose their fees at the beginning of therapy and give reasonable notice of any changes in fees.
10.4 Art therapists represent facts truthfully to clients, third party payers, and supervisees regarding services rendered and the charges for services.
10.5 Art therapists may barter only if (1) it is not clinically contraindicated and (2) the resulting arrangement is not exploitative. Barter is the acceptance of goods, services, or other non-monetary remuneration from clients in return for art therapy services.

Financial matters can be sensitive and, if mishandled, can lead to unnecessary difficulties in the relationship between client and art therapist. The way in which fees are discussed with clients can have lasting impact on the climate of the therapeutic relationship. In thinking about financial issues, art therapists should consider the following questions:

• Are my fees fair and reasonable?
• Should I offer a sliding scale for clients who have financial limitations?
• Do I handle billing in a professional manner?
• Is the practice of bartering for payment, or exchanging services for payment, an ethical practice?
• Can I accept artwork from a client as payment for my services?

5. CLOTHING (PHYSICAL APPEARANCE). Personal appearance issues are sometimes an area of difficulty for art therapists and art therapy students. Some art therapists regard clothing and other aspects of physical appearance as important expressions of their personal identity. Art therapists sometimes take pride in dressing and grooming in a unique manner with a decidedly individual flair. Unique appearance is often not the norm for professionals in healthcare settings. Art therapists are occasionally questioned about the appropriateness of their appearance in a given clinical setting. In recent years, issues have arisen regarding body piercing. While an art therapist may perceive their clothing and physical appearance to be an outward symbol of their creative and unique individualism, it may be viewed as atypical and unprofessional to other professionals in a particular treatment facility. Art therapists have to weigh the potential positive and/or negative effects of their personal appearance in the professional milieu. The purpose in considering appearance is not to support censorship or suppression of individual expression; however, art therapists ought to consider the effects of their appearance in the clinical milieu and reflect upon the following questions:

• What messages do my clothes, hairstyle, and other aspects of my physical appearance convey?
• Does my appearance fit in with what is considered appropriate in the clinical setting where I work?
• How do I define "professional appearance"?

6. LANGUAGE. Art therapists have to consider the effects of language in the clinical context. Some art therapists are relaxed and informal in their use of language. For example, many art therapists encourage their clients to address them by their first name. This is in contrast to some other helping professions. Psychiatrists and physicians generally are referred to by their formal title, as Doctor (last name). Siegel (1990) is a notable exception to this general rule. In *Love, Medicine & Miracles,* Siegel (1990) discusses why he (a physician) made the decision to have patients refer to him by his first name. Neither way of being addressed is better than the other; however, a different relational context is established depending on the language used. Occasionally, art therapists go by nicknames. This can be problematic. In a

discussion of the use of nicknames in professional relationships, Guthiel and Gabbard (1993) point out problems that can occur. They suggest that using nicknames deemphasizes the seriousness of the therapy relationship. Consideration ought to be given to how art therapists want to be addressed, and how they will address their clients.

It can be argued that excessive informality in art therapy contexts can undermine the development of therapeutic relationships. Rinsley (1983) describes the resistance maneuver *leveling* through which clients attempt to relate to therapists as if they were siblings or peers. One way clients may attempt to *level* art therapists is by relating to them as if they were personal friends rather than professional clinicians. This can be a difficult resistance pattern for art therapists to confront because most therapists want to be liked by their clients. Some art therapists tend to establish a nonauthoritarian, non-hierarchical relationship with clients. "However, we must keep in mind that a professional treatment relationship is not synonymous with personal friendship" (Moon, 1998, p. 112). Using appropriate professional language can counteract clients' attempts to relate to art therapists as if they were friends.

Spaniol and Cattaneo (1994) have written an excellent article on the power of language in art therapy relationships. They stress how art therapists can avoid using language in a power-over way. As professionals, art therapists ought to avoid using poor grammar, excessive slang, and profanity, since each of these can have a detrimental effect on the art therapy relationship. The following questions may help art therapists reflect upon their use of language.

- Is it acceptable to use slang words when I am talking with clients?
- Is it acceptable to occasionally swear in the therapy context?
- Should I refer to my clients by their first name, or in a more formal manner?
- What is the best way for my clients to address me in order to establish and maintain the therapeutic relationship?

7. PHYSICAL CONTACT. The issue of whether or not to touch clients is a complex problem for many in art therapy. Some art therapists consider touching a client to be a normal human process and regard the notion of abstention as unacceptable. Other art therapists view physical contact with their clients as forbidden. Some art therapists regard touching a client, student, or supervisee as a humane gesture. Others are afraid that any physical contact with a client may be misinterpreted as intrusive, or exploitive. Of course, the decision of whether or not to touch another human being, or their artwork, is one that must be made thoughtfully and with much consideration

Figure 18. Considering Language–Craypas and Oil Stik
Wendi Boettcher

given to the potential positive and/or negative ramifications. This is an area where art therapists ought not to act solely on the basis of their intuition. It is important for art therapists to think through their reasons for touching or refraining from touching. Physical contact with a client or supervisee does not necessarily create professional boundary problems; however, touching can lead to difficulties. Physical contact between an art therapist and a client is a potent event. Touch can be misconstrued, however, and there are potential legal and ethical ramifications if an art therapist is accused of inappropriately touching a client. In the end, every art therapist ought to address this issue because of the potential impact it can have on the art therapist's capacity to establish and maintain professional boundaries.

There are numerous facets to the issue of touch in art therapy. Many art therapists find the idea of withholding physical contact from their clients objectionable. They view abstinence as cold and alien to their basic nature. Some art therapists, on the other hand, regard physical touch between themselves and their clients as taboo. They argue that touching contaminates therapy relationships, promotes unprofessional interactions, and can easily be misinterpreted and sexualized by clients. The decision of whether or not to touch a client is one art therapists must make carefully and with much forethought given to the potential positive and/or negative therapeutic effects. As Williams (1995) notes, "An art therapist who hugs, ostensibly trying to provide the comfort necessary to help the client create, may in reality be deflecting the power of the symbolic content not only in the relationship, but above all, in the art itself" (p. 107). Art therapists must think deeply about their reasons for touching, or refraining from touching, clients, students, or supervisees. As art therapists consider this question attention ought to be given to their intentions and motivations.

The following questions are intended to help art therapists reflect on issues related to physical contact.

- In what circumstances, if ever, is it acceptable to hug a client?
- What should I do if a client asks me to hold him/her?
- What guidelines should be used to determine if it is acceptable to shake hands with a client? Pat a client on the back? Put an arm around a client's shoulder?
- In what circumstances is it acceptable to touch clients' artworks?

ART MAKING DURING THERAPY SESSIONS

Nearly all therapists and counselors contend with the seven professional boundary areas Guthiel and Gabbard (1993) have identified. However, because of the unique nature of their work, art therapists must also wrestle with the question of whether or not to make art in the company of their clients. Making art, or refraining from making art, alongside clients is a professional boundary dilemma that is unique to art therapists. This is a question that has been widely discussed in the art therapy professional community (Haeseler, 1989; McNiff, 1982; Moon, 1995; Rubin, 1998; Wadeson, 1980). Some art therapists say that there are very few instances in clinical work when they have chosen to not participate in the process of making art with clients (McNiff, 1982). Moon (1995) asserts that the art therapist's art making can be critical in establishing the therapeutic milieu. "The doing of art is my ritual, a reenactment of my personal journey. My willingness and enthusiasm for the ritual is contagious and it both afflicts and affirms, challenges and assures the patient that the journey is worthwhile" (Moon, 1995, p. 47). However, Wadeson (1980) and others argue against art therapists making art alongside clients because they believe it can be an intrusion into the therapeutic process. Wadeson (1980) states:

Usually I don't, for several reasons. First, the field of exploration is the client's life, not mine. It's a matter of role. Second, for those clients who feel inadequate in art, my more experienced drawing might prove intimidating. Third . . . the processing of my picture or sculpture would take up valuable time. (p. 42)

Whether or not art therapists choose to make art alongside their clients has significant impact upon the therapeutic relationship. This is why the question has ethical ramifications. Art therapists can choose to make art with their clients, or choose not to. Either of these approaches can be ethical if undertaken with the best interests of the client having been considered. If the choice is made to create artwork alongside their clients, art therapists ought to be vigilant that their artistic participation does not dilute, interfere with, or in some way negatively influence the therapeutic process for clients. If art therapists choose not to make art with their clients, they have to be attentive to the effects of their nonparticipation. The therapist's watchful stance may interfere with the client's ability to use art expression freely. The choice to not make art alongside clients may increase the power differential between therapist and client and be detrimental to the therapeutic relationship. Consideration ought to be given to these and other aspects of the decision to make art with clients or to refrain from doing so.

When an art therapist is struggling to maintain appropriate boundaries with a particular client, she ought to ask this question: How will my behavior be of help to the client? If she can find no way in which a particular behavior will be of help, it is best to refrain from the course of action. Corey, Corey, and Callanan (1998) note, "To us, behavior is unethical when it reflects a lack of awareness or concern about the impact of the behavior on clients" (p. 225). Art therapists ought to endeavor to always keep the needs of their clients in the foreground of ethical decision making.

Valuable learning about professional boundaries for art therapists can occur during the art process. Establishing and maintaining professional roles requires honest self-assessment. Self-understanding in relation to professional boundaries can be stimulated through carefully selected artistic tasks. In addition to thinking about boundary issues, art therapists can actively explore these issues through artistic self-exploration.

Suggested Artistic Activities

1. In a class or group supervisory session, create several brief vignettes in which an art therapist is confronted with boundary challenging encounters with a client. Write the vignettes on individual pieces of paper and have each member of the class/group select one vignette to use as the subject of an art-

work. Have each member make an art piece that depicts how he/she would handle the situation. Discuss the images and the situations they portray with others in the group. Ask for feedback from others about how you have depicted your response to the client.

2. Create an image of "My Boundaries." Pay attention to the feelings the process of making this artwork stirs in you. Share your image and the feelings it stimulates with a trusted supervisor or peer.

3. Think about your ideas of what professional boundaries are. Write a poem summarizing your views. Share and discuss your poetic creation with a group of peers. Ask for their feedback about the ethical issues your poem may raise.

4. Create a collage on the theme of "a time when my professional boundaries were ineffective or unclear." Discuss with colleagues or a supervisor the issues your collage raises.

5. Create an artwork on the theme of "a time when my professional boundaries were too rigid." Compare this image with the collage you created in Activity 4. Discuss with colleagues or a supervisor the ethical and clinical issues your artwork raises.

6. Create an image of "My Edges." Pay attention to the feelings that the process of making this artwork stirs in you. Share your image and the feelings it stimulates with a trusted supervisor or peer.

7. In a classroom or group supervisory setting, role play situations in which an art therapist struggles to maintain appropriate boundaries. Discuss various strategies regarding how to handle these situations. (See examples below.)

In each of the following role-plays, the leader of the supervisory group, or course instructor, should meet with participants individually to assign the role of either art therapist or client. The participant playing the role of the art therapist should not be given any information about the client role. The person playing the role of the client should not be given any information about the therapist role. After roles have been assigned, each participant should be instructed to think about his or her role and create a piece of artwork from that perspective. Allow thirty to sixty minutes for the art making component of the exercise. When the artworks are completed, the leader/instructor sets the scene by telling observers the scene is the last fifteen minutes of an individual art therapy session. Allow ten minutes for each role-play.

Role Play Instructions

Role Play # 1

Art Therapist—You've been working with a particular client who has been very depressed for over a year. During the last two months the client's symptoms have worsened. You are very concerned the client may be planning to commit suicide. You feel overwhelmed and inadequate to help the client. You will be very vigilant during this session.

Client–You've been seeing an art therapist for over a year. You originally sought therapy because you felt vaguely depressed. Over the past few months your depression has deepened. Making matters worse, you get the feeling your therapist is pulling away from you, and this terrifies you. You have decided to use your art in this session to share your feelings about the therapist.

* * * * *

Role Play #2

Art Therapist–You have been working with a client for several months. You have gradually become aware that you are physically attracted to the client. You are very committed to maintaining your professional boundaries.

Client–You have been seeing an art therapist for several months. You have gradually developed a strong physical attraction to the art therapist. You have decided you would like to move the relationship to a more "personal" level. You will use your art during this session to subtly alter the relationship.

* * * * *

Role Play #3

Art Therapist–You have been seeing a client for several weeks. It is becoming apparent to you that your client is actively using cocaine. You must decide how to handle this situation.

Client–You have been seeing an art therapist for several weeks. Although you are using cocaine for recreation, you do not see this as a problem. It irritates you that the art therapist makes a big deal out of this.

* * * * *

Role Play #4

Art Therapist–You have been seeing a client in art therapy for over one year. You think the therapy has been quite helpful to the client, and you have grown to enjoy your time together in sessions. However, over the last six weeks, she client has "forgotten" to pay you. You have decided to use this session to raise the issue of payment.

Client–You have been seeing an art therapist for over one year. You think the therapy has been quite helpful and you have grown to enjoy your time with the therapist. However, about two months ago, your car's engine blew up and you had to spend a lot of money to get it repaired. You have been unable to pay for your sessions with the art therapist. Since the art therapist has not said anything about this, you assume that it is OK. Still, this is very embarrassing for you. You will use your art during this session to try to convey how you feel.

* * * * *

Role Play #5

Client–You've been seeing an art therapist for a few weeks. Last week, a very close friend of yours died. As the session progresses, you become overcome with sadness. You don't want to talk. You don't want to draw. You just want somebody to hold you. Eventually you ask the art therapist to hold you.

Art Therapist–You've been seeing a client for a few weeks. You really don't know the client all that well yet. Your agenda during this session is to continue to learn about what has been happening in the client's life.

* * * * *

SELF DISCLOSURE

Art therapists contend with difficult recurring questions of how transparent or self-revealing they should be with clients. What are good professional boundaries? What information should be shared with clients about the personal life of the therapist? What information should be kept private? When and why should feelings be shared with clients? Should the art therapist make art alongside clients or should the therapist remain an objective observer of the client's process? These questions and more swirl together and gradually come into focus on the issues of professional boundaries between art therapist and client.

In relation to self-disclosure in art therapy there is a spectrum of possibilities ranging from opaqueness to transparency, with translucence approximately midway between.

OPAQUE	TRANSLUCENT	TRANSPARENT
All aspects of the art therapist's life are with-held from the client.	The art therapist is cautious regarding the sharing of personal information. The question is asked, how will my sharing be helpful to the client?	The art therapy relationshipis viewed as a mutual exchange of self revelations.

The theoretical models that have influenced art therapists' professional development also influences where they place themselves along this spectrum of possibilities. For example, art therapists who practice from a psychoanalytic approach usually maintain an attitude of opaqueness in relation to their clients. Those who have been influenced by a humanistic or relational model of therapy tend to be more open and transparent. How much or how little art therapists reveal to clients about their personal lives has profound implications for their therapeutic work. Commenting on the centrality of the issue of self-disclosure for therapists, Jourard (1964) states:

> If there is any skill to be learned in the art of counseling and psychotherapy, it is the art of coping with the terrors which attend self disclosure, and the art of decoding the language, verbal and non-verbal, in which a person speaks about his [her] inner experience.(p. 24)

Every art therapist must decide on a personal therapeutic style somewhere along this continuum. As art therapists develop their therapeutic style, they often raise questions about "the rules" regarding proper professional self-disclosure. Art therapists "must experience the emptiness of a missed opportunity when they unnecessarily withheld information. Likewise, they must feel the pain of being abused by the client who was not ready or able to respond positively to the gift of the therapist's vulnerability" (Moon, 1994, p. 174). As these experiences of withholding and overexposing happen time and again, art therapists develop a set of inner cues that encourage or warn against self-disclosure.

Regarding the issue of therapist's self-disclosure, Kopp (1972) states, "I am not committed to the encounter group ethos of random openness at every point. I reserve a right to privacy at any given moment, and I respect that right in others (including my clients)" (p. 26). The client is the one seeking therapy from the art therapist; therefore, the clear focus should be on the client's life-images and stories rather than the therapist's. Still, in the spirit of Jourard's notion of mutual exchange, the translucent art therapist is able to form a therapeutic alliance with the client that is based on authenticity and selective self-disclosure.

Regardless of art therapists' level of self-disclosure, it is essential that self-awareness (disclosure of the self to the self) remain a top priority. In order to maintain authenticity, art therapists need to constantly be looking in their own creative mirror. "As in all problems between myself and the other, I must begin by trying to straighten myself out" (Kopp, 1972, p. 26). Art therapists must seek to see themselves honestly. Sometimes this is a pleasant process filled with satisfaction. At other times, it is terribly difficult and threatening. Art therapists may sometimes need to be opaque to their clients but should never be anything less than transparent to themselves.

Alexis' Dilemma

Alexis, an art therapist working in a community mental health agency, has been seeing Barbara, a sixteen-year-old, for several months in individual art therapy sessions. During one session, Barbara becomes very tearful and distraught as she draws a picture of a recent break-up with her boyfriend. She describes him as, "The guy I gave everything to." Alexis is very moved by the drawing and by Barbara's tears. Alexis shares that when she was younger, a man with whom she had slept had also rejected her. The mutual exchange that followed was profound.

Several weeks later, however, Barbara's mother telephones and says she is very concerned that Alexis is, in the mother's words, "encouraging sex outside of wedlock."

- Was it ethical for Alexis to disclose such personal information to Barbara?
- What mistakes, if any, do you think Alexis made?
- Would you have responded to Barbara's drawing differently? How? Why?
- Is it ever ethical for an art therapist to discuss his or her past personal experiences with a client?
- Can you give an example of an art therapist's personal disclosure that might be helpful to a client?
- Are there any things about your life that you should never share with a client?

A Co-therapist's Openness

The following is an abridged version of *A Story of Openness* (Moon, 1995) about a particularly difficult art therapy group consisting of six severely disturbed adolescent girls, an art therapist, and co-therapist. Each of the clients brought her own painful, in some cases, horrific history. The girls all had deep feelings of abandonment, inadequacy, and rage. Many of these feelings centered upon the girls' disturbed relationships with their mothers. It was not surprising that the girls focused intense feelings on the female co-therapist. She became the here-and-now-representative focus of years of hurt, disappointment, loss, and anger. In the group, each girl's anger seemed to stimulate the other's hostility. The girls' anger was most often directed on the co-therapist.

> This came to an abrupt halt about six months into the life of the group. The drawing task of the day was to symbolize an important day in your life. My co-therapist's drawing portrayed herself as a figure in white holding an infant. Several other figures were depicted in attendance, looking at her. Telling the story of her drawing, she said it was the day her first child was born, a wonderful, happy occasion. As the group members talked with her about the drawing, one girl asked why all the people in attendance were drawn in black? There was a long pause. I had the fleeting image of buzzards circling a wounded animal.
>
> Speaking quietly, my co-therapist shared with the group that this was indeed a drawing about the birth of her first child, but not the wonderful occasion she had described at first. This was a drawing of the birth of a child who was born dead—her first child. Tears slid slowly down her cheeks. The girls were weeping silently as well, and so was I. One girl, who had been abandoned at birth, broke the silence by wondering out loud if her real mother ever cries for her. Another shared the anguish she felt as she said good-bye to her own baby when she gave the baby up for adoption.
>
> No buzzards flew in for the kill. For a brief period of time these six angry, isolated girls experienced themselves as supportive, caring pilgrims. My co-therapist was no longer an ogre, a non-person. She became someone with whom they could cry . . . someone who would understand. The group was forever changed by her transparency.
>
> (Moon, 1995, pp. 41-42)

- Was it ethical for the therapist to disclose such personal information to the group?
- Would it have been ethical for the therapist to withhold such personal information from the group?
- What mistakes, if any, do you think were made in this vignette? Why?
- Is this kind of sharing inevitable when therapists create images alongside their clients? Why? Why not?
- Is this an example of why art therapists should not make art in the company of their clients? Why? Why not?
- Is this an example of why art therapists should make art in the company of their clients? Why? Why not?

- Was it beneficial to the clients for the therapist to discuss this past event with the group? Why?
- Can you think of examples of an art therapist's personal disclosure that would be harmful to clients?
- Can you think of examples of an art therapist's personal disclosure that would be helpful to clients?
- Are there things about your life you think should, or should not, be shared with your clients?

Art therapists cannot reasonably develop an appropriate therapeutic presence without addressing the issue of how much or how little personal information they will share with clients. In order to develop a therapeutic persona, art therapists have to be secure within themselves. Engagement in artistic tasks can stimulate self-understanding.

Suggested Artistic Activities

1. Create an image about a situation in which you are revealing to a client some aspect of your personal life. Pay attention to the feelings the process of making this artwork stirs in you. Share your image and the feelings it stimulates with a supervisor or peer.

2. In a class or group supervisory session, create several brief vignettes in which an art therapist is struggling with whether or not to share some personal information with a client. Write the vignettes on individual pieces of paper and then have each member of the class/group select one vignette to use as the subject of a drawing. Have each member create an artwork depicting how he/she would handle the situation. Discuss the artworks and the situations they portray with others in the group. Ask for feedback from others about how you have depicted your response to the client.

3. Think about your position on the transparency–opaque continuum in relation to self- disclosure to clients. Write a poem summarizing your views. Share and discuss your poetic response to the issues with a group of peers. Ask for feedback about the ethical issues your poem raises.

4. Design a billboard that advertises the times when self-revelation with a client is appropriate. Discuss with colleagues or a supervisor the issues your billboard raises.

5. Create an artwork about times when self-disclosure to a client is inappropriate. Compare this image with the billboard you created in Activity # 4. Discuss with colleagues or a supervisor the ethical and clinical issues your artworks raise.

6. In a classroom or group supervision session, role-play situations in which an art therapist might decide to share personal information with a

client. Solicit feedback and discuss how the characters in the role-plays handled the situation.

7. Create role-plays of situations in which an art therapist decides to remain opaque. Compare and contrast the situations presented in Activity # 6 and #7.

8. Create a symbolic image titled "Self Disclosure."

TOUCHING CLIENT ARTWORK

Art therapists must also consider the therapeutic ramifications of touching clients' artworks. Since an artwork is an extension of the artist, physically touching the artwork can become a symbolic touching of the person who made it. When an art therapist touches a client's artwork, the client may interpret this as a benevolent or compassionate gesture, or the client may misinterpret the touch as abusive, manipulative, or intrusive.

In clinical practice, one client might interpret an art therapist's touch of their artwork as a potent and authentic expression of the therapist's care and concern. Another client might misinterpret the art therapist's physical contact with artwork as intrusive or inappropriately intimate. Generally speaking, art therapists should not touch clients' artworks spontaneously or without thorough forethought. Art therapists should touch clients' artworks only when they have a clear rationale for doing so and only if they feel genuinely compelled to do so. Sometimes an art therapist's touch can inhibit the therapeutic process. At other times, an art therapist's physically touching a client's art piece can facilitate the therapeutic relationship.

All art therapists have to develop their own ideas and policies regarding physical contact with clients and their artworks. In order to do this, art therapists need to be secure within themselves and honest about their motivation to touch. Artistic tasks will help art therapists think about and explore issues of physical contact.

Suggested Artistic Activities

1. Create a collage on the theme of "times when touching a client is appropriate." Discuss with colleagues or with a supervisor the issues your collage raises.

2. Create an artwork on the theme of "times when touching a client is inappropriate." Compare this image with the collage created in Activity # 1. Discuss with colleagues or with a supervisor the ethical and clinical issues the artwork raises.

3. In a class or group supervisory session, create several brief vignettes in which an art therapist is either touching, or being touched, by a client. Write the vignettes on individual pieces of paper and then have each member of the class/group select one vignette to use as the subject of a drawing. Have each member create an artwork depicting how he/she would handle the situation. Discuss the images and their corresponding situations.

4. Create an image of a situation when you touched a client's artwork. Pay attention to the feelings the process of making this artwork stirs in you. Share with a supervisor or peer your image and the feelings it stimulates

5. Reflect upon your position on issues about physical contact with clients. Write a poem that summarizes your views. Share and discuss your poetic response to the issues with a group of peers. Ask for feedback about the ethical issues your poem raises.

6. In a classroom or group supervisory setting, role-play situations in which an art therapist might decide to touch a client or the client's artwork. Discuss various strategies regarding how to handle this situation.

7. Create role-plays of situations in which an art therapist decides to withhold physical contact. Compare and contrast the situations presented in Activity # 6 and #7.

ROLE DIFFUSION

In art therapy, role diffusion may be present when art therapists do any number of non-art therapy tasks in their professional lives. There has been much written in the literature of individual psychotherapy regarding the merits of keeping the role of the therapist separate from other associated tasks within the therapeutic milieu. In inpatient psychiatric treatment, it has traditionally been viewed as an ideal for therapists who provide individual psychotherapy to have no other clinical responsibilities beyond the psychotherapy session for the clients on their caseload. This means that an individual client's therapist would not lead a psychotherapy group in which the client is a member. The rationale for this split in roles is based on the belief that the psychotherapist's awareness of "special" information about some clients would preclude the therapist from treating all members of the group equally. Rogers (1965) describes the therapy relationship as an ideal relationship. He says, "In the emotional warmth of the relationship with the therapist, the client begins to experience a feeling of safety as he finds that whatever attitude he expresses is understood in almost the same way that he perceives it, and is accepted" (p. 41). It is easy to see how a therapist's ideal relationship with individual clients would affect the group atmosphere. Clients in the group who were not the therapist's individual therapy clients could develop jealousy or resentment in regard to the specialness of the leader's relationships with some of the group members. Likewise, in the role of group leader, the therapist might need to confront or set limits on clients' behaviors that are hindering group interactions. Such limit setting could complicate the therapist's relationship with clients also seen in individual therapy. In other words, the therapist who attempts to provide both individual therapy and group therapy leadership to the same set of clients experiences role diffusion.

Another example of role diffusion is found in the individual therapist who also serves as a case manager. Case management involves many tasks ancillary to psychotherapy. Case managers may be involved in activities on behalf of their clients, such as negotiating payment for services with insurance companies, coordinating services from a variety of agencies, making behavioral interventions, and other tasks which can be distinguished from classic individual psychotherapy. Art therapists who are working to establish the ideal relationship (Rogers, 1965) find many obstacles when they allow their role as art therapist to become diffused.

It is a difficult time in the health care professions. Art therapists are not immune to the effects of significant changes occurring in mental and physical health services everywhere in the United States. Some of these changes have resulted in art therapists being required by their employers to do many nonart therapy tasks. These various responsibilities challenge the therapists' capacity to avoid role confusion. There may be no way around the reality of such employer demands, but it is important for art therapists to give serious thought and attention to issues of role diffusion in order to provide quality care to clients.

The art therapy profession has established itself as a discipline requiring a masters degree at the level of entry. There are many benefits to this standard, but it is a double-edged sword. Many art therapists are finding themselves in work settings surrounded by colleagues who have received lower levels of academic training. For example, music, horticulture, recreation, occupational, and other action-oriented therapy disciplines do not all require graduate education. In some areas of the country, social workers and counselors practice with only bachelor's level educational preparation. Because of their advanced training, art therapists are often asked to assume administrative positions as supervisors, program directors, and case managers.

In some ways, such administrative positions are attractive to art therapists. The titles "case manager" or "supervisor" are often accompanied by higher salaries, increased professional prestige, and more programmatic power within the treatment system. "Any time one is offered more money, more freedom, and more control the temptation is strong to accept without question" (Moon, 1994, p. 188).

There is a down side to these administrative positions, however. Art therapists who hold administrative positions may experience blurred professional identity as responsibilities for the overall treatment of clients push them away from the practice of art therapy. The art therapist who is also a particular client's case manager must not only provide therapeutic services during the art therapy session, but may also be responsible for deciding many aspects of the client's participation within the treatment milieu. For instance, an art therapist who is also a case manager may be in the position of implementing restrictions on the client's behavior. This may result in the art therapist's role being unclear to the client. Similarly, in an outpatient clinic, the art therapist/case manager may devote much time to nonart therapy tasks such as advocating for a client's needs with funding sources, designing overall treatment plans, enforcing behavioral interventions, and scheduling a variety of therapy sessions. In addition, case managers are usually responsible for documenting all of the therapeutic services a particular client receives, while simultaneously having other administrative chores. These administrative responsibilities inevitably lead to parallel decreases in actual client contact and studio art time, and may result in a gradual isolation from colleagues who were once peers but are now supervisees or implementers of the case management treatment plan.

It is certainly not impossible for therapists to become case managers or clinical supervisors and remain active as art therapists and artists, but it is very easy for these central attributes of an art therapist's professional identity to get "lost in the shuffle." The heart of the art therapy profession is found in the art process and in the therapeutic relationship. These qualities are often absent from the offices and job descriptions of case managers and clinical supervisors.

This is not to suggest that art therapists who become case managers or administrators are bad people who intentionally pulled away, or drifted from their professional foundation. Some may, in fact, be well suited for management positions. For those who want to maintain their identity as art therapists, however, it is important to emphasize that the pressures of case management and supervision are subtle and may be deadening to the creative spirit and to therapeutic relationships. On the other hand, when art therapists are in positions with more authority, they also have a greater chance to exert positive influence on an institution or system. They can serve as art therapy advocates in a way that the typical art therapy clinician cannot.

Art therapists encounter many other forms of role diffusion in clinical settings. Art therapists are often asked to become the "decorators" of the environment around specific holidays. There is nothing inherently wrong in an art therapist using artistic sensibilities in the treatment milieu, but art therapists ought to consider the potential effects of this. For instance, when the

medical director of a psychiatric unit asks an art therapist to help clients dec-
orate for Christmas, the art therapist should ask herself, "Am I being regarded as an arts-and-crafts person rather than as a professional colleague?" If the
answer to this question is "yes," then the art therapist ought to strategize ways
to educate the director about the profession of art therapy in order to reframe
the director's misperceptions. This form of role diffusion undercuts the art
therapist's sense of self as a professional and may undermine self-confidence.
Inevitably, the art therapist's clients will sense this demoralizing dynamic
and this may further erode the therapist's effectiveness. In this example, the
role diffusion is problematic for the art therapist and countertherapeutic for
the therapist's clients.

Another form of role diffusion that art therapists encounter is found in
clinical settings where art therapists are expected to provide activity therapy
services that are beyond the scope of their expertise. In some settings, art
therapists are expected to lead recreation therapy groups, music therapy
groups, drama therapy groups, and other related activities. Leadership of
these activity-oriented groups can cloud an art therapist's work with clients
in art therapy. An example: At a psychiatric hospital, an art therapist co-led
a daily recreation therapy group. The group consisted of fifteen adult psychiatric inpatients, an activity therapist, and the art therapist. While playing
volleyball during a session of the recreation therapy group, a client (who was
also being seen by the art therapist for individual art therapy) became angry
with one of his peers. At one point in the game, the client spiked the volleyball very hard, directly into his peer's face. A fistfight ensued, and the recreation therapist and art therapist had to physically separate and restrain the
two combatants. The relationship between the art therapist and client was
never quite the same after the incident. The client expressed resentment
toward the art therapist for "butting in." The art therapist also harbored less
than positive feelings about the client as a result of the altercation. The therapy relationship was changed because the art therapist's role diffusion.

Section 1.9 of the *Ethical Principles for Art Therapists* states:

> Art therapists do not engage in therapy practices or procedures that are
> beyond their scope of practice, experience, training and education. Art thera-
> pists assist persons in obtaining other therapeutic services if the therapist is
> unable or unwilling to provide professional help, or where the problem or
> treatment indicated is beyond the scope of practice of the art therapist. (p. 4)

Art therapists are working in many different settings, each with their own
particular set of expectations for employees, their level of treatment sophistication, and their unique treatment culture. Many settings where art therapists work challenge the capacity to keep professional roles clear. There is no

doubt that most art therapists will encounter many situations during their career that invite role diffusion. It is important for art therapists to ensure that they are practicing within the scope of their training and education and to maintain clarity about their professional identity as art therapists.

Amy's Problem

Amy has been working as an art therapist at a small private school that specializes in educating children with learning disorders. She has been there for approximately three months. This is her first full-time position after receiving her master's degree. She truly enjoys her work and has been getting along well with colleagues at the school. Recently, the school principal, Mr. Johnson, informed Amy that the drama class is going to be performing Thornton Wilder's *Our Town.* He asked her to "spend a few less hours per week doing individual therapy and help the drama teacher and the class design the set." Amy might make any one of the following responses:

1. I'll be glad to be of help. I love the play, and I am sure the kids will benefit from participating in it.
2. I would like to help, but I have some concerns about seeing fewer clients per week and I am not sure this really falls within the job description of an art therapist. I also wonder what the effect would be on the students to see me in this other role. I would like to talk with my supervisor about this issue before I commit myself.
3. Absolutely not, Mr. Johnson. I worked very hard to put myself through graduate school to be an art therapist, and I am not about to become an amateur set designer.

- Which of the responses above most closely matches how you would handle Amy's situation?
- What do you think about Mr. Johnson's suggestion that Amy see fewer clients in order to devote time to the drama class? What are the ethical problems raised in this situation?
- What do you think the best course of action would be for Amy in this situation?

It is important for art therapists to develop a sense of professional identity. In order to do this, art therapists need to be clear about the scope of their professional responsibilities and they must be secure enough to resist various pulls to extend beyond their role. Issues of professional role can be sorted out and clarified through the following artistic tasks.

Suggested Artistic Activities

1. In a class or group supervisory session, create several brief vignettes in which an art therapist is struggling with issues related to role diffusion. Write the vignettes on individual pieces of paper and then have each member of the class/group select one vignette to use as the subject of an art piece. Have members depict how they would handle the situation. Discuss the artworks and the situations they portray. Ask for feedback from others about how you have depicted your response to the situation.

2. Create an image of yourself in a situation in which you are being asked to fulfill several roles in relation to your clients. Pay attention to the feelings that the process of making this artwork stirs in you. Share your image and the feelings it stimulates with a group of peers. Brainstorm strategies for dealing with such a situation.

3. Think about your position on issues related to role diffusion in art therapy. Write a TV commercial that summarizes your views. Present it to your peers. Engage in discussion about the issues your commercial raises.

4. Create several of "the hats you wear." As you think about your various hats, reflect on whether or not your role as an art therapist is clear to you. Discuss with colleagues or a supervisor your sense of professional identity.

5. In a classroom or group supervisory situation, create and act out role-plays in which an art therapist must deal with issues of role diffusion. Discuss various strategies regarding how to handle these situations.

6. Write a short story about a situation in which an art therapist is involved in role diffusion with his or her clients. Write two endings to the story, one ending depicting a positive resolution to the situation and a second ending depicting a negative resolution to the situation. Read and discuss the story with a group of peers.

MULTIPLE RELATIONSHIPS IN ART THERAPY

Multiple relationships in art therapy (formerly referred to as dual relationships) are a form of role diffusion, but they are different from those described already. The examples of role diffusion just discussed are usually brought on by outside forces, such as the expectations of an employer. In contrast, multiple relationships are usually brought on by the internal wishes of the art therapist. In multiple relationships, art therapists assume two or more roles with a client. An example of a multiple relationship would be when an art therapist provides therapeutic services to a client while simultaneously having a business relationship with the client. These multiple roles can be either simultaneous or sequential. An example of a sequential multiple relationship would be a situation in which an art therapist and client have terminated therapy but continue to see one another in a social relationship. Multiple relationships may entail an art therapist serving in more than one professional capacity. An example of this would be an art therapy educator providing art therapy services to a student. Multiple relationships may also involve an art therapist providing a professional service to an individual while also engaging in a nonprofessional relationship with that individual. Other examples of dual relationships involve art therapists in the following:

- Providing art therapy to a family member or to a friend,
- Giving gifts to clients,
- Receiving gifts from clients,
- Attending a client's wedding or other social function,
- Combining the roles of art therapy supervisor and art therapist,
- Becoming sexually involved with a client, supervisee or student.

In order for art therapists to avoid engaging in multiple relationships it is helpful to keep in mind that therapeutic relationships are not personal relationships. There is nearly always a power differential inherent in the therapist-client dyad. No matter how intimate the relationship, it ought to remain a professional one with clear boundaries between the art therapist and the client.

Section 1.5 of the *Ethical Principles for Art Therapists* states:

> Art therapists refrain from entering into a multiple relationship if the multiple relationship could reasonably be expected to impair the art therapist's competence or effectiveness in performing his or her functions as an art therapist, or otherwise risks exploitation or harm to the person with whom the professional relationship exists.
>
> A multiple relationship occurs when an art therapist is in a professional role with a person and (1) at the same time is in another role with the same person, (2) at the same time is in a relationship with a person closely associated with or related to the person with whom the art therapist has the professional relationship, or (3) promises to enter into another relationship in the future with the person or a person closely associated with or related to the person.
>
> Multiple relationships that would not reasonably be expected to cause impairment or risk exploitation or harm are not unethical.
>
> Art therapists recognize their influential position with respect to clients, and they do not exploit the trust and dependency of clients. (p. 4)

Corey, Corey, and Callanan (1998) note that there are many viewpoints on dual relationships (p. 226). Some authors focus on the difficulties intrinsic to dual relationships. Pope and Vasquez (1991) list a number of problems dual relationships may cause. Among these problems are impairment of the therapist's judgment, exploitation of the client, and distortion of the professional relationship. Other theorists allow some leeway in regard to these issues and tend to see the phenomena of dual relationships as complex and resistant to overly simplified legalistic solutions.

The nature of art therapists' work necessarily involves some forms of multiple relationships. Art therapists often engage in collaborative tasks with clients that inevitably lead to subtle blurring of boundaries. For example, the process of stretching a canvas with a client who has never done this before involves the art therapist in several simultaneous roles:

1. Teacher—to explain the technical aspects of the process;
2. Demonstrator—to illustrate the process by example;
3. Supplier of materials—to provide the stretchers, canvas, staple gun, etc.;
4. Co-worker—to engage in the process along with the client.

All of these roles blur together as the client engages in the process of artistic self-expression. These aspects of art therapy are, by their very nature, forms of multiple relationship and role diffusion, and yet they are central aspects of art therapy. In the broadest sense, dual relationships are inherent in the work of art therapists. In most settings, art therapists cannot remain emotionally and physically detached from clients. Art therapists do not sit behind desks, impassive, as the client engages in artistic expression. Despite the statement (AATA, 2003) "Art therapists refrain from entering into a multiple relationship," (p. 3) some measure of role diffusion is inescapable, and this is not fundamentally unethical. This is not to suggest that the aspirational statements about multiple relationships in the *Ethical Principles for Art Therapists* should be disregarded; however, it must be acknowledged that some aspects of multiple relationships cannot be avoided and that these are not inexorably harmful or unethical.

With the exception of the ethical imperative that therapists not involve in sexual relationships with clients (to be discussed later in this chapter), there is only general agreement regarding the many aspects of multiple relationships in art therapy. Art therapists have the responsibility to observe and regulate themselves and to think deeply about their motivations for involving in relationships in which their roles may become diffused. Corey, Corey, and Callanan (1998) comment, "In rural areas, for instance, mental-health practitioners may find it more difficult to maintain clear boundaries than do those who work in large cities. They may have to blend several professional roles and functions, and they may attend the same church or community activities as the clients they serve" (p. 228).

One example of multiple relationships that many art therapists disagree about is the issue of bartering for services. Some art therapists regard bartering as an integral part of their practice. They believe that if a client cannot afford therapy, they have the right to negotiate a fair exchange that does not include money. One art therapist has told me that she regards bartering as a natural and healthy transaction and that she refuses to govern her work by the standards of capitalism. She often accepts a client's art piece as payment for her therapeutic services. Other art therapists view bartering as acceptable in theory but also see it as a hotbed of potential problems. Still others vehemently disapprove of bartering and consider it unethical and unprofessional.

Art therapists undecided about the pros and cons of bartering for service should consider Hall's (1996) suggestions:

- Evaluate whether the bartering arrangement will put you at risk of impaired professional judgment or have a negative impact on your performance as a therapist.
- Determine the value of the goods or services in a collaborative fashion with the client at the outset of the bartering agreement.
- Determine the appropriate length of time for the barter arrangement.
- Document the bartering arrangement, including the value of the goods or services and a date on which the arrangement will end or be renegotiated (pp. 7, 19).

In addition to Hall's recommendations, Corey, Corey, and Callanan (1998) suggest that it is important to discuss the topic of bartering with colleagues who have experience with this form of payment. Before committing to a barter arrangement, it may be helpful to talk with a supervisor in order to make sure that all of the potential problems with the arrangement have been thought through and/or all of the alternatives to bartering fully explored (p. 236).

MULTIPLE RELATIONSHIP VIGNETTES TO CONSIDER

Helen's Benevolence

Helen is an art therapist who works in a public school in an impoverished neighborhood. She provides art therapy services to children the school guidance counselor classifies as being "at risk." The school does not identify Helen as an art therapist; they call her an arts specialist. One afternoon, one of her clients, an eight-year-old boy named Freddie, comes into the art room crying. When Helen asks him what is wrong, he tells her that another boy, "a bully" has stolen his money. "I was gonna go to a movie after school and now I can't."

At the close of the session, as Freddie is about to leave the art room, Helen takes her wallet from her purse and gives Freddie a five-dollar bill.

- How do you feel about Helen giving Freddie money in this situation?
- Are there any ethical issues that Helen should have thought about prior to giving the five dollars to Freddie?
- Did Helen handle this situation in a professional manner? Why, why not?

Tom's Generosity

Adrienne is a forty-four-year-old widow and mother of three teenagers. She became quite depressed when her husband died suddenly of a heart attack. Adrienne has been a client with Tom, an art therapist, for a little over one year. She has become quite invested in her artistic work, and is a talented artist. Tom very much enjoys working with her. Adrienne enters the art studio one evening quite upset. She tells Tom that her daughter was in a car accident and totaled the car. She says she is going to have to take out a loan to get a new car and can no longer afford to be in art therapy. Adrienne states that she needs to end their relationship immediately and then burst into tears.

After several minutes Adrienne calms down. She begins to work on her painting. Tom is troubled by the prospect of discontinuing this relationship in such an abrupt manner. As the session proceeds, he suggests that perhaps Adrienne might trade one of her paintings in lieu of paying for several art therapy sessions.

- How do you feel about Tom's handling of this situation?
- Are there therapeutic issues that Tom should explore with Adrienne regarding their barter arrangement?
- What impact might Adrienne's artistic skills have had on Tom's clinical judgements in regard to this situation?
- Would it have been ethical for Tom to allow the relationship with Adrienne to simply end after the session discussed above?
- Did Tom handle this situation in a professional manner? Why? Why not?

Joanne's Music

Joanne is an art therapist in private practice. She has been seeing Sam, a twenty-seven-year-old professional musician, in individual art therapy sessions for several months. As their relationship has developed, Joanne has become increasingly aware of the number of interests that she and Sam have in common. Among these common interests are Joanne's own musical interests and aspirations. She sings, plays keyboards, and has always wanted to try performing professionally.

During a session, Sam tells Joanne that one of the members of his band has decided to move to another city and the band is looking for another member. Joanne tells Sam that she would be interested in trying out for the band. Joanne reasons that becoming a member of the group would be good for Sam, because they would have even more contact, and at the same time this would be an exciting and challenging experience for her.

- In this situation, is it ethical for Joanne to become a member of Sam's band?
- Are there therapeutic issues that Joanne should explore with Sam regarding the impact this could have on their relationship?
- Do you think Joanne has handled this situation in a professional manner?
- Would it be ethical for Joanne to continue to see Sam in therapy if she becomes a member of the band?
- Would it be ethical for her to see Sam in therapy if the band members decide against her joining their group?
- In this situation, is Joanne acting in the best interests of Sam, or is she acting in response to her own needs?
- If you were Joanne's supervisor, what would you advise her regarding this situation?

Dan and Rhonda

Dan is an art therapist who works in a community mental health agency. He first met Rhonda when she came to the agency seeking treatment for her depression and was referred to an art therapy group Dan leads. During the course of her involvement in the group, Rhonda works through some painful abandonment issues pertaining to her childhood. After nearly two years in the group, Rhonda decides to terminate her involvement.

Several months after Rhonda terminates therapy, Dan receives a letter from her. In the letter, Rhonda shares that she has been having strong feelings about him ever since she left therapy. The letter says that she thinks about Dan a lot and that she wonders if they could see one another.

Initially, Dan is surprised by the content of the letter but he also recognizes he too has affectionate feelings toward Rhonda. He recognizes that he has suppressed his feelings for therapeutic reasons. After thinking it over, Dan telephones Rhonda and suggests that they meet at a local art gallery to talk about their relationship.

- How do you feel about Dan's handling of this situation?
- Are there ethical issues that Dan is not addressing?
- Does the fact that Dan has suppressed his feelings about Rhonda raise any professional or ethical questions?
- What do you think Dan should do next?

GIFTS IN ART THERAPY

Clients frequently offer art therapists gifts. Gifts may be in the form of artworks made for the art therapist or they may be presents purchased for special occasions. It is essential for art therapists to explore their feelings, expectations, and fears relative to the giving and receiving of gifts from clients before such situations arise. "It is recommended that therapists avoid the exchange of gifts with clients or families, for such encounters tend to alter the essential relationship" (Moon, 1992, p. 107). Clients often wish to concretize the special bond they feel with their therapist through giving a gift. Art therapists can avoid unnecessary discomfort for clients and for themselves by making their policy regarding gift giving and receiving clear at the beginning of the therapy relationship.

The act of giving or receiving a gift, or refusing to do so, can have far-reaching meanings in the context of the art therapy relationship. While the general rule of abstention is helpful, it probably cannot apply to each and every circumstance. It is important for art therapists to think deeply about their relationships with clients before accepting or rejecting an offered gift. In therapy relationships, there may be no such thing as a "free gift with no strings attached."

All art therapists face circumstances in which they may be tempted to form dual relationships with clients. Art therapists have to develop their own ideas and policies regarding multiple relationships. Consideration should be given to what is appropriate in their community and clinical contexts. In order to do this, art therapists need to be self-aware and honest about their motivations. The following artistic tasks will help art therapists think about and explore dual relationship issues.

Suggested Artistic Tasks

1. Create a collage on the theme of multiple relationships. As you think about your finished collage, reflect on whether or not you are engaged in any multiple relationships in your current clinical work. Discuss with colleagues or a supervisor how to handle these relationship issues.

2. In a class or group supervisory session, create several brief vignettes in which an art therapist is wrestling with whether or not to engage in a multiple relationship with a client. Write the vignettes on individual pieces of paper and then have each member of the class/group select one vignette to use as the subject of an art piece. Ask each member to create an artwork depicting how he/she would handle the situation. Discuss the drawings and the situations they portray with others in the group. Ask for feedback from others about how you have depicted your response to the client.

3. Create an image of yourself engaging in a multiple relationship with one of your clients. Pay attention to the feelings the process of making this artwork stirs in you. Share your image and the feelings it stimulates with a supervisor or peers.

4. Think about your position related to a multiple relationship situation in art therapy. Write a poem that expresses your views. Share and discuss your poetic response to the issue with a group of peers. Ask for their feedback about the issues your poem addresses.

5. In a classroom or group supervisory session, create role-play situations in which an art therapist must deal with a circumstance that involves a multiple relationship with a client. Discuss various strategies regarding how to handle this situation.

6. Create a cartoon storyboard detailing a situation in which you discover that one of your art therapy colleagues is engaging in what you consider to be an inappropriate multiple relationship with a client. Depict how you would handle this situation.

SEXUAL RELATIONSHIPS AND ISSUES THAT ARISE IN ART THERAPY

In the first chapter of this text, three modes of moral thinking were discussed: deontological, teleological, and antinomian. Throughout the book, I have suggested that there are limitations to the deontological, legalistic, approach to ethical decision-making for art therapists. I have also expressed the view that the antinomian perspective, which provides for no principles or rules whatsoever, does not offer art therapists much in the way of help as they think through professional ethical dilemmas. By a process of elimination then, I have supported the teleological approach to resolution of ethical problems in art therapy. This system of reasoning stresses that professional conduct must be evaluated in relation to the end or ends that it serves.

Perhaps the one exception to the overall situational tone of this text is in relation to the issue of sexual contact between an art therapist and a client. In relation to this topic, deontological reasoning must guide the discussion. Sexual relationships between art therapists and their current clients are implicitly prohibited in the *Ethical Principles for Art Therapists* (2003). The code of ethics of every helping profession contains specific statements that prohibit sexual intimacy in the therapeutic relationship (American Psychological Association, 1995; American Association of Marriage and Family Therapists, 1991; American Counseling Association, 1995; National Association of Social Workers, 1996; National Organization of Human Service Professionals, 1995; American Music Therapy Association, 1998). "The existing codes are explicit with respect to sexual harassment and sexual relationships with clients, students, and supervisees" (Corey, Corey, and Callanan, 1998, p. 248).

It is certain that art therapists must refrain from engaging in sexual relationships with their clients, students, and supervisees. However, the *Ethical Principles for Art Therapists* does not address the many indirect ways that eroticism and sexuality are at times present in art therapy contexts. It is essential to acknowledge that relationship between art therapists and their clients, students, or supervisees may contain varying measures of erotic or sexual material. The erotic elements in art therapy are not merely limited to sexual intercourse. It is important that art therapists be self-aware and self-accepting regarding their sexual feelings and that they make conscious decisions as to how to handle erotic issues in the context of therapy, supervisory, and educational relationships.

Art therapists are human and as such are prone to experience a variety of sexual feelings. Some examples follow: an art therapist feeling sexually attracted to a client, an art therapy supervisor and supervisee experiencing mutual attraction, or an art therapy instructor feeling attracted to a student. These feelings are normal and may be a natural component of art therapy relationships; however, they should not be acted upon. It is important for art therapists to monitor their behavior in order to guard against the potential for engaging in inappropriate relationships. If this monitoring is not done, art therapists run the risk of inadvertently behaving seductively with their clients. They may influence clients to focus on romantic or sexual feelings toward them, or they may engage in physical contact that is primarily intended to arouse or satisfy their sexual desires. Clearly, such behaviors are unethical.

The question arises: If it is natural for an art therapist to occasionally experience sexual feelings toward a client, supervisee, or student, how can sexual misconduct be avoided? In order to prevent unethical behavior it is necessary to explore the clinical, ethical, educational, and professional issues related to sexuality in art therapy relationships in training and supervisory sessions. These issues ought to be addressed in both undergraduate and graduate level art therapy education programs with students. Art therapy practitioners may seek opportunities to explore these issues in clinical supervision, continuing education programs, and conference seminars. As discussed earlier in this text, personal therapy may also be a means to deal with art therapists' sexual needs, feelings, and motivations. In each of these contexts it must be stressed that there is a deep distinction between having sexual feelings toward a client, student, or supervisee, and acting out these feelings. A sexual feeling is just a feeling; it is neither good nor bad. How art therapists' sexual feelings are translated into behaviors is an ethical and professional matter of the utmost concern. A sexual relationship between an art therapist and his or her client is potentially damaging to both the client and the art therapist. It is unprofessional and unethical for art therapists to act out sexual feelings toward their clients.

Being an art therapist does not make a person faultless or immune to human feelings. All human beings make mistakes and art therapists are no exception. It is extremely important for art therapists to commit themselves to thinking deeply about their feelings and to behaving in a manner that is most helpful to their clients, students, and supervisees. Readers interested in exploring this subject in more depth are referred to Schaverien's (1995) examination of the female art therapist's desires. Many art therapists encounter circumstances in which they experience sexual feelings toward a client. In order to avoid inappropriate action, art therapists need to be self-aware and honest about their sexual feelings. The following artistic tasks are intended to help art therapists think about and explore such issues.

Suggested Artistic Tasks

1. Imagine you are conducting an art therapy session and your client is subtly suggesting that he/she would like to engage in sexual activity with you. Do a drawing depicting how you would handle this situation. Discuss with peers or a supervisor your drawing and the situation it portrays. Ask for feedback about how you have depicted your response to the client.

2. Create an image of yourself acting out a sexual fantasy with one of your clients. Reflect upon the feelings that the process of making this artwork stirs in you. Share your image and the feelings it stimulates with a trusted supervisor or peer.

3. Think about your position on giving and receiving gifts from clients in art therapy. Write a poem that expresses your views.

4. Create a collage on the theme of things that you find to be erotically stimulating. As you reflect upon your collage, think about how these things are, or are not, present in your current clinical work. Discuss with peers or a supervisor how you would handle a sexually provocative encounter with a client.

5. In a classroom or group supervisory session, role-play situations in which an art therapist must deal with a client who gives him/her a gift.

6. In a classroom or group supervisory session, role-play situations in which an art therapist must deal with her own sexual feelings toward a client.

Chapter VIII

RESPONSIBILITY TO ART THERAPY
RESEARCH PARTICIPANTS

A core quality of the art therapy profession is creativity. This creativity is seen in art therapists' abilities to establish therapeutic relationships, engage in artistic work, publish their work in journal articles and texts, and form and maintain local and national professional organizations. Creativity is also evidenced in art therapists' research endeavors. From the earliest days of art therapy in America, there has been interest in researching the field. Mary Huntoon, for example, engaged in recognized research beginning in 1947 at the Winter Hospital in Topeka Kansas (Casado, 1980). "In the first publication specific to our field, Volume 1, Number 1, of the *Bulletin of Art Therapy*, there is evidence of an interest in research" (Knapp, 1992a). Throughout the years, interest in art therapy research has intensified (Anderson, 1983; Gantt, 1986; Junge, 1989; Malchiodi, 1995; McNiff, 1987; Rosal, 1989; Rubin, 1984; Tibbetts, 1995; Wadeson, 1978, 1992, 1995). In 1998, *Art Therapy: Journal of the American Art Therapy Association* dedicated two consecutive issues to art therapy research. In the first of these two publications, Rosal (1998) states, "Art therapists are becoming increasingly aware that research is and will continue to be an important component of our field (p. 47).

The increasing interest in research has sparked many debates among art therapists. Tibbetts (1995) articulated trepidation that a large number of art therapists reject the notion art therapy research is important. Some art therapists are unconvinced that there is a need for research at all. "The debate is centered on the issue of *how we know what we know* about art therapy" (Rosal, 1998, p. 47). Some art therapists think research will serve the profession by substantiating the therapeutic power and benefits of art therapy. In art therapy's professional history, research has sometimes seemed to be motivated by the discipline's attempt to justify itself according to the scientific, medical, and psychological communities' frames of reference. Many art therapists have felt as if they did not fit into the quantitative-qualitative dichotomy that in recent times has defined the world of research in the behavioral sciences. Other art therapists argue that therapeutic art processes are too complicated to be counted or measured objectively. Wolf (1995) went so far as to posit art therapy research might "contribute to the diminution of our credibility" (p. 259).

Regardless of where art therapists stand, the philosophic debates regarding art therapy research have served to sharpen thinking about the necessity, relevance, and forms of research. Although the need for, and forms of, art therapy research may be controversial for some time in the professional community, it is clear research will continue in educational settings and in the field of practice. With this in mind, it is important to examine ethical principles influencing art therapy research processes. This chapter aims to illustrate basic principles of ethical research for art therapists.

Section 8, Responsibility to Research Participants, of the *Ethical Principles for Art Therapists* addresses issues related to research in the following way:

> Art therapy researchers respect the dignity and protect the welfare of participants in research. Researchers are guided by laws, regulations, and professional standards governing the conduct of research.
>
> 8.2 To the extent that research participants may be compromised by participation in research, investigators seek the ethical advice of qualified professionals not directly involved in the investigation and observe safeguards to protect the rights of research participants.
>
> 8.3 Researchers requesting participants' involvement in research inform them of all aspects of the research that might reasonably be expected to influence willingness to participate. Investigators take all reasonable steps necessary to ensure that full and informed consent has been obtained from participants who are also receiving clinical services, have limited understanding and/or communication, or are minors.
>
> 8.4 Researchers respect participants' freedom to decline participation in, or to withdraw from, a research study at any time with no negative consequences to their treatment.
>
> 8.5 Information obtained about a research participant during the course of an investigation is confidential unless there is an authorization previously obtained in writing. When there is a risk that others, including family members, may obtain access to such information, this risk, together with the plan for protecting confidentiality, is to be explained as part of the procedure for obtaining informed consent.

Art therapy researchers are obliged to respect the dignity and safeguard the well being of participants in research. Since graduate art therapy educational programs routinely require research and seasoned practitioners are experiencing the need for outcome-based research findings in their work settings, inquiry into the ethics of art therapy research demands increasing attention.

McNiff (1998) asserts:

> Research can be integrated with practice at every level in order to promote knowledge, enrichment and creative renewal. . . . I also believe that creative arts therapy can make unique contributions to the larger context of human understanding as researchers in other disciplines begin to explore ways of expanding their investigations through the arts. (p. 11)

To engage in research means to study thoroughly. To "re-search" is to "search again" through a process of organized and systematic inquiry. However, Knapp (1992b) notes, "Research with human subjects is not spectator sport; it is a complex, hands on experience with its own set of rules, expectations and potential pitfalls" (p. 39).

As art therapists begin to plan and prepare to conduct research, Allen (1992) suggests the following:

1. Examine your own image of what research must be. Create an image of a researcher. Do this through drawing and writing. Find out about your own fears and expectations.
2. Take a basic research methods course, usually offered on the undergraduate level in the psychology department of most colleges. Audit the course if you want to relieve anxiety and save money.
3. Do personal research with art therapy methods. Make art yourself and see what happens. Keep a journal of your results for planning studies with other subjects.
4. Consider what your motives are. If your research desire is directly related to job security, try to hook up with an existing project in your institution. It is much easier than starting from scratch and is a good learning experience.
5. Start study and support groups to sustain yourself as you undertake research. It helps to share both results and disappointments.
6. Hire experts to collaborate with and to advise you. You don't need to be an expert on every aspect of research.

These specific suggestions can enhance art therapists' success as researchers. Allen (1992) asserts, "It helps to know as much as possible about ourselves and what research means to us before embarking on a research project" (p. 26).

After having considered Allen's suggestions, the next area of focus for art therapy researchers is consideration of the well-being of research participants. In order to protect the welfare of participants in research, and guard against unethical research practices, art therapists ought to consider the following areas as they plan their research projects:

1. Rationale and Intention: A rationale for the research project should be articulated in a clear and concise statement of the rationale for the research project. This includes attention to the specific goals of the study, what is expected to be learned from the project, and what significance the study has to the art therapy profession.
2. Process and Protocol: A comprehensive and clear explanation of the methods and procedures that will be used to conduct the project is essential.
3. Participant Description: A thorough and accurate description of the subject population should be developed. Reasons for conducting research with a particular population should be delineated.
4. Potential Benefits and Risks: The potential benefits of the project for the participant and for society in general should be carefully assessed. Likewise, attention should be given to the potential physical, psychological, or social risks to participants. A thoughtful account of the risk/benefit ratio for the research project ought to be developed.
5. Informed Consent: Procedures for obtaining informed consent should be developed and utilized. (See discussion of informed consent below.)
6. Protections Against Risk: Realistic plans that will safeguard the welfare of participants should be developed. These may include procedures related to appropriate advance screening of participants, availability of medical services, and accessibility of appropriate psychological aid.

As in therapy relationships, one of the most important research considerations is the issue of informed consent. In all art therapy research activities, the student or practitioner must obtain informed consent from each project participant. In the case of those not able to give informed consent (e.g., children, or persons who are mentally handicapped), informed consent must be obtained from their guardians or legal representatives. Art therapy researchers should use a written informed consent document. A copy of the informed consent form should be given to the person signing the form and the art therapist should keep the original on file.

In clear and non-technical language, research participants must be informed of:

• The fact they are participating in a research study
• Goals/intent of the study
• Expected length of time of the participants' involvement

- How, and for what purposes, participants' images and/or artworks may be used or exhibited during or at the conclusion of the project
- Processes involved in the project
- Foreseeable benefits to the participant
- Foreseeable risks to the participant
- Extent, if any, to which confidentiality of information and privacy of the participants will be maintained
- Who to contact with appropriate questions about the research, participant's rights, and research-related injury to the participant
- The voluntary nature of participation and the fact that participants may withdraw consent at any time.

There are two customary procedures that art therapy researchers may use to obtain informed consent:

1. The participant or a legal representative signs a written informed consent document that incorporates the elements listed above.
2. The participant or a legal representative signs a document indicating the participant had the elements listed above explained to her/him and she/he understood the oral description and agrees to participate in the research activity.

A sample consent form is included as Appendix IV in *A Guide to Conducting Art Therapy Research (pp. 239-241)*, published by the American Art Therapy Association (1992).

THE RIGHTS OF IMAGES IN ART THERAPY RESEARCH

Art therapy researchers are obligated to protect the welfare of all participants in research. It is imperative to keep in mind the participants in art therapy research are not only the human subjects, but the image/artwork subjects as well. A fundamental principle for conducting ethical art therapy inquiry is for researchers to pay attention to the artistic aspects of the research process. Artistic images and procedures are as much the subject of inquiry as are the human beings involved in the project. If they are regarded as autonomous entities, images and artworks require careful and respectful treatment as the focus of research. The discipline of regarding our research of artworks and images in this way will serve to expand and deepen our care and respect for the artist-persons who are also the subject of our investigations. As art therapy students and practitioners contemplate ethical questions related to research projects, equal consideration can be given to the rights of all research participants, including not only the human subject, but also the artistic, imaginal "other."

EXPANDING ART THERAPY RESEARCH

Art therapy research has sometimes been motivated by art therapists' wish to justify the discipline in the terms of the scientific frame of reference. There are many ways to engage in art therapy research beyond the realm of quantification procedures that force a structure of empirical fundamentalism onto the process of exploration. Linesch (1992) states, "It is my belief that a wide range of research methodologies offers exciting opportunities for art therapy research. Such a range will allow art therapists to maintain a fundamental commitment to the creative process while engaging in rigorous scholarly work" (p. 134). Many meaningful issues in art therapy practice call for methods of investigation based on principles of artistic and experiential knowing.

Practicing art therapists and art therapy students have a deep well of experiences that may offer important opportunities for expanding the practice of research within other professions. Art therapists can make significant and unique contributions to the effort to understand human existence as they continue to explore ways of broadening their research investigations through artistic methods.

The practice of empirical research methods aimed at producing measurable outcomes, regarded by many in the art therapy community as crucial to practice, should not be diminished. Quantifiable research studies can serve to illustrate the complicated artistic and therapeutic issues inherent in art therapy. These studies can focus attention on how the arts are helpful to clients. There are many questions and problems in art therapy can be legitimately studied through statistical inquiry. It is important that these research projects be conducted in such a way as to positively contribute to the understanding of the fundamental processes of artistic expression in therapy.

In order to ensure that research approaches are ethical, the particular method of inquiry for any given research study should be carefully considered and chosen. Linesch (1992) argues, "It seems imperative that those of us who are concerned about art therapy research within our field acknowledge the complexity of the issues and utilize the diversity for growth rather than rigid divisiveness" (p. 134). A single form of research cannot be applied to every art therapy research question with equal effectiveness.

Chapter IX

ART THERAPISTS' RESPONSIBILITY TO THE ART THERAPY PROFESSION

Art therapists often find themselves working in isolation from other art therapists. In many clinical settings, people from other professional disciplines, who may have little or no genuine understanding of art therapy, surround art therapists. Art therapists working in private practice may have little collegial contact with other professionals. Those who work in community agencies are likely to be the only art therapists on their respective staffs. The result of such professional isolation can be burnout, loss of enthusiasm, role diffusion, disinterest in the latest research findings, and a sense of disenfranchisement from the larger art therapy community. Professional isolation is one reason it is important to become identified with, and active in, regional and national professional associations.

The American Art Therapy Association (AATA) is a body of professionals committed to the belief that making art is healing and life enhancing. Attending the annual national AATA conference is important for art therapists because this is one time during the year when art therapists can be with a large number of other people who share the underlying view that making art is therapeutic. The annual conference can be, in the best possible sense, like a family reunion. Art therapists have the opportunity to see friends and colleagues with whom they have little or no contact throughout the year. The experience can be one of renewal, where a sense of pride and excitement about being an art therapist is generated.

The focus of this chapter is the ethical aspects of being a member of a professional community. As professionals, art therapists have responsibilities to:

- Participate in the activities of local professional associations and the American Art Therapy Association;
- Promote the goals of art therapy;
- Adhere to the practice standards of the profession;

- Participate in activities that contribute to the betterment of society;
- Assist in the development of laws and regulations relevant to the practice of art therapy which serve the public interest;
- Ascribe due credit to those who have contributed to one's publications, and appropriately cite persons who merit credit for creative or original ideas;
- Take sensible precautions to ensure that one's publications are advertised and promoted in an accurate manner;
- Prevent the misuse or distortion of one's art therapy research discoveries by any practitioner, employer, or institution, and;
- Treat one another with courtesy and respect.

PARTICIPATION IN ART THERAPY PROFESSIONAL ASSOCIATIONS

In art therapy there are two formal levels of professional association, the national *American Art Therapy Association* (AATA) and the local *Affiliate Chapters* of the AATA. It is a good idea for graduate art therapy students to begin to identify with both the local and national association early on in their training in order to begin to foster professional relationships. The AATA provides many benefits to its members, including subscription to *Art Therapy: The Journal of the American Art Therapy Association*, a quarterly *Newsletter*, eligibility for professional liability insurance, ongoing professional development through regional symposia and the national conference, and discounted registration fees for the conference. Most affiliate chapters of AATA also provide a periodic newsletter, informal regional gatherings, formal meetings, educational offerings, opportunities for supervision, and collegial networking. These organizations are the primary supporters of continuing education and professional community building. The goals of the American Art Therapy Association and its local affiliate chapters are summarized in its Mission Statement.

> The American Art Therapy Association, Inc. (AATA) is an organization of professionals dedicated to the belief that the creative process involved in the making of art is healing and life enhancing.
>
> Its mission is to serve its members and the general public by providing standards of professional competence, and developing and promoting knowledge in, and of, the field of art therapy.

In the years that the American Art Therapy Association has been in existence, much has been done to systematize the art therapy discipline.

Standards of art therapy graduate education have been established. Arduous registration procedures and systems have been devised, and a national certification examination has been created. The American Art Therapy Association has been empowered to govern and nurture the development of the profession on a national scale. A rigorous process of educational program approval has been delineated and the majority of practicing art therapists has ratified the *Ethical Principles for Art Therapists*. A credentialing corporation has been founded, by-laws written, and consequences for non-compliance with the above have been defined. In many regards, art therapy has become an institution.

There are both positive and negative results of this evolving process of formalization. A troublesome result of formalizing the discipline is the tendency to want to establish a uniform set of theories, philosophies, and approaches. As art therapy attempts to more clearly define itself, there is the temptation to impose a narrow set of common understandings.

The formalization of art therapy has, in part, been in an effort to establish professional respectability in the eyes of other disciplines. There is certainly nothing inherently wrong with respectability; however, some art therapists have suggested that the field has been too concerned with justifying itself in the eyes of other professions. Because of the desire to be approved of by other disciplines, there have been times when some art therapy theorists have sometimes been criticized for exploring perspectives that other professions do not endorse. Historically, one of the virtues of the art therapy profession has been our capacity to embrace difference. The first word of our professional name, ART, implies an eagerness to work with contrast, harmony, and dissonance, and to integrate disparate parts into a new consonant whole. This is what artists have done from the beginning of time. It is a task of all ethical art therapists, and institutions of art therapy, to hold in tension the possibility of multiple truths about this profession.

In order to avoid undue theoretical constriction, "the institutions of art therapy must, in the near future, reevaluate their by-laws, standards, and unspoken mores. The windows and doors of the building must be opened, for the air is getting stale within. I worry about our suffocating one another"(Moon, 1994, p.193). The AATA Board of Directors and the AATA committees are comprised of individual art therapists. The only way for art therapists to be assured that the windows and doors of the building will be open is through active participation. Deborah Good, president of the AATA from 1998 to 1999, echoed this sentiment, "As AATA members, you have a strong voice in the continual formation of our association" (Good, 1999, p.3), and by extension, I might add, the formation of the profession.

PROMOTING THE GOALS OF ART THERAPY

The following is a summary of the goals of AATA as outlined in Section 2 of the Bylaws of the American Art Therapy Association. The goals of art therapy are to provide for, and promote:

• Educational opportunities within the field of art therapy;
• Public awareness of the field;
• Progressive development of the therapeutic use of art;
• The advancement of research and standards of clinical practice;
• Maintenance of criteria for training future art therapists;
• Appropriate opportunities for the exchange of information;
• The coordination of the therapeutic use of art in institutional and private practice settings;
• The awarding of scholarships and research grants.

A central issue in the art therapy professional community has been the effort to establish professional status of art therapy in mental and physical health settings. For many years, this effort was thwarted by the difficulties inherent in defining the profession. These difficulties have been overcome through the efforts of AATA members who hammered out an encompassing definition:

> Art therapy is the therapeutic use of art making, within a professional relationship, by people who experience illness, trauma, or challenges in living, and by people who seek personal development. Through creating art and reflecting on the art products and processes, people can increase awareness of self and others, cope with symptoms, stress, and traumatic experiences; enhance cognitive abilities; and enjoy the life-affirming pleasures of making art.
>
> Art therapists are professionals trained in both art and therapy. They are knowledgeable about human development, psychological theories, clinical practice, spiritual, multicultural and artistic traditions, and the healing potential of art. They use art in treatment, assessment and research, and provide consultations to allied professionals. Art therapists work with people of all ages: individuals, couples, families, groups, and communities. They provide services, individually and as part of clinical teams, in settings that include mental health, rehabilitation, medical and forensic institutions; community outreach programs; wellness centers; schools; nursing homes; corporate structures; open studios and independent practices.
>
> (AATA, 2004 Membership Directory, p. iv.)

Feder and Feder (1984) note, "The commonly accepted attributes of a profession constitute a base in a substantial body of knowledge, a lengthy training period, exclusivity, and control over its members as well as over entry into the practice" (p.233). Progress in the drive toward professionalism in art therapy can be seen in the rigorous standards for educational training programs, the academic standards required of students involved in art therapy education, and the demanding requirements for credentialing. In the relatively recent past, a separate Art Therapy Credentials Board and a national certification examination have been added to establish a way to measure a minimum knowledge base for art therapists. At the time of this writing, there continue to be keen debates as to whether or not the certification examination is helpful to the status of the profession, or simply another bureaucratic (and expensive) hoop through which to jump.

Generally, it is true that what is good for art therapy is good for art therapists. Individual art therapists are personally and professionally enriched by participation in educational events that promote their growth. Art therapists benefit from increased public awareness of the field. As the discipline continues to develop its theoretical and practical fund of knowledge related to the therapeutic use of art, practitioners' professional self-regard is heightened. All art therapists can potentially benefit from new research in the field. As the standards of clinical practice continue to be defined, communicated, and implemented, professional practitioners naturally become more self-confident. Hence, working to advance the overall goals of art therapy serves each and every individual art therapist as well.

Figure 19. Gathering Together–Charcoal
Lolita Nogan

ADHERENCE TO THE STANDARDS OF THE PROFESSION

The standards of practice for art therapists are clearly outlined by the American Art Therapy Association. The Art Therapy Credentials Board, Inc. (ATCB) is a separate and independent organization that grants credentials. It is important that art therapists understand these are two separate and distinct but related organizations. The AATA is a membership organization dedicated to the mission and goals discussed in earlier sections of this text. The Art Therapy Credentials Board (ATCB) is comprised of a board of directors who design and implement registration standards and administer the national certification examination. These organizations have two entirely separate corporate structures and their missions are markedly different. Both serve art therapy practitioners by establishing and maintaining high standards. However, maintenance of standards of competence is a responsibility that is shared by all art therapists, not just the professional associations.

It is ethically imperative that art therapy students and practitioners be familiar with all relevant standards documents. Ignorance of a particular standard does not excuse one from the obligation to adhere to it. Art therapy education programs must diligently work to inform students of these standards; however, it is ultimately the individual's obligation to know the content of the standards of the profession.

The sequence of credentialing that art therapists follow is:

1. Complete a baccalaureate degree in art therapy or a related field.
2. Complete the Master of Arts Degree or Master of Science Degree in Art Therapy
3. Become a member of the American Art Therapy Association (this can occur prior to # 1 above).
4. Complete 1000 hours of supervised clinical experience (postgraduation from an AATA "approved" graduate program), or completion 2000 hours of supervised clinical experience (postgraduation from a graduate program that is not an approved AATA educational site). At least a Registered Art must provide half of the supervision Therapist (ATR).
5. Apply for registration (ATR) with the Art Therapy Credentials Board (ATCB).
6. After receipt of the ATR, the art therapist is eligible to take the national certification examination.Successful completion of this exam constitutes Board Certification (ATR-BC).

Information regarding the standards for registration and the national certification examination may be obtained by contacting the ATCB.

Art Therapy Credentials Board
The Center for Credentialing and Education
3 Terrace Way, Suite B
Greensboro, North Carolina 27403-3660
(877) 213-2822
email: info@atcb.org
website: www.atcb.org

ASSISTING IN THE DEVELOPMENT OF LAWS AND REGULATIONS RELEVANT TO ART THERAPY

Art therapists have ethical obligations in relation to state laws and mandates regulating the practice of art therapy. At the time of this writing, several states have enacted licensure laws that include art therapy as one of the disciplines subject to regulation. Some states have legislation pending that may affect art therapists. Other states have legislation that excludes art therapists.

There has been debate among art therapists regarding the positive effects of licensure laws. Some art therapists believe that licensure by an official State Licensing Board bestows an air of professional status upon art therapists. Others regard licensure as an essential means to ensure professional survival in relation to receiving third-party payments. Still other art therapists view the licensure process as an important mechanism to protect the consumer. Practitioners in these camps argue that licensure is a professional imperative. They believe that without licensure, art therapy jobs may disappear and the discipline may cease to exist. On the other side of the debate are art therapists who question the validity of licensure systems. Still others argue that art therapy's sense of professional identity must come from within, rather than be imposed by external licensing boards. Regardless of what an art therapist's position is on this controversial topic, it is nevertheless important to be informed about the state laws and regulations relevant to art therapy.

Art therapists can be constructive agents of change within communities. They can help local and state organizations and legislative bodies find solutions for societal problems such as child abuse, domestic violence, delinquency, prejudice against the mentally ill, and mistreatment of the elderly. These are but some of the difficulties that must be addressed through appropriate legislation and regulation, and art therapists can serve as advocates for such causes. Art therapists have an ethical responsibility to work toward the formidable task of convincing those who influence federal and state funding to allocate an equitable amount of their budgets to humanitarian causes such as those listed above.

It is clear that the leadership of AATA believes the organization and its individual members have a responsibility to help shape public policy guidelines and prioritize issues and goals. Commenting on individual responsibility, Lindberg (1999), the legislative consultant to AATA, states, "The best advocacy effort is built on a foundation of education and constituent contact. Interested AATA members will be trained in the art of educating Members of Congress and other federal policy makers. Ideally, AATA members from the congressional districts and states will contact their respective elected officials" (p. 15). Art therapists have an ethical responsibility to be positive agents of change within their communities.

ISSUES RELATED TO PUBLICATION

When shared with the art therapy community, the development of art therapy theories, philosophies, methodologies, techniques, and research advance the field of art therapy. Art therapists share their ideas in a variety of ways, both formally and informally. Among the mechanisms available are making presentations at professional conferences, conducting in-service workshops, publishing in professional journals, contributing to edited collections, and authoring books. This can be hard work, for as Malchiodi (1992) notes, ". . . it is paramount that writing about art therapy theory, practice, and research be articulate and exacting, especially if art therapists want to demonstrate a unique knowledge base which is distinctly separate from other related disciplines" (p. 64). Art therapists beginning the process of collecting their ideas soon discover there is no surer way to organize their thoughts than by trying to explain or teach them to someone else.

It is important for art therapy authors and presenters to do a thorough and accurate review of the existing literature relevant to the specific topic with which they are dealing (Malchiodi, 1992, p. 62). It is virtually impossible to contribute something new to the field if one is not fully aware of previous work documented in the literature of the profession. It is imperative that art therapists ascribe due credit to those who have contributed to their publications, and appropriately cite persons who merit credit for creative or original ideas. In order to do this in a consistent and ethical manner, the profession of art therapy has adopted the format of the American Psychological Association as a guide to professional writing. It is important that art therapy authors become familiar with, and adhere to, the style specifications presented in the Publication Manual of the American Psychological Association (1994).

It is crucial that art therapists attempt to precisely, fluently, and eloquently describe the profession. As art therapy continues to develop as a valuable discipline, there will be many opportunities to publicly articulate its worth. It is important for authors to hold sacred the power their words have in giving form to the art therapy discipline.

Once an art therapist's article or book has been published, it is necessary to take sensible precautions to ensure that one's publications are advertised and promoted in an accurate, appropriate, and ethical manner. Art therapy authors must also work to prevent the misuse or distortion of their art therapy techniques, methods, theories, and research discoveries by any practitioner, employer, or institution.

PROFESSIONAL COURTESY

Underlying each of these responsibilities to the art therapy profession is the notion that art therapists treat one another with courtesy and respect. Narrowly defined, professional courtesy is, "the respect extended to colleagues, peers, teachers, and supervisors when utilizing their original work in one's written publication or oral presentation" (Malchiodi, 1994, p. 242). A broader definition of professional courtesy might extend beyond the bounds of literary and public citation. Professional courtesy, in its broader view, could be an attitude of respect and considerate regard extended to colleagues, peers, teachers, and supervisors in most (if not all) circumstances.

The collective history of art therapy in America is enriched by near legendary word-of-mouth accounts of the haggling, arguing, and eventual compromises that occurred during the early gatherings of the pioneers of the field. Some book reviews and letters to the editor in art therapy newsletters and journals serve as testimonials to the passions of art therapists. At times, such passionate expressions about particular viewpoints can lead to the temptation to make disparaging remarks about colleagues. To extend professional courtesy means adopting an attitude of respect and consideration, sometimes even towards persons with whom one vehemently disagrees.

Chapter X

DEALING WITH AN ETHICAL VIOLATION

All art therapists are the guardians of the profession. They have an ethical obligation to protect the welfare of clients, supervisees, students, the public, and the profession at large. Art therapists also have a responsibility to take action when they become aware of unethical behavior on the part of a professional colleague. If, in an art therapist's judgment, the nature of a colleague's actions constitutes unethical practice, it is the art therapist's responsibility to protect the standards of ethical practice and to see that unethical behavior is addressed.

Art therapists have a deep desire to help others. This core value can lead to internal conflict when an art therapist is confronted with a situation in which he/she has ethical concerns regarding another art therapist's behavior. A frequently asked question from art therapy students and practitioners is "What is my responsibility when I become aware of an art therapist who is behaving in an unethical manner?"

In order to begin discussion of this question, consider the following situations:

- You are aware of an art therapy peer who maintains a private practice and does not keep ongoing progress notes or formal records of interactions with clients. You have asked the art therapist about this, and the justification given is the view that documentation is a waste of time and energy. What should you do?
- You are a student in a graduate art therapy program. You have heard that an art therapy professor at your school is having a sexual relationship with one of your peers. When you ask your peer about this, the response is that they are both consenting adults and that it is none of your business. What would you do?
- During an individual supervision session, your clinical supervisor makes what you consider to be an extremely inappropriate interpretation of your client's artwork. When you express your discomfort with the super-

visor's approach, she reminds you that you need her recommendation in order to become registered as an art therapist. How would you handle this?

• You become aware that an art therapy student is writing fictitious client progress notes in order to look good in the eyes of her supervisor. What should you do?

Most art therapists are, by nature, tolerant and accepting of others. However, such acceptance can cause inner turmoil when an art therapist becomes aware of a situation in which another art therapist may be behaving unethically. Even in situations where there is no doubt that a colleague is involved in unethical behavior, art therapists still may have questions regarding how best to respond it.

When individuals become a member of the American Art Therapy Association they agree to abide by the AATA Ethical Principles for Art Therapists. "It is the ethical responsibility of each member to act in accordance with these principles and to comply with all applicable laws, regulations, and licensing requirements that govern the practice of therapy in each member's state" (AATA, 2003, p. 14).

Disagreements and conflicts are inevitable in any profession. Situations periodically arise in which one or more people believe that an art therapist may have violated the AATA Ethical Principles for Art Therapists or the ATCB Code of Professional Practice. Ethical complaints regarding an art therapist's behavior are directed to the Art Therapy Credentials Board if the complainant is seeking disciplinary action against the art therapist. Section VII, Disciplinary Procedures of the *Code of Professional Practice* ATCB (2005) states:

> Any person concerned with possible violation of ATCB Standards of Conduct, or other ATCB standard, policy or procedure, may initiate a complaint by identifying the persons alleged to be involved and the facts concerning the alleged conduct in as much detail and specifically as possible with available documentation in a written statement the Ethical Standards should bring this to the attention of the Committee in the form of a written complaint. (p. 7)

In the *Code of Professional Practice* (ATCB 2005) disciplinary procedures and potential sanctions are outlined (see Appendix B). The process of filing a formal complaint can be somewhat intimidating, however, and some art therapists may resist. The following strategic considerations may be of help to art therapists who have concerns regarding the ethicality of another art therapist's behavior.

1. Discuss your concerns with the art therapist in question. Attempt to do so in a nonjudgmental, nonaccusatory manner. This is not always easy, but it is essential to be clear that the ultimate purpose of the discussion is to help the art therapist and her/his clients. If, after this discussion, you are still concerned regarding the art therapist's behavior, proceed to the next step.

2. Discuss your general concerns, without naming the art therapist, with a supervisor, mentor, or experienced colleague whose wisdom and opinions you value. Ask for his/her feedback and input regarding the behaviors that are of concern. If the supervisor or mentor agrees that your concerns are valid, proceed to the next step. If your supervisor or mentor does not concur with your view, take some time to think through the issues further. If, after careful consideration, you are still concerned about the art therapist's behavior proceed to the next step.

3. Discuss your concerns again with the art therapist in question. Maintain a non-judgmental, nonaccusatory manner, but be clear that you have serious ethical concerns regarding the art therapist's behavior. Attempt to be supportive of the art therapist in question. It is most helpful to be specific regarding the behaviors you consider problematic. Appeal to the art therapist's desire to provide his or her clients with high-quality, effective therapeutic service. You may suggest that he or she seek supervision or personal therapy. You might also suggest ways that you could be a source of support to the art therapist as he/she wrestles with the issue.

4. If the art therapist is able to see the validity of your concerns and is able to develop a plan of action in response, you may have fulfilled your ethical obligation to the profession. If the art therapist becomes defensive and exhibits no motivation to examine the issues, then you must take additional steps.

5. If, after having discussed your concerns with the art therapist in question and with your supervisor or mentor, you remain concerned about the ethicality of the art therapist's behavior, you are obligated to bring the matter to the attention of the Art Therapy Credentials Board in the form of a written complaint.

In general, ethical concerns are best dealt with at the level closest to the situation. Ideally, ethical violations are dealt with directly among colleagues without the formal intervention of professional associations. However, it is clearly the responsibility of every art therapist to confront unethical practice by other art therapists, even if that necessitates registering a complaint with the ATCB. In fact, failure to confront a recognized ethical violation is considered to be an ethical violation itself.

Again, each member of AATA is ethically obliged to uphold the standards of practice and to address violations of the ethical principles by other members of the association. Art therapists credentialed by the ATCB are expected to adhere to the *Code of Professional Practice* and to cooperate with the Ethics Officer, and to respond to inquiries by the Disciplinary Hearing Committee in a thorough and timely manner. This means that when an art therapist becomes aware of unethical behavior(s) by an art therapy colleague, he/she must address the behavior.

As stated earlier in this chapter, because of the core values of acceptance and non-judgment, it is often difficult and uncomfortable for art therapists and others in the helping professions to determine that a colleague's behavior is unethical. At the same time, however, it may be easier to see shortcomings in others' behavior than to monitor and reflect upon one's own conduct. While it is important for art therapists to serve the profession by reporting apparent violations of the ethical standards of the discipline, it is equally important for art therapists to continually monitor their own behavior.

At some point in their careers, art therapists may face situations in which they need to deal with their concerns regarding the unethical behavior of colleagues. The following artistic tasks will help art therapists think about and explore these issues.

Suggested Artistic Tasks

1. In a class or group supervisory session, create an artwork that depicts feelings you have had or would expect to have when confronting another art therapist with an allegation of unethical behavior. Discuss the images and the situations they portray with others in the group.

2. Create an image representing how you would feel if you were accused of an ethical violation. Pay attention to the feelings that the process of making this artwork stirs in you. Share your image and the feelings it stimulates with a trusted supervisor or peers.

3. Think about what behaviors you believe to be serious enough to warrant making a formal ethics complaint. Write a poem that reflects your feelings about one such behavior. Share and discuss your poetic creation with a group of peers. Ask for their feedback about the ethical issue(s) your poem addresses.

4. Create a collage on the theme of "two unethical behaviors art therapists are particularly likely to commit." Discuss with colleagues or with a supervisor the issues your collage raises.

5. In a classroom or group supervisory setting, role-play situations in which one art therapist confronts another about ethical concerns. Discuss various strategies regarding how to handle these situations.

6. In a classroom or group supervisory setting, enact role-plays of situations in which an art therapist ignores a colleague's unethical behavior. Discuss, compare and contrast the situations presented in Activities #5 and #6.

Chapter XI

ADVERTISING AND PUBLICITY

Ad-ver-tise (ad'ver tiz') vt. - tising, tised: To warn, call attention to; to tell about or praise (a product, service, etc.) publicly, as through newspapers, handbills, radio, television, etc., so as to make people want to buy it; to make known or give notice of; to call the public's attention to things for sale or rent (*Webster's New World Dictionary*, 1988, p. 19-20).

Art therapists have the right to call attention to, tell about, and publicly praise their services through newspapers, handbills, business cards, radio, and television in order to make people aware of art therapy as a treatment option. Advertising, however, ought to be done in an ethical, professional, and appropriate manner.

The profession of art therapy is a relative newcomer in relation to other helping professions such as psychiatry, psychology, nursing, and social work. At the time of this writing, the American Art Therapy Association is approaching its thirty-fifth year. There are only a few thousand art therapists nationwide. Hence, art therapy is not nearly as well known as many of the other healthcare disciplines. An important aspect of art therapists' work is to inform the public about their services. In a sense, art therapists must become promoters of, and advocates for, the profession. As is the case with other helping professions, advertising is an essential component of economic survival.

It is appropriate for art therapists to engage in advertising so that laypersons may make informed decisions regarding professional services. In order to advertise in an ethical manner, it important for art therapists consider the following areas:

- Information regarding professional competence, education, training, and experience must be presented accurately.
- Information should be presented in such a way as to maintain the dignity of the profession.

- Information about art therapy services should not mislead the public or misrepresent the profession.
- Information about an individual art therapy practitioner should accu rately portray the individual's scope of practice.
- No unsupportable claims regarding services should be made.

Issues regarding advertising are addressed in section 11 of the *Ethical Principles for Art Therapists.*

11.0 Advertising

Art therapists accurately represent their professional competence, education, training, and experience.

Art therapists do not use a name that is likely to mislead the public concerning the identity, responsibility, source, and status of those under whom they are practicing, and do not hold themselves out as being partners or associates of a firm if they are not.

Art therapists do not use any professional identification (such as a business card, office sign, letterhead, or telephone or association directory listing) if it includes a statement or claim that is false, fraudulent, misleading, or deceptive. A statement is false, fraudulent or deceptive if it: (a) fails to state any material fact necessary to keep the statement from being misleading; (b) is intended to, or likely to, create an unjustified expectation; or (c) contains a material misrepresentation of fact.

Art therapists correct, whenever reasonable, false, misleading, or inaccurate information and representations made by others concerning the therapist's qualifications, services, or products.

Art therapists make certain that the qualifications of persons in their employ are represented in a manner that is not false, misleading, or deceptive.

11.6. Art therapists may represent themselves as specializing within a limited area of art therapy only if they have the appropriate education, training, and experience to practice in that specialty area.

11.7. AATA credentialed, professional, associate, and other members in good standing may identify such membership in AATA in public information or advertising materials, but they must clearly and accurately represent the membership category to which they belong.

11.8. Art therapists do not use the ATR[8] and/or ATR-BC following their name unless they are officially notified in writing by the Art Therapy Credential Board, Inc., that they have successfully completed all applicable registration and certification procedures. Art therapists may not use the initials "AATA" following their name as if it were an academic degree.

11.9. Art therapists may not use the AATA initials or logo without receiving written permission from the Association.

DEALING WITH THE NEWS MEDIA

Many art therapists have used newspapers, radio, and television news stories and interviews to inform the public about art therapy. While it has been said that any publicity is good publicity, experience suggests that this is not always the case in relation to the art therapy profession. Consider the following description of an actual television interview.

In September of 1991, a local television station contacted the art therapist at a psychiatric hospital. The station wanted to videotape an interview with the art therapist for broadcast during a weekly program feature on health issues. An appointment was made to tape the session in one of the art therapy rooms at the hospital. The art therapist had a few days to think about how to present art therapy and to prepare for the interview. The therapist decided against doing too much didactic presentation and chose instead to engage the interviewer in an art therapy experience.

The actual taping of the session lasted nearly an hour. The physician who was the interviewer was generally receptive to the art therapy experiential process. The art therapist left the session feeling pretty good about the entire experience and was told that the segment would air in a few days.

What the art therapist failed to consider, however, was that the hour interaction would be edited down to a three-minute segment for broadcast. The therapist also did not anticipate the effect of the news anchor person's casual on-air interactions with the physician/interviewer prior to, and following, the taped segment.

When the story aired, the news segment opened with the following interaction among the news anchors and the medical specialist.

Anchor Woman: Mention medical treatments and most of us think of drugs and surgery, but there are other alternatives.

Anchor Man: And our medical specialist, [name deleted] joins us now with a look at art therapy.

Medical Specialist: Sounds a little strange doesn't it, but then that probably fits my personality. He looked toward the newswoman, smiled, and said, "Do you think?" There was a brief pause, then he said, "You lie, you are laughing." (laughter)

Anchor Woman: I do not, I am trying to be nice. (laughter)

Medical Specialist: No, art . . . art therapy really can be quite effective for treating a variety of psychological problems. And last night I got to spend some time with an art therapist at a local hospital.

* * * * *

This light bantering was an aspect of their on-the-air ambiance. It is likely that none of the three TV personalities meant any disrespect toward the art therapy profession. However, the effect of this lead-in to the videotaped segment was to create a sense of frivolity and shallowness that seemed to trivialize the feature that followed. The broadcast then cut away to the edited videotape for approximately three minutes. The tape editor did a fairly good job of capturing the essence of what had transpired between the process, the artistic media, and the people involved.

During the interview, the physician/interviewer engaged in several artistic tasks and was guided by the art therapist in exploring the meaning of the images. The editor selected a brief interaction focused on the interviewer's depiction of himself as a tree. Generally, when viewed in isolation from what preceded and followed, the videotape was an adequate thumbnail sketch of art therapy in a psychiatric context. However, at the conclusion of the video segment, the following interaction occurred:

Medical Specialist: This was really intriguing to go through this, and . . . and even though it was an exercise that I was doing as part of a report for television, I really started . . . I was amazed, I really started to learn some things about myself and I thought it was a pretty good tree." He then turned to the anchor woman, grinned and said, "So, [delete name] I brought it with . . . and uh . . . and I'm gonna give you the tree. I think maybe I ought to be able to sell it commercially, but you can take it home and frame it. (Laughter)

Anchor Woman: . . . and I need art in my house.

Anchor Man: (Chuckles)

Medical Specialist: There ya' go.

Anchor Woman: I do need art in my house, and I think that this probably . . . this . . . I look at this, I see you.

Medical Specialist: Do you? (Laughter)

Anchor Woman: I look at this, I see *you*, now. (much laughter) That branch system, that is you. (Laughter)

Medical Specialist: It really is an effective therapy, especially for some kids.

(The trio sobers for a brief time)

Anchor Man: Why would that be especially good for kids.

Medical Specialist: Well, it's especially good for like for a five or a six-year- old who really has difficulty in most instances expressing things verbally. But you give them a blank piece of paper like this and some chalk, or some crayons, or some paint and they really get busy. And you can open them up by just doing what . . . what the art therapist was doing with me. By talking about, well, why did you do, what do you see in this, what does this represent, what would be the context of this? Really intriguing, and it was fun to do.

Anchor Woman: And then over time you can chart progress then by the way the pictures change?

Medical Specialist: Right. I'll bring you a new tree in a couple months. (Chuckle)

Anchor Woman: OK thank you. I need one for the other wall now. Thank you. (dissolves into laughter)

* * * * *

The bantering between the TV personalities seemed to trivialize the story. Unfortunately, this transformed a potentially positive public education opportunity into a fluffy tidbit on the local news. The before, and after, interactions clearly undermined the integrity of the interview.

When interviewed for television broadcasts, art therapists should consider the following items prior to giving their consent:

1. Who will be the interviewer? When possible, the art therapist should familiarize herself with the on-camera style of the interviewer in order to anticipate how the interviewer will interact with her.

2. What is the intent of the interview? Is the station genuinely interested in informing the public about art therapy? Are they interested in providing "fluff" to their newscast? Are they seeking a sensationalized angle on the story?

3. How will the segment be introduced? It is advisable to talk about this with the interviewer ahead of time in order to stress the seriousness of the work.

4. How will the segment be concluded? How will they segue to the next story? While it is unlikely that the art therapist will have any control over the flow of the newscast, it can be helpful to express concerns in order to sensitize the interviewer(s) to these issues.

5. What is the TV station's history with other such interviews? Have such stories been handled respectfully, playfully, sensationally, etc.?

6. Art therapists must keep in mind the potency and scope of broadcast media. Depending upon the size and location of a particular television viewing area, an interview with an art therapist may be seen by hundreds of thousands of people. For most of those people all they will ever know about art therapy will be what they observe on the television. Art therapists ought to be cautious, careful, and thoughtful as they consider doing a television interview.

Art therapists often receive requests from newspapers to be the subject of human interest or health-related feature stories. Newspaper stories are an excellent way to provide information to the general public. It is important for

art therapists to think through what they want to convey in an interview prior
to the event. In some instances, articles are clear, well written, and informa-
tive. In other instances, art therapists are misquoted, and on occasion stories
are fabricated. These experiences lead to the following points to consider for
art therapists being interviewed by newspaper journalists:

1. Who will be the reporter? The art therapist should become familiar with
   other articles by the interviewer in order to get a feel for how the interviewer will write the story.
2. What is the intent of the story? Is the newspaper genuinely interested in
   informing the public about art therapy? Is the newspaper interested in
   demythologizing therapy, or in seeking an exciting angle on the story?
3. Where will the story be placed in the paper? It is advisable to talk about
   this with the reporter ahead of time in order to stress the seriousness of
   the work. How will the story be headlined? The art therapist may have
   little control over these things, but it can still be helpful to express concern about them in order to sensitize the reporter to such issues.
4. What is the newspaper's history with other healthcare interviews? Have
   such stories been handled respectfully, playfully, sensationally, etc.?
5. Who will read the story? Art therapists must keep in mind the power of
   the printed word. Depending upon the size and location of a particular
   newspaper, a story about an art therapist may be read by thousands of
   people. For most of the readership, all they will ever know about art
   therapy will come from what they read in the paper. It is important for
   art therapists to be cautious, careful, and thoughtful as they consider
   doing a newspaper interview.

Many art therapists, at some point in their career, will consider advertising their services or be asked to grant news interviews. Art therapists have to
develop guidelines and policies regarding advertising and publicity that are
appropriate to their contexts. The following artistic tasks will help art therapists think about and explore these issues.

Suggested Artistic Activities

1. Imagine you are an art therapist who is asked to be interviewed by a
   reporter from the media. Create an art piece that depicts the feelings
   the interview might stimulate. Discuss the images with others.
2. Create an image of a billboard advertising art therapy services. Pay
   attention to the feelings that the process of making this artwork stirs.
   Share the image and the feelings it stimulates with peers or a supervisor. Ask for feedback regarding the information the ad conveys.

3. Consider your ideas about what constitutes good advertising and false or misleading advertising. Write a poem that reflects your feelings about one such ad. Share and discuss your poetic creation with a group of peers. Ask for feedback about the ethical issue(s) your poem addresses.

4. Create a collage on the theme of "how art therapists should advertise their services." Discuss with colleagues or a supervisor the issues your collage raises.

5. In a classroom or group supervisory session, role-play situations in which an art therapist must struggle with a news interview in which he/she is badly misquoted. Discuss various strategies regarding how to handle such situations.

6. Create and videotape commercials about art therapy. Show the videos in class or in a supervision group and discuss the feelings and ideas these commercials stimulate.

Chapter XII

ART THERAPISTS IN PRIVATE PRACTICE

Beginning in the mid 1980s and continuing to the present day, the nature of healthcare institutions and third-party reimbursement organizations in the United States has undergone dramatic changes. One by-product of the changing healthcare marketplace has been an increase in the numbers of art therapists choosing to work in private practice and in other contexts independent of larger umbrella institutions. Typically, art therapists who are working as independent practitioners possess some practical experience and clinical maturity prior entering private practice. Art therapists in private practice ought to be secure in their clinical expertise and need to have developed some business acumen if they are to be successful.

When art therapists decide to work as independent practitioners, they assume full responsibility for the delivery of services to their clients (Wirtz, Sidun, Carrigan, Wadeson, Kennedy, & Marano-Geiser, 1994). Likewise, they assume full liability for their practice as well. In 1993, the American Art Therapy Association published guidelines for independent practitioners that were eventually incorporated into the AATA Ethics Document.

Independent practitioners of art therapy should be Credentialed Professional Members of the American Art Therapy Association. In addition to maintaining their registration (ATR), they must have had at least two years or 3,000 hours of full-time practice or 3,000 hours of paid clinical art therapy experience. It must be emphasized that this was meant to be a minimum requirement. Clearly, the more experience an art therapist has prior to entry into private practice, the better. Art therapists are advised against entering independent practice until they have gained significant clinical experience. The nature and pressures of private practice demand a certain amount of clinical experience that many novice art therapists do not possess. In addition to supervised clinical experience, independent art therapists need to have considerable life experience before they strike out on their own.

Beyond the minimum two years of full-time practice, one of the hallmarks of professional maturity is the capacity of the art therapist to identify cases and situations beyond the scope of their expertise. In such circumstances, it is imperative that the independent art therapist seek qualified psychological or medical consultation and/or refer the client to a more qualified therapist. In cases in which medication is required, the art therapist must obtain appropriate medical consultation for the client. Mature art therapists know the boundaries of their qualifications and do not attempt to provide services other than those for which they have been adequately trained.

There are many federal, state, and local laws that relate to the independent practice of art therapy. Relevant statutes vary from state to state and it is the responsibility of the individual independent practitioner to know of and adhere to these laws. An increasing number of states have licensure laws regarding independent art therapy practice to which practitioners must conform.

Among the many responsibilities of art therapists in private practice are those related to the maintenance of a safe, predictable, and serviceable environment in which they provide their services. The following environmental components are imperative:

- proper ventilation
- adequate lighting
- access to water supply
- knowledge of hazards or toxicity of art materials and the effort needed to safeguard the health of clients
- storage space for art projects and secured areas for any hazardous materials
- monitored use of sharps
- allowance for privacy and confidentiality
- compliance with any other health and safety requirements according to state and federal agencies which regulate comparable businesses.

Art therapists in private practice have to pay particular attention to the issues of informed consent, discussed in Chapter II. Areas of informed consent that are especially relevant to independent practitioners concern the limits of confidentiality, the sharing of information in supervision, and the art therapist's duty to report suspected abuse.

Although independent art therapists may have more freedom regarding treatment planning and documentation of service than their colleagues who work within traditional healthcare systems, they still are obliged to develop treatment plans and document clients' experiences within art therapy sessions. Although the specific forms of planning may vary, it is advisable for art therapy treatment plans to address the following areas:

1. How the art therapist intends to aid the client in achieving a positive level of functioning and quality of life;
2. Specific schedule, duration, and nature of art therapy sessions;
3. Problems, goals, and actions that address the client's needs, dysfunctions, and strengths;
4. Reference to how and when particular goals have been met;
5. Mechanisms for systematic review, evaluation, modification, and appropriate alteration.

Art therapists in private practice have to document their work with clients. The specific form of art therapy documentation will vary depending upon the independent practitioner's context. Regardless of context the following areas ought to be addressed in some manner:

1. Brief statement of the problems, goals, and actions addressed during the session;
2. Description of media used during the session;
3. Description of processes involved in the session;
4. Description, or depiction, of images/artworks created by the client during the session;
5. Observations regarding client's affect, behavior, and thought process;
6. Appropriate reference to relevant verbal content of the art therapy session;
7. Summary of aspects of the session relevant to the stated problems, goals, and actions.

At the conclusion of the art therapy relationship, independent art therapists ought to write a discharge/transfer summary containing a description of the client's overall response to therapy and any recommendations for treatment in the future.

An important characteristic of mature art therapists is the ability to know when it is appropriate to terminate the therapy relationship. This truly is an art and not a science. Generally, an art therapist should begin to talk about termination as the client nears fulfillment of the goals specified in the treatment plan. It is essential to note that the termination phase of art therapy is a process, not an event. Ideally, this phase of the art therapy process consists of the internalization and consolidation of the gains made during treatment. It is a process of readying to leave the art therapy journey, to take a different path that inevitably separates the client from the art therapist. The termination phase often is a time when clients struggle with the concept that meaningful relationships in life do not necessarily last forever. However, it is important for clients to learn they can take relationships with them in the form of memories and experiences shared with the art therapist. Ideally, clients develop the awareness that they can recreate the experience of the relationship with the art therapist by creating new quality relationships in other, non-treatment settings.

During termination, the arts provide a means to express the sense of loss experienced as the relationship with the art therapist comes to an end. These feelings are often too difficult to put into words but may be profoundly expressed in images. In addition, the artifacts of the journey—the sculptures, paintings, and drawings—serve as the tangible objects clients take with them from the experience. These are the observable external representations of invisible internal experiences.

Moustakas (1995) describes the final phase of therapy in this way: "The aim is to bring together the *what* of the person's experience and the *how* in such a way that its nature and meanings are embraced" (p. 211). The client and the art therapist must put much effort into understanding the essence of meaning in their time together. This is not a simple process of summing-up, but rather is a creative "re-imagining" of the core meanings of their time together.

It is ethically imperative for art therapists to maintain an attitude of support and acceptance in regard to the inevitable end of the therapy relationship. It is a safe to assume that many art therapy clients have not had successful termination experiences in the past. It is more likely they have experienced unhealthy versions of the process. The last major piece of work between the art therapist and the client is the crafting of a healthy process of letting go.

As the institutional healthcare environments continue to change in the future, many art therapists may decide to enter private practice. Independent practitioners have many important decisions to make regarding their career paths. The following artistic tasks will help art therapists sort through and explore some of these issues.

Suggested Artistic Activities

1. Create an image of yourself as an independent art therapy practitioner.
2. Create an image what your "ideal" studio or office space would look like. Consider what regard as the pros and cons of private practice. Pay attention to the feelings that the process of making this artwork stirs in you. Share your image, ideas, and feelings with a trusted supervisor or peer group.
3. Think about your ideas regarding what constitutes adequate treatment planning. Create an image that symbolizes the qualities of what you regard as a good treatment plan. Reflect upon your image. Does your image contain the aspects listed in this chapter? How? Why?

4. Write a poem that expresses your feelings about being an independent practitioner. Share and discuss your poem with a group of peers. Ask for their feedback about the issues your poem raises.

5. Create a collage on the theme of "art therapy documentation". Discuss with colleagues, or a supervisor, the issues your collage raises.

6. In a classroom or group supervisory situation, role-play situations in which an art therapist is struggling with bringing up the subject of termination with a client she has grown close to. Act out the client's reaction to the art therapist initiating this discussion. Explore various strategies regarding how to handle the situation.

7. Create an image of two termination experiences you have had in your own life, one of them positive, the other negative. Discuss with peers the emotional differences in these two situations.

Chapter XIII

MULTICULTURAL AND DIVERSITY ISSUES IN ART THERAPY

The focus of this chapter is on ethical concerns that emerge in relation to issues of diversity and multiculturalism in art therapy. Section 1.1 of the *Ethical Principles for Art Therapists* (AATA, 2003) states, "Art therapists do not discriminate against or refuse professional service to anyone on the basis of age, gender identity, race, ethnicity, culture, national origin, religion, sexual orientation, disability, socioeconomic status, or any basis proscribed by law" (p. 3). While the aspirational nature of this statement is appreciated, it does little to ensure or support the development of multicultural awareness and sensitivity in art therapists. It is not possible to provide a comprehensive examination of multiculturalism and diversity issues in art therapy in this text due to the complexity of the issues. Art therapists are encouraged to deepen their knowledge of these subjects by exploring other sources on their own. I will, however, raise questions regarding the ways art therapists' cultural backgrounds and underlying suppositions are liable to affect their art therapy practice.

> Coming to grips with the complicated roles that ethnic and cultural diversity play in their work is a significant and formidable task confronting many art therapists. Our very definitions of human development are ethnoculturally based. Eastern cultures, for example, tend to define the person as a social being and categorize development as growth in the capacity for empathy. By contrast, many Western cultures begin by positing the individual as a psychological being and defining development as growth in the capacity for differentiation. (Hiscox and Calish, 1998, p. 9).

In the broadest sense, all interactions among people are multicultural. Each individual's family represents a culture that is unique from all others. Art therapists and their clients bring beliefs, attitudes, biases, mores, and values to the therapeutic situation. Corey, Corey, and Callanan (1998) note that therapists can err in both directions regarding attention to cultural differences. "One mistake is to deny the importance of these cultural variables in counseling; another is to overemphasize cultural differences to the extent that practitioners lose their naturalness and fail to make contact with their clients" (p. 318). The first of these mistakes is perhaps an extension of the American valuation of assimilation into the dominant culture. Historically, this value was summarized and euphemized in the phrase, "the great American melting pot." Recently, however, there has evolved an increased emphasis on acknowledging and honoring differences within and among cultural groups.

ESSENTIAL CONCEPTS

Corey, Corey, and Callanan (1998) state, "Culture, ethnicity, minority group, multiculturalism, multicultural counseling, diversity, ethnic-sensitive practice, racism, stereotypes, and the culturally encapsulated counselor are critical concepts for multicultural counseling" (p. 319). In this brief examination of multicultural issues in art therapy, it is important to consider the relevance of these essential concepts to the practice of art therapy.

For the purposes of this text, I will refer to culture in the broad sense as being comprised of, and affected by, racial, ethnic, gender, religious, economic, and geographic factors. Culture is also associated with sexual orientation, physical or emotional disability, age, social, and educational variables. This broad perspective of culture is important for art therapists because culture affects the ways in which people adjust to their physical, psychological, and social environment.

Ethnicity refers to the sense of self that comes from common ancestry, race, experience, and history. Ethnic identity is a potent unifying force that stems from unique experiences solidified through common social and cultural heritage.

In the United States and much of the Western world, the dominant culture is white, middle or upper class, and male. Minority groups are any category of people who have been oppressed and discriminated against by the larger, dominant society. Minority groups have typically experienced a pervasive sense of powerlessness and domination. It is important to note that *minority* has more to do with the experience of oppression than numerical yardsticks.

Generally speaking, multiculturalism refers to any interaction among two or more groups of people with different cultural backgrounds. Practicing art therapy from a multicultural perspective denotes taking into account the

complexity of dealing with individuals who have a set of cultural ʟ
values that influence their behavior. In addition, practicing from a ı.
tural perspective means art therapists must attempt to recognize theı.
values, beliefs, and biases that affect their behavior. Art therapists' and theı.
clients' values, beliefs, and behaviors are shaped by a number of factors
including gender, race, ethnicity, political views, economic status, geographic
region, religion, sexual orientation, physical appearance, disabilities, and
age. Multiculturalism provides a way of thinking about the world that highlights the complex diversity of a pluralistic society, while at the same time
proposing avenues of common concern that tie culturally different people to
one another (Pedersen, 1991).

Figure 20. Exploring Difference—Painted Wood

The term, "multicultural art therapy" suggests an awareness of a relationship in which the art therapist and the client are of different cultural groups.
Because of this cultural difference, the art therapist and the client are likely
to view the world differently. Each may have very different ideas about social
and emotional reality. Thus, multicultural art therapy entails making a con-
certed effort to integrate cultural awareness, cultural sensitivity, acceptance
of diversity, and knowledge of multicultural issues into the practice of art
therapy.

Due to rapid innovations in information technologies over the last decade, the world has become, for communications purposes, a smaller place. Telecommunications satellites and the Internet have revolutionized the flow and exchange of information worldwide. Not that long ago, it would have taken weeks to send and receive a letter from the United States to some remote places on the planet. Today, nearly every elementary school child in America can log on to the World Wide Web and communicate almost instantly with human beings around the globe. The long-term effects of this shrinkage are nearly unfathomable.

The experience of the world as a "global village" has made cultural diversity an actuality. Art therapists must attend to the issues inherent in providing therapy to diverse people. Art therapists who are sensitive to multicultural issues endeavor to identify and honor the influence of sociocultural forces on their clients. These forces, no doubt, play their part in the etiology, manifestation, explanation, and resolution of some forms of mental and emotional dysfunction. The real challenges for art therapists lay in understanding cultural beliefs and social norms and protecting them from being categorized as pathological simply because they do not match the dominant view of "normal."

Culture influences every aspect of life. Human behavior, thought, emotion, and spirituality are all shaped by the cultural context within which they evolve. Hiscox and Calish (1998) state, "Culture includes such features as attitudes, forms of emotional expression, patterns of relating to others and ways of thought" (p. 9). The sum of all cultures is an organized and integrated aggregate of patterned qualities, histories, experiences, and traits that form a mosaic-like portrait of the world. Individuals within a specific culture share some experiences in common with the larger community while maintaining some measure of autonomy. A specific culture, in turn, occupies a particular place within the larger mosaic and again shares some commonalties with other cultures while retaining its own cultural distinctness. Culture has undeniable impact upon one's experience of, and perspective on, emotional, inter-, and intra-psychic experience. Each tile in the mosaic portrait of the world is singular and offers a unique quality to the portrait as a whole. Each tile affects and is affected by the larger connected portrait of which it is an element.

Art therapists who work with clients from cultural backgrounds different than their own are faced with theoretical and practical problems in their efforts to understand and respect imagery and visual forms. There may be culture-specific meanings for visual symbols and images, as well as culture-specific differences in artistic style and form. On the other hand, as Calish and Hiscox (1998) note, art therapists are also presented with the opportunity to transcend the limitations of language and cultural roadblocks through the use of artistic media. While recognizing this opportunity, it is important for art therapists not to rely upon the false assumption that art is a "universal" language.

ART THERAPISTS MULTICULTURAL SELF-ASSESSMENT

In order to avoid unethical behavior related to cultural insensitivity, it is essential for art therapists to deepen their understanding of their own cultural presuppositions and assumptions. Multicultural awareness is the base upon which appreciation of difference is built. Being culturally self-aware helps art therapists begin to understand both differences and commonalties among cultures. The following is a brief Multicultural Self-Assessment intended to help art therapists examine their thoughts on professional and ethical issues in art therapy related to multiculturalism. It is a survey in which art therapists must select the answer that most closely matches their beliefs and attitudes. In some instances, readers may find it difficult to rate their reaction to the statements. It is fine to choose more than one response if necessary. I encourage art therapists to share their responses with classmates or peers in supervision groups and to compare their views with others. This will help the class or groups engage in discussion of the issues. Participants in this exercise are encouraged to write five additional statements based on their own experiences and to discuss them with others in the class or group.

Instructions: Indicate the response that most closely matches your beliefs regarding the statements below. Use the following code:

5 = Strongly agree
4 = Agree
3 = Undecided
2 = Disagree
1 = Strongly disagree

1. An ethical art therapist helps her minority clients assimilate into the dominant culture._____
2. Minority clients should only receive art therapy services from art therapists of the same background._____
3. Art is a universal language and therefore all art therapists are multiculturally sensitive. _____
4. Art therapists must take seriously the cultural and ethnic differences between themselves and their clients. _____
5. Therapeutic relationships are more difficult to establish when the art therapist and the client have different sexual orientations. _____

6. Female clients who have been sexually abused should never be seen by a male art therapist._____

7. Art therapists who are Caucasian, well-educated, caring, and self-aware are more likely to impose their values on clients than art therapists who are from an ethnic minority. _____

8. Art therapists who have not received education regarding cultural differences have no business providing services to clients from diverse populations._____

9. Art therapists should be forced to document that they have received specialized training in multicultural art therapy as a condition of registration with the American Art Therapy Association._____

10. At this time in my art therapy career I think that I am well prepared to provide art therapy services to diverse client populations._____

11. _____
12. _____
13. _____
14. _____
15. _____

Since art therapy is a form of psychological and rehabilitative treatment that has developed in the West, many art therapists are susceptible to what Corey, Corey, and Callanan (1998) term, "cultural tunnel vision" (p. 320). Among the attributes of cultural tunnel vision are the tendency to view one's reality as *the* reality, insensitivity to differences among people, and an underlying belief that one's way of thinking is correct and need not be subject to adaptation to alternative ways of thinking. To greater or lesser degrees, all art therapists suffer from cultural tunnel vision. It takes a concentrated effort for art therapists to monitor their biases so they do not hinder the formation of positive art therapy relationships. Art therapists, regardless of cultural background, must critically examine their own prejudices, attitudes, and expectations about the art therapy process.

The *Ethical Principles for Art Therapists* (AATA, 2003) addresses issues of multicultural awareness in section 6:

6.0 Art therapists are aware of and respect cultural, individual, and role differences, including those based on age, gender, gender identity, race, ethnicity, culture, national origin, religion, sexual orientation, disability, language, and socioeconomic status and consider these factors when working with members of such groups. Art therapists try to eliminate the effect on their work of biases based on those factors, and they do not knowingly participate in or condone activities of others based upon such prejudices.

Art therapists take reasonalble steps to ensure that they are sensitive to differences that exist among cultures. They are earnest in their attempts to learn

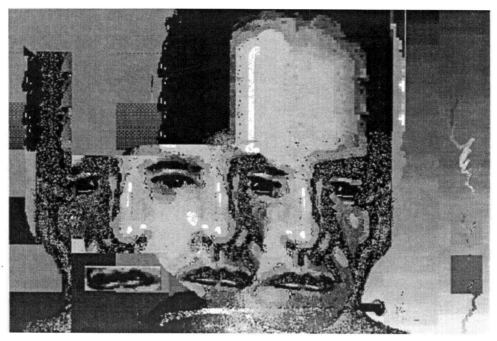

Figure 21. Examining Attitudes–Computer Graphic
John Meza

about the belief systems of people in any given cultural group in order to provide culturally relevant interventions and treatment.

Art therapists are aware of their own values and beliefs and how they may affect cross-cultural therapy interventions.

6.3 Art therapists obtain education about and seek to understand the nature of social diversity and oppression with respect to race, ethnicity, national origin, color, gender, sexual orientation, class, age, marital status, political belief, religion, and mental or physical disability.

Art therapists acquire knowledge and information about the specific group(s) with which they are working and the strengths inherent in that cultural group. They are sensitive to individual differences that exist within the cultural group and understand that individuals may have varying responses to group norms. When working with people from cultures different from their own, art therapists engage in culturally sensitive supervision, seek assistance from members of that culture, and make a referral to a professional who is knowledgable about the culture when it is in the best interest of the client to do so. (pp. 8-9)

Providing art therapy services from a monocultural perspective, as if all clients were the same, does not reflect reality and can result in unethical and inappropriate practice. Art therapists in the United States live in a nation where the provision of health services has often been adversely influenced by institutionalized racism. Art therapists who work in health care systems and institutions may wish to critically examine their facilities with an eye toward determining the presence of overt or covert racism. It is important for art therapists to reflect upon the implications of institutional racism on their capacity to ethically serve clients.

One way for art therapists to sensitize themselves to issues of cultural diversity and to avoid behaving unethically is by increasing awareness of their culture of origin. Deepening understanding of one's own cultural background is the foundation for exploring and comprehending ways that cultures differ from one another. Becoming culturally self-aware also helps art therapists begin to understand cultural commonalties. The following artistic tasks are intended to help art therapists increase awareness of their personal and larger cultural contexts.

Suggested Artistic Activities

1. Portrait of My Personal Culture—Research your own cultural background. Resources for this investigation may be conversations with relatives; personal memories from childhood; interviews with people from the neighborhood where you grew up; letters, diaries, or other written accounts of culture; scrapbooks; picture albums; library resources; etc. Create an artwork that presents a portrait of your culture. This could be a painting, drawing, dance, poem, short story, or fable that highlights important qualities of your cultural context. Pay special attention during your research to the attitudes, stigmas, and beliefs about mental illness and therapy that are held by your culture. Try to discover the role the arts played in your culture. Share your art piece with peers.*

2. In a class or peer supervision group, write a list of your values that you owe primarily to your culture. Using chalk or tempera paint, create an abstract image that represents your cultural values. Share and discuss your image with peers. Look for ways in which your values differ from those of others in the group.

3. In a class or supervision group, create a "bias box" by covering the inside of a cardboard (or small wooden) box with colors, images, words and stereotypes you associate with cultures other than your own. Try to not censor yourself as you are working on the box. When finished, step back and examine what you have done, paying attention to the emotional impact of these associations. If possible, share your bias box with someone who is from

---

* Indicates activities adapted from the Multicultural Isses in Art Therapy courses taught by Catherine Moon at the Harding Graduate Art Therapy Program and Marywood University Graduate Art Therapy Program.

one of the cultures you have depicted. Examine the impact that the box has on him or her.

4. Take a look at a peer's "bias box" that contains references to your cultural background. Reflect on how these images, words, and stereotypes make you feel. Write a poem that expresses your reactions to the box.

5. Oppression Sketchbook/Journal—The purposes of this task are to record instances of oppression and privilege and to help in consciousness-raising. The creation of an oppression sketchbook involves making sketches and notations about events of everyday life. Keep a sketchbook/journal that records events and situations you encounter in which you observe or experience oppression or unearned privileged. Make a quick sketch or write a brief poem or commentary about the experience. Share your journal with a peer or classmates.

6. Art and Culture—This task is to be an exploration of the visual arts from the vantagepoint of a particular culture. Explore the role and significance of the visual arts in that culture. Examine the culture-specific meanings for symbols and images and the culturally conditioned differences in style and form. Consider the practical implications of this in art therapy. What impact does this knowledge have on designing art therapy activities that are congruent with the client's definition and experience of art? Create an art piece in response to the research you have done and the ideas it has generated.

7. Multicultural Festival—This task is designed to foster a sense of celebration about the enriching nature of diversity. Each student or member of a supervision group is asked to contribute one item from their own cultural background and one item from a cultural background other than their own. One contribution is to be a food item, and the other contribution is to be a story, song, dance, ritual, tradition, artwork, or other cultural gift to be shared with others in the group. Set aside a significant block of time to share the items in a meaningful way.

EMBRACING DIVERSITY IN ART THERAPY

Art therapists are susceptible to ethnocentric biases and may unintentionally fail to understand clients of a different age, race, sexual orientation, or social class. If art therapists do not integrate awareness of diversity factors into their work, they may be violating their clients' cultural integrity and infringing on basic human rights. An example of such an infringement is seen in the following vignette:

Alex is a thirty-year-old Caucasian art therapist working in a geriatric nursing home. The nursing home has a large population of clients who immigrated to the United States from Germany in the years just prior to World War II. Alex enjoys his interactions with elderly clients but often feels frustrated when working with men of German descent.

During one particularly exasperating session, one of the clients, an eighty-seven-year-old, tells Alex, "Leave me alone young man. I get along just fine without whimpering like you."

After the session, Alex laments to his supervisor, "They never share any feelings in my men's expressive art group. They say that it's childish. What am I doing wrong? Why are they so resistive?"

Alex's supervisor responds by asking, "What do you do when the men won't draw or talk about their feelings?"

"I try to be a role model. I assure them it's healthy to express themselves . . . that it's OK to cry, or laugh, or be angry. But they don't pay any attention."

* * * * *

Alex has failed to understand the cultural background of the men in his group. They grew up in a period when it was not considered appropriate for men to "share their feelings" openly. While Alex values self-expression and emotional intimacy, the men in his group may value stoicism, hard work, and keeping one's problems to ones' self. In a very real sense, Alex's asking them to share their feelings is antithetical to their view of what it means to be a man.

Violations and infringements of this sort inevitably impede the development of a genuine therapeutic relationship. It is nearly impossible to establish an authentic therapeutic relationship if the art therapist is unable to understand and honor the cultural background of the client. The failure to deal with diversity factors leads to unethical practice (Ivey, 1990). In order to work effectively, art therapists must attempt to relate to the person as a whole. Art therapists know they cannot treat the depression or anxiety a client is experiencing without attending to the "bigger picture" of the client's life. Nor can they help a stroke victim regain the use of a hand without paying attention to the feelings the client has about the impairment. Depression and anxiety must be seen in the context of the whole person, and an impaired hand must be seen as attached to a human being. In a similar way, clients cannot be separated from their cultural context. As a discipline, art therapy and all its members are ethically compelled to embrace cultural diversity. The following three cases address some of the issues described in this chapter.

The Anger of Su Ling

Su Ling, a sixteen-year-old Asian high school student who has lived with her family in America for the past year and a half, was referred to Andrea, a Caucasian art therapist who works in a community counseling agency. Her mother brought Su Ling to the agency because she had been becoming increasingly defiant at home. Her mother stated that, "Su Ling's friends are bad, not good for her." During her second art therapy session, Su Ling drew a picture of her father holding a pair of scissors in one hand and shredded blue jeans in the other. Andrea asked Su Ling to tell a story about the drawing. Su Ling began to weep silently.

After a few minutes, Andrea said, "If my father ever did that, I would have really been enraged." Su Ling then left the room and refused to come back into the art studio. Later that day, Andrea wrote a progress note in Su Ling's chart. "The client is passively resistive to therapy at this time."

- Did the art therapist's actions indicate an understanding of the roles family members play in Su Ling's culture?
- What might have been the impact of the art therapist's comment, "If my father ever did that, I would have been enraged" ?
- Did the art therapist's note accurately reflect the client's behavior?
- What would you have written in the chart about this encounter?
- How would you have responded to Su Ling's drawing?

Antonio's Family Drawing

A court appointed social worker admitted a seven-year-old African American boy, Antonio, to the children's unit at a psychiatric hospital. He had been having difficulties at school, disrupting the class, disobeying rules, and getting into fights with other boys. John, a Caucasian art therapist, was assigned to administer an art therapy assessment of Antonio. One of the tasks John asked of Antonio was to depict his family doing something together. Although Antonio was very angry about being in the hospital, he liked to draw and participated willingly in the assessment process. His drawing of the family doing something together depicted a woman, a small boy, and a large man sitting in front of what appeared to be a jail cell door. John asked Antonio to explain the drawing, but Antonio refused.

When John wrote the narrative report of the assessment, he described the drawing as Antonio and his mother visiting Antonio's father in prison. He speculated that the absence of Antonio's father from the home had perhaps led to Antonio's escalating aggressive behaviors at school.

- Do you see any evidence of racial bias in John's interpretation of Antonio's drawing?
- What racial stereotypes may have been at work in this case?
- How might a multiculturally sensitive art therapist have interpreted Antonio's family drawing?
- What assumptions did the art therapist make in this case that were insensitive to cultural diversity issues?
- Given your cultural background and values, how would you have worked with Antonio if he were your client?

Donna's Dilemma

Donna, a white, newly married art therapist in private practice, has been treating Elaine, a depressed twenty-seven-year-old lesbian woman, for several months. Initially the therapy seemed to be going well. Donna and Elaine appeared to have established an authentic relationship and Elaine had reported feeling somewhat better. However, things began to take a turn for the worse shortly after Donna returned from her honeymoon. Elaine seemed to be sinking further into a dark pit of paralyzing depression. During one session, as she worked on a painting of a dark, foreboding cave, Elaine told Donna, "I just don't think I can trust you anymore."

Donna was taken aback. "Why, Elaine?"

"Well, I really thought . . . even though we never talked about it or anything . . . I really thought you were . . . you know, one of us."

Donna grimaced involuntarily. "You thought I was gay?"

"Yes, and now that I know you aren't, I'm not sure you can understand where I am coming from."

Donna, a little flustered by this, replied, "Why would it make any difference if I am gay or straight?"

Elaine bristled, "If you have to ask, I can't tell you."

Elaine did return to a few more art therapy sessions with Donna but then abruptly terminated the relationship.

- Do you detect any signs of bias from Donna?
- In what ways was Donna culturally sensitive or insensitive?
- Should Donna have referred Elaine to another art therapist? Why, or why not?

SUMMARY

A number of authors (Calish & Hiscox, 1998; Cattaneo, 1994; McNiff, 1984; Moreno & Wadeson, 1986; Waller, in Gilroy, & Dalley, 1989) have implored art therapists to learn about their own and other cultures. They suggest this as a way to increase awareness of how cultural context affects the way art therapists work with clients who are culturally similar to them and clients who are of a different cultural background. Art therapists face unique challenges when working with people of a different age, race, gender, sexual orientation, social class, or culture. For art therapists, one of the most significant of these challenges is not to force their view of reality onto their clients. Corey, Corey, and Callanan (1998) note, "Imposing one's own vision of the world on clients not only leads to negative therapeutic outcomes but also constitutes unethical practice" (344).

Cultural sensitivity, cultural awareness, and appreciation of diversity can be developed through contact and experience with an assortment of cultural events, ethnic groups, and selected readings, as well as through intentional efforts to increase awareness of one's own cultural background. "As art therapists, we bring our complete beingness into the therapy session—our varied histories and stories" (Riley-Hiscox, 1999, p. 148). It is ethically imperative that art therapy services be rendered in an appropriate manner for the client being served. This means that art therapists cannot universally apply their skills in the same way with every client and in every clinical situation. Henley (1999) notes, "in practicing art therapy, we must remain sensitive to the effects that powerful art has on different members of a group" (p. 144). There must be a conscientious effort to reflect upon core attitudes, values, and clinical assumptions, so that an appropriate, culturally sensitive therapeutic plan can be designed for each unique client.

FIVE TENETS OF ETHICAL MULTICULTURAL ART THERAPY

1. In order to appreciate and honor differences in clients' cultures, art therapists must be aware of and value their own cultural backgrounds.
2. Art therapists need to be aware of how their own cultural and aesthetic biases influence their assumptions and values about clients' artworks and behaviors.
3. Art therapists need to be sensitive to their clients' cultural backgrounds, and cognizant of culture-specific meanings associated with colors, forms, and symbols.
4. Art therapists must be aware that an individual client's dysfunction develops in a sociocultural context. The cultural context influences the

particular nature and form of the dysfunction, as well as what constitutes normal behavior.

5. Art therapists must develop treatment plans and interventions appropriate to working with people from different cultural backgrounds.

Chapter XIV

EVOLVING ETHICAL CHALLENGES

With the emergence of digital imaging technology, individual access to personal computers, and the establishment of the World Wide Web and Internet as common aspects of daily life have come entirely new potential applications of art therapy that were nearly unimaginable not too long ago. Along with these potentials, a new set of ethical dilemmas has come to light. Art therapy by electronic means is a new and evolving application and, as such, it presents opportunities for service, as well as ethical predicaments not encountered in the past. Art therapists are advised to use caution as the ethical ramifications of providing art therapy services via the Internet and other electronic means emerge.

For example, it is conceivable that an art therapist living in New York could provide a form of art therapy by interacting with a client residing in Utah via email, video conferencing, instant messaging, or live video streaming. The client's artwork could be viewed by the art therapist during the process of creation, or downloaded in finished form.

There is no doubt that communication technologies will continue to evolve and the capacity of art therapists to establish connections with potential clients all over the world will continue to develop. Such technologies offer the positive possibilities of providing art therapy services to clients who live in remote locations, or who are limited in their capacity to travel to a therapist's office. One can envision other applications emerging that will allow art therapists to provide or receive supervision electronically. With the development of new applications of art therapy, however, there are also potential problems to be addressed. Among these problems are:

1. Risks to the privacy of clients
2. Laws and regulations regarding the provision of therapeutic services of the state in which the art therapist resides.
3. Laws and regulations regarding the provision of therapeutic services of the state(s) or country in which the art therapist's client(s) reside.

4. Concerns regarding the ability of an art therapist to make an appropriate referral to another therapist when it would be in the best interest of the client.

5. Concerns regarding the ability of an art therapist to facilitate admission to a hospital or other treatment facility when it would be in the best interest of the client (for example, if a client expressed suicidal ideation).

6. Concerns regarding the art therapist's potential inability to appropriately assess the client in terms of facial expression, tone of voice, eye contact, posture, and other nonverbal expressions that require face-to-face interaction.

RISKS TO THE PRIVACY OF CLIENTS

Art therapists who are considering offering services through electronic means must be aware of the privacy and security issues inherent in such services. It is clear that the Internet does not provide foolproof security. Computers are vulnerable to attacks from hackers and identity theft is a significant problem associated with the rise in computer use. An art therapist providing art therapy services electronically must be sufficiently knowledgeable regarding security safeguards. In addition, art therapists must inform potential clients of the risks to their privacy and the limits of confidentiality inherent in electronic communications. Art therapists are advised to familiarize themselves with the rules and standards of the Health Insurance Portability and Accountability Act of 1996 relating to security and privacy of health information.

LAWS AND REGULATIONS REGARDING THE PROVISION OF THERAPEUTIC SERVICES

Art therapists who provide services through electronic means are responsible for taking reasonable steps to ensure that any such services are in accordance with all applicable laws and regulations of the state in which they reside, and are aware of the licensing requirements and applicable laws and regulations of the states in which their clients reside.

REFERRAL

Art therapists who provide services through electronic means should be prepared to make an appropriate referral to another therapist when it would be in the best interest of the client. The process of referral is a common one among therapists, but this is complicated when an art therapist does not reside in the same area as his or her client. Art therapists are advised to educate themselves regarding the availability of appropriate referral sources in a client's area in the event that such a referral would be in the best interest of the client.

ADMISSION TO A HOSPITAL OR OTHER TREATMENT FACILITY

In the course of therapy, it is sometimes necessary for an art therapist to arrange for a client to be admitted to a hospital or other secure treatment facility in order to ensure the safety of the client. An admission may be warranted if a client indicates that he or she is considering suicide, or is in some way potentially dangerous to others. Arranging for an emergency admission may be quite complicated when an art therapist does not reside in the same area as his or her client. Art therapists are advised to educate themselves regarding the availability of appropriate facilities in a client's area in the event that an admission to a secure facility would be in the best interest of the client.

ASSESSMENT

Traditionally, the nature of our work as art therapists entails an ongoing process of assessing clients' emotional well-being. Art therapists continually monitor a host of nonverbal cues that clients give. Among these clues are clients' facial expressions, tone of voice, eye contact, posture, grooming, and the ways they interact with art materials. All of these nonverbal modes of communication require face-to-face interaction. One of the shortcomings of instant messaging, email, and other electronic media is the absence of access to the aforementioned nonverbal cues. In the absence of access to such communications, art therapists should develop plans to compensate for the lack of face-to-face interaction.

Although the provision of art therapy by electronic means is in the early stages of development, section 14 of the *Ethical Principles for Art Therapists* addresses the issues raised by evolving technologies in the following:

14.1. Art therapists who offer services or information via electronic transmission inform clients of the risks to privacy and the limits of confidentiality.

14.2. Art therapists who provide services through electronic means are governed by the AATA Ethical Principles for Art Therapists.

14.3. Art therapists are responsible for taking reasonable steps to ensure that any services through electronic means are in accordance with all applicable laws and regulations, and are aware of the licensing requirements of the states in which their clients reside.

CHAPTER SUMMARY

Serious questions will continue to surface as the art therapy discipline explores the evolving application of art therapy services by electronic means. As an art therapy educator I have encountered some of these as colleges and universities have encouraged me to develop on-line art therapy courses. There are parallel concerns between distance learning educational modalities and art therapy by electronic means. I have resisted suggestions to develop on-line art therapy courses because art therapy is ultimately a discipline rooted in relationship building through art making. Perhaps I am limited by my lack of technological sophistication, but I cling to the notion that I want to be in the company of students, and I have found no way to do this satisfactorily via the Internet. Just as I want to be in the presence of students, so too, when providing art therapy services, I want to be in the room with clients.

Despite my reservations, I am convinced that applications of art therapy by electronic means will continue to emerge. It behooves art therapists to think deeply about the ethical issues associated with providing art therapy through electronic means. Among the ethical issues are: privacy of clients' health information, legal concerns regarding licensure and individual state standards, potential referral resources, potential facility resources, and methods of ongoing client assessment.

Chapter XV

FINAL THOUGHTS

Why should I teach him the language of painting,
since there seems to be absolutely nothing which he
is desperate to talk about? (Vonnegut, 1987, p. 181)

As I near the end of my work on this second edition of *Ethical Issues in Art Therapy*, I find myself revisiting the goals of this book and imagining (hoping really) that I have succeeded. As in the earlier work, I wanted to raise some difficult questions related to ethical dilemmas in art therapy, and update the text in light of revisions to the Ethics Document of the American Art Therapy Association. While art therapists share many common ethical concerns with other helping professionals, there are ethical dilemmas that are absolutely unique to art therapists. I wanted to provide art therapists with a helpful model for thinking about ethical issues. Art therapists and therapists from other disciplines who use visual arts, music, drama, movement, or poetry have had to struggle with unique ethical quandaries without much systematic support from professional literature. I have endeavored to present ways to think through and resolve the complex ethical problems art therapists inevitably encounter in their professional lives.

I have avoided offering my views on how specific ethical questions should be answered. The reader may be assured that I do have many opinions but I have no interest in my views being taken as guidelines for anyone else's behavior. In those instances where I did present my beliefs regarding a particular issue, I did so in an effort to demonstrate a model of ethical reasoning. I hope this will encourage art therapists to give form to their own positions. If other art therapists' solutions to these quandaries happen to concur with mine, that's fine. If not, that's fine too. So be it.

Despite the fact that I referred often to the *Ethical Principles for Art Therapists* (AATA, 2003), and the fact that I had a significant hand in their creation, I must reiterate that those principles, while quite helpful, are inadequate to cover every circumstance. I hope the discussion of deontological,

213

teleological, and antinomian approaches to ethical problem solving were helpful. Ultimately, art therapy students and practitioners must grapple with questions of moral professional behavior. Every art therapist must decide how the ethical principles apply to a specific problem. This can be confusing, anxiety producing, hard, and lonely work. I trust this book has helped to clarify issues, soothe anxieties, ease the burden of puzzling through ethical issues, and assured art therapists that they are not completely alone in their work.

In an effort to provide opportunities for stimulating discussion and debate in the classroom or supervisory group, I have offered many examples of ethical dilemmas. I have faith that lively debates will grow out of art therapists working with this text. I envision course instructors being challenged and encouraged to mine the depths of their own experiences as they help students struggle with professional morality issues. What fun!

Most chapters include a list of suggested artistic tasks aimed at helping art therapy students and practitioners review the material and begin to creatively formulate or clarify their own positions on key issues. I would enjoy receiving feedback from readers about how these suggested exercises worked. I am also very interested in readers' reactions to, and criticisms of, this book. I invite you to send your comments and feedback to the publisher's address and they will forward the information on to me.

Art therapists who came to this book in search of simple or rote answers to ethical questions were undoubtedly disappointed. As I said at the outset, ethical issues in art therapy are, more times than not, a spectrum of shades of gray. When I began this project, I was concerned about the absence of a text addressing the ethical predicaments unique to art therapy. I have been surprised at how many ethical issues are peculiar to our discipline. Hopefully, this book begins to fill the void in the literature on ethics and art therapy.

All of us are routinely confronted with moral problems in our professional lives. There are hidden dangers ahead if we do not think deeply about our behavior. It is crucial to contend with these quandaries before they occur, as they happen, and after the fact, in order to shape and understand our professional ethics.

While the ethical problems referred to in this book were written from the viewpoint of a visual arts therapist, I hope that poetry therapists, music therapists, dance movement therapists, and drama therapists will be able to recast the issues into their professional context.

One of the reasons for making art is to depict what is genuine and true about life. The work of the expressive arts therapist is all about using one's creativity to get beneath the surface of things. In a very real sense, the anguish, zest, and untamed intensity of existence is the essential subject of inquiry for creative arts therapists. Going about this work in an ethical and moral manner is terribly important.

I know the words in this text inevitably fail to convey the depth of my passion for art therapy and my commitment to deepening and expanding our discussion of ethical practice. I worry that this exploration of ethical issues in our profession may have only skimmed the surface. Ethical reasoning in art therapy is a subject that demands serious and prolonged academic exploration. Still, I hope that the stories and ideas I have shared here will stimulate your interest. If I have done this skillfully and with integrity, perhaps you will be drawn into the work of reflecting on your behavior. Perhaps you will write the next article or book about ethical issues in art therapy.

While writing this text, I simultaneously worked on a handful of paintings. During this time, I felt a deep responsibility to my mentors, to each of the clients I have worked with over the years, and to the artworks they have created. As I stood before the blank canvas or sat before the computer, I was intensely aware of the seriousness of the effort. The canvas surfaces reminded of inner questions that had to be addressed. The computer screen dared me to write about the way I think through ethical problems in the therapeutic studio.

I regard our work as art therapists as sacred. Every time an angry client conveys her woundedness in paint, I believe she finds some of the nourishment and courage her life longs for. The therapy is not about helping rid her of suffering; it is found in helping her creatively work with, explore, embrace, and express her anguish. The effort in this writing has not been to rid art therapists of the anxiety of ethical decision making, but rather to immerse them in the difficult process of ethical reasoning.

It would be presumptuous of me to claim that this book has completely explored all of the subtleties, ambiguities, and complexities of ethical issues in art therapy. Still, if presumption is an act of imagination, then perhaps I am free to imagine that I have adequately presented a text that touches upon the major themes and ethical issues of art therapy. I hope students new to the field and seasoned practitioners alike will be better prepared to deal with the ethics of their practice as a result of having read this book. I believe the strengths of this text come from the real-life clinical and educational encounters I've had with clients, students, and artworks, in a variety of settings.

My presentation of key ethical issues in art therapy is nearly complete. I have introduced ethical dilemmas that may present frightening images and professional uncertainties. I must add one more notion to this mix, without love, none of this matters. Art therapists work with processes and images that emerge from the deepest parts of human beings. It is not an overstatement to describe this work as an act of love. In fact, it may be an understatement to define it as anything less than love. Doing art therapy, making art, and being with people who are suffering require great effort. Thinking about how to do these things ethically is hard work. Striving to be an ethical art therapist challenges human inertia, and calls us toward self-transcendence. Facing and responding to such challenges for the sake of clients' welfare are acts of love and courage. It is not always easy for art therapists, or anyone for that matter, to behave in an ethical manner in today's world. This book is not enough to ensure that every member of the art therapy professional community will always make optimal ethical decisions. It is not enough to write about deontology, teleology, antinomianism, confidentiality, clients' rights, images' rights, and all of the other subjects of this book. Each of these topics is nothing outside the context and discipline of love.

One More Suggested Artistic Task

Reflect upon the ideas, issues, and feelings this book has raised for you. Create an art piece that synthesizes, or integrates, your reactions to the text. Share it with others.

APPENDICES

Appendix A

AMERICAN ART THERAPY ASSOCIATION ETHICAL PRINCIPLES FOR ART THERAPISTS

(Approved by AATA Board of Directors: March 29, 2003)

INTRODUCTION

AATA MISSION STATEMENT

The American Art Therapy Association, Inc., is an organization of professionals dedicated to the belief that the creative process involved in the making of art is healing and life-enhancing.

Its mission is to serve its members and the general public by providing standards of professional competence and developing and promoting knowledge in and about the field of art therapy.

PREAMBLE

This Ethics Document is intended to provide principles to cover many situations encountered by art therapists. Its goals are to safeguard the welfare of the individuals and groups with whom art therapists work and to promote the education of members, students, and the public regarding ethical principles of the art therapy discipline.

In this Ethics Document, the term *reasonable* means the prevailing professional judgment of art therapists engaged in similar activities in similar circumstances, given the knowledge the art therapist had or should have had at the time.

This Ethics Document applies to art therapists' professional activities across a wide variety of contexts, such as in person, postal, telephone, and Internet and other electronic transmissions. These activities shall be distinguished from the private conduct of art therapists, which is not within the purview of this document.

The development of a vigorous set of ethical principles for art therapists' work-related behavior requires a personal commitment and constant effort to act ethically; to encourage ethical behavior by students, supervisees, employees, and colleagues; and to consult with others concerning ethical problems. This ethics document defines and establishes principles of ethical behavior for current and future members of this association and informs credentialing bodies, employers of art therapists, and the general public that members of the American Art Therapy Association, Inc., are required to adhere to the Ethical Principles for Art Therapists.

ETHICS COMMITTEE STATEMENT OF PURPOSE

The Ethics Committee is the committee charged by the American Art Therapy Association, Inc. (AATA), to educate the membership regarding issues of ethical practice and to maintain and encourage adherence to its Ethical Code and Principles of Practice.

ETHICAL PRINCIPLES FOR ART THERAPISTS

The Board of Directors of the American Art Therapy Association (AATA) hereby promulgates, pursuant to Article VIII, Sections 1, 2, and 3 of the Association Bylaws, a Revised Code of Ethical Principles for Art Therapists. Members of AATA abide by these principles and by applicable laws and regulations governing the conduct of art therapists and any additional license or certification that the art therapist holds.

PRINCIPLES

1.0 RESPONSIBILITY TO CLIENTS

Art therapists endeavor to advance the welfare of clients, respect the rights of those persons seeking their assistance, and make reasonable efforts to ensure that their services are used properly.

1.1 Art therapists do not discriminate against or refuse professional service to anyone on the basis of age, gender identity, race, ethnicity, culture, national origin, religion, sexual orientation, disability, socioeconomic status, or any basis proscribed by law.

1.2 At the outset of the client-therapist relationship, art therapists discuss and explain client rights, roles of both client and therapist, and expectations and limitations of the art therapy process.

1.3 Where the client is a minor, any and all disclosure or consent required is obtained from the parent or legal guardian of the minor client, except where otherwise mandated by law. Care is taken to preserve confidentiality with the minor client and to refrain from disclosure of information to the parent or guardian that might adversely affect the treatment of the client.

1.4 Art therapists respect the rights of clients to make decisions and assist them in understanding the consequences of these decisions. Art therapists advise their clients that decisions on the status of therapeutic relationships are the responsibility of the client. It is the professional responsibility of the art therapist to avoid ambiguity in the therapeutic relationship and to strive for clarity of roles at all times.

1.5 Art therapists refrain from entering into a multiple relationship if the multiple relationship could reasonably be expected to impair the art therapist's competence or effectiveness in performing his or her functions as an art therapist, or otherwise risks exploitation or harm to the person with whom the professional relationship exists.

A multiple relationship occurs when an art therapist is in a professional role with a person and (1) at the same time is in another role with the same person, (2) at the same time is in a relationship with a person closely associated with or related to the person with whom the art therapist has the professional relationship, or (3) promises to enter into another relationship in the future with the person or a person closely associated with or related to the person.

Multiple relationships that would not reasonably be expected to cause impairment or risk exploitation or harm are not unethical.

Art therapists recognize their influential position with respect to clients, and they do not exploit the trust and dependency of clients.

1.6 Art therapists refrain from engaging in an activity when they know or should know that there is a substantial likelihood that their personal problems will prevent them from performing their work-related activities in a competent manner.

1.7 Art therapists refrain from taking on a professional role when (1) personal, professional, legal, financial, or other interests and relationships could reasonably be expected to impair their competence or effectiveness in performing their functions as art therapists, or (2) expose the person or organization with whom the professional relationship exists to harm or exploitation.

1.8 Art therapists terminate therapy when it becomes reasonably clear that the client no longer needs the service, is not likely to benefit, or is being harmed by continuing the service.

1.9 Art therapists do not engage in therapy practices or procedures that are beyond their scope of practice, experience, training, and education. Art therapists assist persons in obtaining other therapeutic services if the therapist is unable or unwilling to provide professional help, or where the problem or treatment indicated is beyond the scope of practice of the art therapist.

1.10 Art therapists, prior to termination, provide pre-termination counseling and suggest alternate service providers as appropriate, except where precluded by the actions of clients or third-party payers.

1.11 Art therapists strive to provide a safe, functional environment in which to offer art therapy services. This includes:
proper ventilation;
adequate lighting;
access to water;
knowledge of hazards or toxicity of art materials, and the effort needed to safeguard the health of clients;
storage space for artwork and secured areas for any hazardous materials;
allowance for privacy and confidentiality;
compliance with any other health and safety requirements according to state and federal agencies which regulate comparable businesses.

2.0 CONFIDENTIALITY

Art therapists protect confidential information obtained from clients, through artwork and/or conversation, in the context of the professional relationship while clients are in treatment and post-treatment.

2.1 Art therapists treat clients in an environment that protects privacy and confidentiality.

2.2 Art therapists inform clients of the limitations of confidentiality.

2.3 Art therapists do not disclose confidential information for the purposes of consultation and supervision without client's explicit consent unless there is reason to believe that the client or others are in immediate, severe danger to health or life. Any such disclosure must be consistent with laws that pertain to the welfare of the client, family, and the general public.

2.4 In the event that an art therapist believes it is in the interest of the client to disclose confidential information, he/she seeks and obtains written consent from the client or client's guardian(s) when possible before making any disclosures, unless there is reason to believe that the client or others are in immediate, severe danger to health or life.

2.5 Art therapists disclose confidential information when mandated by law in a civil, criminal, or disciplinary action arising from such art therapy services. In these cases client confidences may be disclosed only as reasonably necessary in the course of that action.

2.6 Art therapists maintain client treatment records for a reasonable amount of time consistent with state regulations and sound clinical practice, but not less than seven years from completion of treatment or termination of the therapeutic relationship. Records are stored or disposed of in ways that maintain confidentiality.

3.0 ASSESSMENT METHODS

Art therapists develop and use assessment methods to better understand and serve the needs of their clients. They use assessment methods only within the context of a defined professional relationship.

3.1 Art therapists who use standardized assessment instruments are familiar with reliability, validity, standardization, error of measurement, and proper application of assessment methods used.

3.2 Art therapists use only those assessment methods in which they have acquired competence through appropriate training and supervised experience.

3.3 Art therapists who develop assessment instruments based on behavioral science research methods follow standard instrument development procedures. They specify in writing the training, education, and experience levels needed to use such instruments.

3.4 Art therapists obtain informed consent from clients regarding the nature and purpose of assessment methods to be used. When clients have difficulty understanding the language or procedural directives, art therapists arrange for a qualified interpreter.

3.5 In selecting assessment methods and reporting the rèsults, art therapists consider any factors that may influence outcomes, such as culture, race, gender, sexual orientation, age, religion, education, and disability. They take reasonable steps to ensure that the results of their assessments are not misused by others.

3.6 Art therapists take reasonable steps to ensure that all assessment artwork and related data are kept confidential according to the policies and procedures of the professional setting in which these assessments are administered.

4.0 CLIENT ARTWORK

Art therapists regard client artwork as the property of the client. In some practice settings client artwork, or representations of artworks, may be considered a part of the clinical record retained by the therapist and/or agency for a reasonable amount of time consistent with state regulations and sound clinical practice.

4.1 Client artwork may be released to the client during the course of therapy and upon its termination. The client is notified in instances where the art therapist and/or the clinical agency retain copies or photographic reproductions of the artwork in the client file as part of the clinical record.

4.2 Art therapists obtain written informed consent from the client or, where applicable, a legal guardian in order to keep client artwork, copies, slides, or photographs of artwork, for educational, research, or assessment purposes.

4.3 Art therapists do not make or permit any public use or reproduction of client art therapy sessions, including dialogue and artwork, without written consent of the client.

4.4 Art therapists obtain written informed consent from the client or, where applicable, a legal guardian before photographing clients' artwork or video taping, audio recording, otherwise duplicating, or permitting third-party [two-word adjectives are hyphenated before a noun] observation of art therapy sessions.

4.5 Art therapists use clinical materials in teaching, writing, and public presentations if written authorization has been previously obtained from the clients. Reasonable steps are taken to protect client identity and to disguise any part of the artwork or video tape that reveals client identity.

4.6 Art therapists obtain written, informed consent from the client before displaying client art in any public place.

5.0 PROFESSIONAL COMPETENCE AND INTEGRITY

Art therapists maintain high standards of professional competence and integrity.

5.1 Art therapists keep informed of developments in their field through educational activities and clinical experiences.

5.2 Art therapists diagnose, treat, or advise on problems only in those cases in which they are competent, as determined by their education, training, and experience.

5.3 Art therapists cooperate with other professionals, when indicated and professionally appropriate, in order to serve their clients effectively

5.4 Art therapists, because of their potential to influence and alter the lives of others, exercise reasonable care when making public their professional recommendations and opinions through testimony or other public statements.

5.5 Art therapists do not engage in any relationship with clients, students, interns, trainees, supervisees, employees, research participants, or colleagues that is exploitative by its nature.

5.6 Art therapists do not distort or misuse their clinical and research findings.

5.7 Art therapists do not knowingly engage in behavior that is harassing or demeaning to persons with whom they interact.

6.0 MULTICULTURAL AWARENESS

Art therapists are aware of and respect cultural, individual, and role differences, including those based on age, gender, gender identity, race, ethnicity, culture, national origin, religion, sexual orientation, disability, language, and socioeconomic status and consider these factors when working with members of such groups. Art therapists try to eliminate the effect on their work of biases based on those factors, and they do not knowingly participate in or condone activities of others based upon such prejudices.

6.1 Art therapists take reasonable steps to ensure that they are sensitive to differences that exist among cultures. They are earnest in their attempts to learn about the belief systems of people in any given cultural group in order to provide culturally relevant interventions and treatment.

6.2 Art therapists are aware of their own values and beliefs and how they may affect cross-cultural therapy interventions.

6.3 Art therapists obtain education about and seek to understand the nature of social diversity and oppression with respect to race, ethnicity, national origin, color, gender, sexual orientation, class, age, marital status, political belief, religion, and mental or physical disability.

6.4 Art therapists acquire knowledge and information about the specific cultural group(s) with which they are working and the strengths inherent in that cultural group. They are sensitive to individual differences that exist within the cultural group and understand that individuals may have varying responses to group norms.

6.5 When working with people from cultures different from their own, art therapists engage in culturally sensitive supervision, seek assistance from members of that culture, and make a referral to a professional who is knowledgeable about the culture when it is in the best interest of the client to do so.

7.0 RESPONSIBILITY TO STUDENTS AND SUPERVISEES

Art therapists instruct their students using accurate, current, and scholarly information and will foster the professional growth of students and advisees.

7.1 Art therapists as teachers, supervisors, and researchers maintain high standards of scholarship and present accurate information.

7.2 Art therapists are aware of their influential position with respect to students and supervisees, and they avoid exploiting the trust and dependency of such persons. Art therapists, therefore, shall not engage in a therapeutic relationship with their students or supervisees.

7.3 Art therapists take reasonable steps to ensure that students, employees, or supervisees do not perform or present themselves as competent to perform professional services beyond their education, training, and level of experience.

7.4 Art therapists who act as supervisors are responsible for maintaining the quality of their supervision skills and obtaining consultation or supervision for their work as supervisors whenever appropriate.

7.5 Art therapists do not require students or supervisees to disclose personal information in course- or program-related activities, either orally or in writing, regarding sexual history, history of abuse and neglect, psychological treatment, and relationships with parents, peers, spouses or significant others, except when (1) the program or training facility has clearly identified this requirement in its admissions and program materials or (2) the information is necessary to evaluate or obtain assistance for students whose personal problems could reasonably be judged to be preventing them from performing their training or professional related activities in a competent manner or whose personal problems could reasonably be judged to pose a threat to the students or others.

8.0 RESPONSIBILITY TO RESEARCH PARTICIPANTS

Art therapy researchers respect the dignity and protect the welfare of participants in research.

8.1 Researchers are guided by laws, regulations, and professional standards governing the conduct of research.

8.2 To the extent that research participants may be compromised by participation in research, investigators seek the ethical advice of qualified professionals not directly involved in the investigation and observe safeguards to protect the rights of research participants.

8.3 Researchers requesting participants' involvement in research inform them of all aspects of the research that might reasonably be expected to influence willingness to participate. Investigators take all reasonable steps necessary to ensure that full and informed consent has been obtained from participants who are also receiving clinical services, have limited understanding and/or communication, or are minors.

8.4 Researchers respect participants' freedom to decline participation in, or to withdraw from, a research study at any time with no negative consequences to their treatment.

8.5 Information obtained about a research participant during the course of an investigation is confidential unless there is authorization previously obtained in writing. When there is a risk that others, including family members, may obtain access to such information, this risk, together with the plan for protecting confidentiality, is to be explained as part of the procedure for obtaining informed consent.

9.0 RESPONSIBILITY TO THE PROFESSION

Art therapists respect the rights and responsibilities of professional colleagues and participate in activities that advance the goals of art therapy.

9.1 Art therapists adhere to the ethical principles of the profession when acting as members or employees of organizations.

9.2 Art therapists attribute publication credit to those who have contributed to a publication in proportion to their contributions and in accordance with customary professional publication practices.

9.3 Art therapists who author books or other materials that are published or distributed appropriately cite persons to whom credit for original ideas is due.

9.4 Art therapists who author books or other materials published or distributed by an organization take reasonable precautions to ensure that the organization promotes and advertises the materials accurately and factually.

9.5 Art therapists value participation in activities that contribute to a better community and society.

9.6 Art therapists recognize the importance of developing laws and regulations pertaining to the field of art therapy that serve the public interest, and with changing such laws and regulations that are not in the public interest.

9.7 Art therapists cooperate with the Ethics Committee of the American Art Therapy Association, Inc., and truthfully represent and disclose facts to the Ethics Committee when requested.

9.8 Art therapists take reasonable steps to prevent distortion, misuse, or suppression of art therapy findings by any institution or agency of which they are employees.

10.0 FINANCIAL ARRANGEMENTS

Art therapists make financial arrangements with clients, third-party payers, and supervisees that are understandable and conform to accepted professional practices.

10.1 When art therapists pay, receive payment from, or divide fees with another professional, other than in an employer-employee relationship, the payment to each is based on the services provided (clinical, consultative, administrative, or other) and is not based on the referral itself.

10.2 Art therapists do not financially exploit their clients.

10.3 Art therapists disclose their fees at the beginning of therapy and give reasonable notice of any changes in fees.

10.4 Art therapists represent facts truthfully to clients, third-party payers, and supervisees regarding services rendered and the charges for services.

10.5 Art therapists may barter only if (1) it is not clinically contraindicated and (2) the resulting arrangement is not exploitative. Barter is the acceptance of goods, services, or other non-monetary remuneration from clients/patients in return for art therapy services.

11.0 ADVERTISING

Art therapists engage in appropriate publicity regarding professional activities in order to enable laypersons to choose professional services on an informed basis.

11.1 Art therapists accurately represent their professional competence, education, training, and experience.

11.2 Art therapists do not use a name that is likely to mislead the public concerning the identity, responsibility, source, and status of those under whom they are practicing, and do not hold themselves out as being partners or associates of a firm if they are not.

11.3 Art therapists do not use any professional identification (such as a business card, office sign, letterhead, or telephone or association directory listing) if it includes a statement or claim that is false, fraudulent, misleading, or deceptive. A statement is false, fraudulent, misleading, or deceptive if it: (a) fails to state any material fact necessary to keep the statement from being misleading; (b) is intended to, or likely to, create an unjustified expectation; or (c) contains a material misrepresentation of fact.

11.4 Art therapists correct, whenever reasonable, false, misleading, or inaccurate information and representations made by others concerning the therapist's qualifications, services, or products.

11.5 Art therapists make certain that the qualifications of persons in their employ are represented in a manner that is not false, misleading, or deceptive.

11.6 Art therapists may represent themselves as specializing within a limited area of art therapy only if they have the appropriate education, training, and experience to practice in that specialty area.

11.7 AATA credentialed, professional, associate, and other members in good standing may identify such membership in AATA in public information or advertising materials, but they must clearly and accurately represent the membership category to which they belong.

11.8 Art therapists do not use the ATR® and/or ATR-BC following their name unless they are officially notified in writing by the Art Therapy Credential Board, Inc., that they have successfully completed all applicable registration and certification procedures. Art therapists may not use the initials "AATA" following their name as if it were an academic degree.

11.9 Art therapists may not use the AATA initials or logo without receiving written permission from the Association.

12.0 INDEPENDENT PRACTITIONER

An independent practitioner of art therapy is a Credentialed Professional Member of the American Art Therapy Association, Inc. (AATA), who is practicing art therapy independently and who is responsible for the delivery of services to clients where the client pays the therapist directly or through insurance for art therapy services rendered.

12.1 Independent practitioners of art therapy maintain their registration with the Art Therapy Credentials Board, Inc. (ATCB), and have, in addition to registration, at least two full years of full-time practice or 3,000 hours of paid clinical art therapy experience.

12.2 Independent practitioners of art therapy obtain qualified medical or psychological consultation for cases in which such evaluation and/or administration of medication is required.

12.3 Independent practitioners of art therapy must conform to laws that pertain to the provision of independent mental health practice.

12.4 Independent practitioners of art therapy confine their practice within the limits of their training. The art therapist neither claims nor implies professional qualifications exceeding those actually earned and received. The therapist is responsible for correcting any misrepresentation of these qualifications.

13.0 REFERRAL AND ACCEPTANCE

13.1 Independent practitioners of art therapy, upon acceptance of a client, specify to clients their fee structure, payment schedule, session scheduling arrangements, and information pertaining to the limits of confidentiality and the duty to report.

13.2 Independent practitioners of art therapy design treatment plans and document activity to assist the client in attaining maintenance of the maximum level of functioning and quality of life appropriate for each individual.

13.3 Independent practitioners of art therapy terminate art therapy when the client has attained stated goals and objectives, or fails to benefit from art therapy services.

13.4 Independent practitioners of art therapy communicate the termination of art therapy services to the client.

14.0 ART THERAPY BY ELECTRONIC MEANS

Art therapy by electronic means is a new and evolving application of art therapy. As such, it presents opportunities for service, as well as ethical dilemmas not encountered in the past. Art therapists are advised to use caution as the ethical ramifications of providing art therapy services via the Internet and other electronic means emerge.

14.1 Art therapists who offer services or information via electronic transmission inform clients of the risks to privacy and the limits of confidentiality.

14.2 Art therapists who provide services through electronic means are governed by the AATA Ethical Principles for Art Therapists.

14.3 Art therapists are responsible for taking reasonable steps to ensure that any services through electronic means are in accordance with all applicable laws and regulations and are aware of the licensing requirements of the states in which their clients reside.

15.0 ABIDING BY THE ETHICAL PRINCIPLES FOR ART THERAPISTS

By accepting membership in the American Art Therapy Association, Inc. (AATA), art therapists agree to abide by the AATA Ethical Principles for Art Therapists. It is the ethical responsibility of each member to act in accordance with these principles and to comply with all applicable laws, regulations, and licensing requirements that govern the practice of therapy in each member's state. These principles are written to provide a basis for education and a foundation for ethical practice.

15.1 The AATA Bylaws, Article VIII, Section 1, authorizes the Ethics Committee to be a standing committee of the Association. The committee educates the membership as to the Ethical Principles for Art Therapists and has the responsibility to recommend and implement these principles as adopted by the Board of Directors of the Association and as may be amended from time to time.

15.2 Art therapists who have had their professional credentials revoked by the Art Therapy Credentials Board as a result of an ethics violation shall have their AATA membership terminated.

16.0 COMPLAINTS

16.1 Conflicts and disagreements are inherent in any organization and in any human interaction. Situations may occur in which one or more individuals believe that one or more AATA members may have violated the AATA Ethical Principles for Art Therapists.

16.2 Individuals who believe Art therapy Credentials Board (ATCB) ethical standards or state licensing regulations have been violated should file complaints directly with those entities.

Effective date: 8/30/03

Appendix B

ART THERAPY CREDENTIALS BOARD CODE
OF PROFESSIONAL PRACTICE

I. PREAMBLE

The Art Therapy Credentials Board, Inc. (ATCB) is a non-profit organization which seeks to protect the public by issuing registration and board certification credentials to practitioners in the field of art therapy who meet certain established standards. The Board is national in scope and includes both academicians and practitioners who work to establish rigorous standards which have a basis in real world practice.

Registration and board certification, hereinafter sometimes referred to as credentials, are offered to art therapists from a wide variety of practice disciplines, who meet high standards for the practice of art therapy.

Obtaining and maintaining ATCB credentials shall require adherence to ATCB's Standards of Conduct, included within this Code of Professional Practice. The Code of Professional Practice is designed to provide art therapists with a set of Ethical Considerations (Part II) that should guide them in their practice of art therapy, as well as Standards of Conduct (Part IV) to which every credentialed art therapist must adhere. ATCB may suspend, revoke, withhold, or decline to grant the credentials of any person who fails to adhere to the Standards of Conduct.

ATCB does not guarantee the job performance of any person. ATCB does not express an opinion regarding the competence of, or warrant the job performance of, any registered or board certified art therapist. Rather, registration or board certification constitutes recognition by ATCB that, to its best knowledge, an art therapist meets and adheres to certain minimum academic, preparation, professional experience, continuing education, and professional standards.

II. ETHICAL CONSIDERATIONS

The Art Therapy Credentials Board endorses the following general ethical principles, which should guide the conduct of all art therapists who seek to obtain or maintain credentials under the authority of ATCB. In addition, the specific ethical standards found in section II.B. should be considered by all independent practitioners, as defined therein. These principles are closely based upon standards adopted by The American Art Therapy Association, but they have been adapted to meet the goals and mission of ATCB, and are intended to stand as an independent expression of the ethical principles that guide the work of those who hold or seek ATCB credentials. ATCB does not warrant that the adherence to these ethical principles will guarantee compliance with the standards adopted by The American Art Therapy Association or will guarantee compliance with any ethical or disciplinary procedures of any state licensing, registration, or certification program.

A. GENERAL ETHICAL PRINCIPLES

1.0 STANDARDS. RESPONSIBILITY TO CLIENTS.

Art therapists aspire to advance the welfare of all clients, respect the rights of those persons seeking their assistance, and make reasonable efforts to ensure that their services are used appropriately.

1.1 Art therapists do not discriminate against or refuse professional services to anyone on the basis of race, gender, religion, national origin, age, sexual orientation, or disability.

1.2 At the outset of the client-therapist relationship, art therapists should discuss and explain to clients the rights, roles, expectations, and limitations of the art therapy process.

1.3 Art therapists respect the rights of clients to make decisions and assist them in understanding the consequences of these decisions. Art therapists advise their clients that decisions on whether to follow treatment recommendations are the responsibility of the client. It is the professional responsibility of the art therapist to avoid ambiguity in the therapeutic relationship and to ensure clarity of roles at all times.

1.4 An art therapist continues a therapeutic relationship only so long as he or she believes that the client is benefiting from the relationship. It is unethical to maintain a professional or therapeutic relationship for the sole purpose of financial remuneration to the art therapist or when it becomes reasonably clear that the relationship or therapy is not in the best interest of the client.

1.5 Art therapists do not engage in therapy practices or procedures that are beyond their scope of practice, experience, training, and education. Art therapists should assist persons in obtaining other therapeutic services if the therapist is unable or unwilling to provide professional help, or where the problem or treatment indicated is beyond the scope of practice of the art therapist.

1.6 Art therapists do not abandon or neglect clients receiving services. If an art therapist is unable to continue to provide professional help, he or she should assist the client in making reasonable alternative arrangements for continuation of services.

2.0 PROFESSIONAL COMPETENCE AND INTEGRITY

Art therapists maintain high standards of professional competence and integrity.

2.1 Through educational activities and clinical experiences, art therapists keep informed and up-dated with regard to developments in their field or which relate to their practice.

2.2 Art therapists assess, treat, or advise on problems only in those cases in which they are competent as determined by their education, training, and experience.

2.3 Art therapists do not knowingly provide professional services to a person receiving treatment or therapy from another professional, except by agreement with such other professional, or after termination of the client's relationship with the other professional.

2.4 Art therapists, because of their potential to influence and alter the lives of others, exercise special care when making public their professional recommendations and opinions through testimony or other public statements.

2.5 Art therapists seek appropriate professional consultation or assistance for their personal problems or conflicts that may impair or affect work performance or clinical judgment.

2.6 Art therapists do not distort or misuse their clinical and research findings.

2.7 An art therapist may file a complaint with ATCB when the art therapist has reason to believe that another art therapist is or has been engaged in previously unreported conduct that violates the law or the Standards of Conduct contained in this Code. This does not apply when the belief is based upon information obtained in the course of a therapeutic relationship with a client; however, this does not relieve an art therapist from the duty to file any reports required by law.

2.8 An art therapist may notify ATCB of any previously unreported disciplinary sanctions imposed upon another art therapist by another professional credentialing agency or organization, when such sanctions come to his or her attention.

3.0 RESPONSIBILITY TO STUDENTS AND SUPERVISEES

Art therapists instruct their students using accurate, current, and scholarly information and at all times foster the professional growth of students and advisees.

3.1 Art therapists as teachers, supervisors, and researchers maintain high standards of scholarship and present accurate information.

3.2 Art therapists do not permit students, employees, or supervisees to perform or to hold themselves out as competent to perform professional services beyond their education, training, experience, or competence.

3.3 Art therapists who act as supervisors are responsible for maintaining the quality of their supervision skills and obtaining consultation or supervision for their work as supervisors whenever appropriate.

4.0 RESPONSIBILITY TO RESEARCH PARTICIPANTS

Art therapists who are researchers seek to respect the dignity and protect the welfare of participants in research.

4.1 Researchers should be aware of and comply with federal and state laws and regulations, agency regulations, and professional standards governing the conduct of research.

4.2 Researchers should make careful examinations of ethical acceptability in planning studies. To the extent that services to research participants may be compromised by participation in research, investigators should seek the ethical advice of qualified professionals not directly involved in the investigation and observe safeguards to protect the rights of research participants.

4.3 A researcher requesting a participant's involvement in research should inform him or her of all risks and aspects of the research that might reasonably be expected to influence willingness to participate, and should obtain a written informed consent, reflecting an understanding of the said risks and aspects of the research, signed by the participant, or, where appropriate, by the participant's parent or legal guardian. Researchers should be especially sensitive to the possibility of diminished consent when participants are also receiving clinical services, have impairments which limit understanding and/or communication, or when participants are children.

4.4 Researchers respect participants' freedom to decline participation in or to withdraw from a research study at any time. This principle requires special thought and consideration when investigators or other members of the research team are in positions of authority or influence over participants. Art therapists, therefore, should avoid relationships with research participants outside of the scope of the research.

4.5 Information obtained about a research participant during the course of an investigation should be treated as confidential unless there is an authorization previously obtained in writing. When there is a risk that others, including family members, may obtain access to such information, this risk, together with the plan for protecting confidentiality, should be explained as part of the above stated procedure for obtaining a written informed consent.

5.0 RESPONSIBILITY TO THE PROFESSION

Art therapists respect the rights and responsibilities of professional colleagues and participate in activities which advance the goals of art therapy.

5.1 Art therapists adhere to the standards of the profession when acting as members or employees of organizations.

5.2 Art therapists attribute publication credit to those who have contributed to a publication in proportion to their contributions and in accordance with customary professional publication practices.

5.3 Art therapists who author books or other materials which are published or distributed appropriately cite persons to whom credit for original ideas is due.

5.4 Art therapists who author books or other materials published or distributed by an organization take reasonable precautions to ensure that the organization promotes and advertises the materials accurately and factually.

5.5 Art therapists are encouraged, whenever possible, to recognize a responsibility to participate in activities that contribute to a better community and society, including devoting a portion of their professional activity to services for which there is little or no financial return.

5.6 Art therapists are encouraged, whenever possible, to assist and be involved in developing laws and regulations pertaining to the field of art therapy which serve the public interest and with changing such laws and regulations that are not in the public interest.

5.7 Art therapists cooperate with any ethics investigation by any professional organization or government agency, and truthfully represent and disclose facts to such organizations or agencies when requested or when necessary to preserve the integrity of the art therapy profession.

5.8 Art therapists endeavor to prevent distortion, misuse, or suppression of art therapy findings by any institution or agency of which they are employees.

6.0 FINANCIAL ARRANGEMENTS

Art therapists seek to ensure that financial arrangements with clients, third party payers, and supervisees are understandable and conform to accepted professional practices.

6.1 Art therapists should not offer or accept payment for referrals.

6.2 Art therapists do not exploit their clients financially.

6.3 Art therapists represent facts truthfully to clients, third party payers, and supervisees regarding services rendered and the charges therefore.

7.0 ADVERTISING

Art therapists should engage in appropriate informational activities to enable lay persons to choose professional services on an informed basis.

7.1 Art therapists accurately represent their competence, education, training, and experience relevant to their professional practice.

7.2 Art therapists assure that all advertisements and publications, whether in directories, announcement cards, newspapers, or on radio or television, are formulated to accurately convey, in a dignified and professional manner, information that is necessary for the public to make an informed, knowledgeable decision.

7.3 Art therapists should not use a name which is likely to mislead the public concerning the identity, responsibility, source, and status of those under whom they are practicing, and should not hold themselves out as being partners or associates of a firm if they are not.

7.4 Art therapists should not use any professional identification (such as a business card, office sign, letterhead, or telephone or association directory listing) if it includes a statement or claim that is false, fraudulent, misleading or deceptive. A statement is false, fraudulent, misleading or deceptive if it: fails to state any material fact necessary to keep the statement from being misleading; is intended to, or likely to, create an unjustified expectation; or contains a material misrepresentation of fact.

7.5 An art therapist corrects, whenever possible, false, misleading, or inaccurate information and representations made by others concerning the therapist's qualifications, services, or products.

7.6 Art therapists make certain that the qualifications of persons in their employ are represented in a manner that is not false, misleading, or deceptive.

7.7 Art therapists may represent themselves as specializing within a limited area of art therapy only if they have the education, training, and experience which meet recognized professional standards to practice in that specialty area.

B. INDEPENDENT PRACTITIONER. SPECIFIC ETHICAL CONSIDERATIONS.

8.0 INDEPENDENT PRACTITIONER. GENERAL.

The Independent Practitioner of Art Therapy is an art therapist who is practicing art therapy independently and who is responsible for the delivery of services to clients where the client and/or third party payer pays the clinician directly or through insurance for art therapy services rendered.

8.1 When appropriate, independent practitioners of art therapy obtain qualified medical or psychological consultation for cases in which such evaluation and/or administration of medication is required. Art therapists do not provide services other than art therapy unless certified or licensed to provide such other services.

8.2 Independent practitioners of art therapy conform to relevant federal, state, and local statutes and ordinances which pertain to the provision of independent mental health practice. Laws vary from state to state. It is the sole responsibility of the independent practitioner to conform to these laws.

8.3 Independent practitioners of art therapy confine their practice within the limits of their training. Art therapists neither claim nor imply professional qualifications exceeding those actually earned and received by them. The art therapist is responsible for avoiding and/or correcting any misrepresentation of these qualifications. Art therapists adhere to state laws regarding independent practice and licensure, as applicable.

9.0 INDEPENDENT PRACTITIONER. ENVIRONMENT.

Independent practitioners of art therapy seek to provide a safe, functional environment in which to offer art therapy services. This includes, but is not limited to: proper ventilation, adequate lighting, access to water supply, knowledge of hazards or toxicity of art materials and the effort needed to safeguard the health of clients, storage space for art projects and secured areas for any hazardous materials, monitored use of sharps, allowance for privacy and confidentiality, and compliance with any other health and safety requirements according to state and federal agencies which regulate comparable businesses.

10.0 INDEPENDENT PRACTITIONER. ACCEPTANCE AND FINANCIAL ARRANGEMENTS.

An independent practitioner of art therapy should sign and issue a written professional disclosure statement to a client upon the establishment of a professional relationship. Such statement should include, but need not be limited to, the following information: education, training, experience, professional affiliations, credentials, fee structure, payment schedule, session scheduling arrangements, information pertaining to the limits of confidentiality and the duty to report, and the name, address, and telephone number of ATCB along with information regarding the function of ATCB. It is suggested that a copy of the statement be retained in the client's file. Independent practitioners of art therapy seek to ensure that financial arrangements with clients, third party payers, and supervisees are understandable and conform to accepted professional practices.

10.1 Independent practitioners of art therapy do not offer or accept payment for referrals.

10.2 Independent practitioners of art therapy do not exploit clients financially.

10.3 Independent practitioners of art therapy disclose their fees at the commencement of services and give reasonable notice of any changes in fees.

10.4 Independent practitioners of art therapy represent facts truthfully to clients, third party payers, and supervisees regarding services rendered and the charges therefore.

11.0 INDEPENDENT PRACTITIONER. TREATMENT PLANNING.

Independent practitioners of art therapy design treatment plans:

a. To assist the client in attaining maintenance of the maximum level of functioning and quality of life appropriate for such individual;
b. In compliance with federal, state, and local regulations and any licensure requirements governing the provision of art therapy services in the state;
c. That delineate the type, frequency, and duration of art therapy involvement;
d. That contain goals that reflect the client's current needs and strengths, formulated, when possible, with the client's understanding and permission;
e. That provide for timely review, modification, and revision.

12.0 INDEPENDENT PRACTITIONER. DOCUMENTATION.

Independent practitioners of art therapy should document activity with clients so that the most recent art therapy progress notes reflect, at a minimum, the following:

a. The client's current level of functioning.
b. The current goals of any treatment plan.
c. Verbal content of art therapy sessions relevant to client behavior and goals.
d. Artistic expression relevant to client behavior and goals.
e. Changes (or lack of change) in affect, thought process, and behavior.
f. Suicidal or homicidal intent or ideation.

12.1 Upon termination of the therapeutic relationship, independent practitioners of art therapy should write a discharge/transfer summary that includes the client's response to treatment and future treatment recommendations.

13.0 INDEPENDENT PRACTITIONER. TERMINATION OF SERVICES.

Independent practitioners of art therapy terminate art therapy when the client has attained stated goals and objectives or fails to benefit from art therapy services.

13.1 Independent practitioners of art therapy communicate the termination of art therapy services to the client.

III. ELIGIBILITY FOR CREDENTIALS

As a condition of eligibility for and continued maintenance or renewal of any ATCB credential, each applicant, registrant or certificant agrees to the following:

A. Compliance with ATCB Standards, Policies and Procedures

No person is eligible to apply for or maintain credentials unless in compliance with all ATCB eligibility criteria as stated in the ATR and ATR-BC applications, as well as all other ATCB rules and standards, policies and procedures, including, but not limited to, those stated herein, and including timely payment of fees and any other requirements for renewal of credentials. Each applicant, registrant or certificant bears the burden for showing and maintaining compliance at all times. ATCB may deny, revoke, decline to renew, or otherwise act upon credentials when an applicant, registrant, or certificant is not in compliance with all ATCB standards, policies and procedures.

B. Complete Application

1.ATCB may make administrative requests for additional information to supplement or complete any application for credentials or for renewal of existing credentials. An applicant shall truthfully complete and sign an application in the form provided by ATCB, shall provide the required fees, and shall provide additional information as requested. The applicant shall notify ATCB within 60 days of occurrence of any change in name, address, telephone number, and any other facts bearing on eligibility for credentials, including but not limited to: filing of any civil or criminal charge, indictment or litigation involving the applicant; disposition of any civil or criminal charge, indictment or litigation involving the applicant, including, but not limited to, dismissal, entry of a judgment, conviction, plea of guilty, plea of nolo contendere, or disciplinary action by a licensing board or professional organization. An applicant, registrant, or certificant shall not make and shall correct immediately any statement concerning his or her status which is or becomes inaccurate, untrue, or misleading.

2. All references to "days" in ATCB standards, policies and procedures shall mean calendar days. Communications required by ATCB shall be transmitted by certified mail, return receipt requested, or other verifiable method of delivery. The applicant, registrant, or certificant shall provide ATCB with confirmation of compliance with ATCB requirements as requested by ATCB through its President or Management Director.

C. Property of ATCB

The examinations, certificates, and cards of ATCB, the name Art Therapy Credentials Board, the mark ATR, the mark ATR-BC, the term Registered Art Therapist, the term Registered Art Therapist-Board Certified, and all abbreviations relating thereto, are all the exclusive property of ATCB and may not be used in any way without the express prior written consent of ATCB. In case of suspension, limitation, relinquishment or revocation of ATCB credentials, or as otherwise requested by ATCB, a person previously holding an ATCB credential shall immediately relinquish, refrain from using, and correct at his or her expense any and all outdated or otherwise inaccurate business cards, stationery, advertisements, or other use of any certificate, logo, emblem, and the ATCB name and related abbreviations.

D. Pending Litigation

An applicant, registrant, or certificant shall notify ATCB of the filing in any court of an information, complaint, or indictment charging him or her with a felony or with a crime related to the practice of art therapy or the public health and safety, or the filing of any charge or action before a state or federal regulatory agency or judicial body directly relating to the practice of art therapy or related professions, or to a matter described in Section IV. Such notification shall be within 60 days of the filing of such charge or action, and shall provide documentation of the resolution of such charge within 60 days of resolution.

E. Criminal Convictions

Any person convicted of either (i) a felony, or (ii) any crime substantially related to or impacting upon art therapy, the therapist's professional qualifications or public health and safety shall be ineligible for credentials for a period of five years from and after completion of sentence by final release from confinement (if any), or satisfaction of fine imposed, whichever is later. Convictions of this nature include but are not limited to those involving rape, sexual abuse of a patient or child, actual or threatened use of a weapon or violence, and prohibited sale, distribution or possession of a controlled substance.

IV. STANDARDS OF CONDUCT

The Art Therapy Credentials Board adopts the following standards of conduct, which shall guide the conduct of all art therapists who seek to obtain or maintain credentials under the authority of ATCB. These standards are closely based upon standards adopted by The American Art Therapy Association, but they have been adapted to meet the goals and mission of ATCB, and are intended to stand as an independent expression of the standards of conduct that shall guide the work of those who hold ATCB credentials.

1.0 CONFIDENTIALITY

Art therapists shall respect and protect confidential information obtained from clients including, but not limited to, all verbal and/or artistic expression occurring within a client-therapist relationship.

1.1 Art therapists shall protect the confidentiality of the client-therapist relationship in all matters.

1.2 Art therapists shall not disclose confidential information without the client's explicit written consent unless there is reason to believe that the client or others are in immediate, severe danger to health or life. Any such disclosure shall be made consistent with state and federal laws that pertain to welfare of the client, family, and the general public.

1.3 In the event that an art therapist believes it is in the interest of the client to disclose confidential information, he or she shall seek and obtain written authorization from the client or the client's legal guardian, before making any disclosures, unless such disclosure is required by law.

1.4 Art therapists shall disclose confidential information when mandated by law and/or in an ATCB disciplinary action. In these cases client confidences may be disclosed only as reasonably necessary in the course of that action.

1.5 Art therapists shall maintain client treatment records for a reasonable amount of time consistent with state regulations and sound clinical practice. Records shall be stored or disposed of in ways that maintain confidentiality.

1.6 Where the client is a minor, any and all disclosure or consent shall be made to or obtained from the parent or legal guardian of the minor client, except where otherwise provided by state law. Care shall be taken to preserve confidentiality with the minor client and to refrain from disclosure of information to the parent or guardian which might adversely affect the treatment of the client, except where otherwise provided by state law.

2.0 PUBLIC USE AND REPRODUCTION OF CLIENT ART EXPRESSION AND THERAPY SESSIONS

Art therapists shall not make or permit any public use or reproduction of a client's art therapy sessions, including verbalization and art expression, without express written consent of the client or, where appropriate, the client's parent or legal guardian.

2.1 Art therapists shall obtain written informed consent from a client, or where applicable, a parent or legal guardian before photographing the client's art expressions, video taping, audio recording, or otherwise duplicating, or permitting third party observation of art therapy sessions.

2.2 Art therapists shall use clinical materials in teaching, writing, and public presentations only if a written authorization has been previously obtained from the client who produced the material, or, where appropriate, a parent or legal guardian. Once authorization has been granted, the therapist shall ensure that appropriate steps are taken to protect client identity and disguise any part of the art expression or videotape which reveals client identity.

2.3 Art therapists shall obtain written, informed consent from a client or, when appropriate, the client's parent or legal guardian before displaying the client's art in galleries, mental health facilities, schools, or other public places.

3.0 PROFESSIONAL RELATIONSHIPS

Art therapists shall not engage in any relationship with current or former clients, students, interns, trainees, supervisees, employees, or colleagues that is exploitative by its nature or effect. Art therapists shall make their best efforts to avoid, if it is reasonably possible to do so, entering into non-therapeutic or non-professional relationships with current or former clients, students, interns, trainees, supervisees, employees, or colleagues or any family members or other persons known to have a close personal relationship with such individuals such as spouses, children, or close friends. In the event that the nature of any such relationship is questioned, the burden of proof shall be on the art therapist to prove that a non-therapeutic or non-professional relationship with current or former clients, students, interns, trainees, supervisees, employees, or colleagues is not exploitative or harmful to any such individuals.

3.1 Art therapists shall not engage in exploitative relationships with clients. Exploitative relationships include, but are not limited to, borrowing money from or loaning money to a client, hiring a client, engaging in a business venture with a client, engaging in a romantic relationship with a client, or engaging in sexual intimacy with a client.

3.2 Art therapists shall take appropriate professional precautions to ensure that their judgment is not impaired, that no exploitation occurs, and that all conduct is undertaken solely in the client's best interest.

3.3 Art therapists shall not use their professional relationships with clients to further their own interests.

3.4 Art therapists shall be aware of their influential position with respect to students and supervisees, and they shall avoid exploiting the trust and dependency of such persons. Art therapists, therefore, shall not provide therapy to students or supervisees contemporaneously with the student/supervisee relationship.

3.5 Art therapists shall not engage in exploitative relationships with their students or supervisees. An exploitative relationship is a relationship between an art therapist and a student or supervisee which, in fact or by its inherent nature, contains the potential for abuse by the art therapist of the trust and dependency of the student or supervisee and the inherently influential position of the art therapist over the student or supervisee. Exploitative relationships between art therapists and students or supervisees include, but are not limited to, borrowing money from or loaning money to the student or supervisee, engaging in a romantic relationship with a current student or supervisee, or engaging in sexual intimacy with a current student or supervisee.

V. GROUNDS FOR DISCIPLINE

ATCB may deny or revoke credentials or otherwise take action with regard to credentials or an application for credentials under the following circumstances:

A. Failure to observe and comply with the Standards of Conduct stated above in Section IV;

B. Failure to meet and maintain eligibility for ATCB credentials;

C. Irregularity in connection with any ATCB examination;

D. Failure to pay fees required by ATCB;

E. Unauthorized possession of, use of, or access to ATCB examinations, certificates, cards, and logos, the name Art Therapy Credentials Board, the term ATCB, and abbreviations relating thereto, the terms Registered Art Therapist, Registered Art Therapist - Board Certified, the abbreviations ATR and ATR-BC, and any variations thereof, and any other ATCB documents and materials;

F. Obtaining, maintaining, or attempting to obtain or maintain credentials by a false or misleading statement, failure to make a required statement, fraud, or deceit in an application, reapplication, or any other communication to ATCB;

G. Misrepresentation of status of ATCB credentials;

H. Failure to provide any written information required by ATCB;

I. Failure to cooperate with ATCB or any body established or convened by ATCB at any point from the inception of an ethical complaint through the completion of all proceedings regarding that complaint;

J. Habitual use of alcohol or any drug or any substance, or any physical or mental condition, which impairs competent and objective professional performance;

K. Gross or repeated negligence in the practice of art therapy or other professional work;

L. Limitation or sanction (including but not limited to discipline, revocation or suspension by a regulatory board or professional organization) in a field relevant to the practice of art therapy;

M. The conviction of, or plea of guilty or plea of *nolo contendere* to, (i) any felony or (ii) any crime related to the practice of art therapy, the therapist's professional qualifications, or public health and safety. Convictions of this nature include but are not limited to those involving rape, sexual abuse of a patient or child, actual or threatened use of a weapon or violence, and the prohibited sale, distribution or use of a controlled substance;

N. Failure to timely update information, including any violation of this Section, to ATCB;

O. Failure to maintain confidentiality as required in the Standards of Conduct, by any ATCB policy or procedure, or as otherwise required by law; or

P. Other violation of an ATCB standard, policy or procedure stated herein or as stated in the ATCB candidate brochure or other material provided to applicants, registrants, or certificants.

VI. APPOINTMENT OF DISCIPLINARY HEARING COMMITTEES

A. The ATCB Board of Directors by a majority vote may appoint an Ethics Officer and a Disciplinary Hearing Committee, to consider alleged violations of the Standards of Conduct contained in this Code or any other ATCB standard, policy or procedure. The ATCB Board of Directors shall appoint the chair of the Disciplinary Hearing Committee.

B. The Disciplinary Hearing Committee shall be composed of three members, including the chair. The membership of each of these Committees shall be drawn from ATCB registrants and certificants, except that one member of the Disciplinary Hearing Committee shall be a public member who shall not be a ATCB registrant or certificant.

C. The initial appointments to the disciplinary hearing committee shall be for terms of years as determined by the ATCB Board of Directors to result in staggered expiration dates. Thereafter, a committee member's term of office on the committee shall run for three years and may be renewed.

D. A committee member may serve on only one committee and may not serve on any matter in which he or she has an actual or apparent conflict of interest or his or her impartiality might reasonably be questioned. When a party to a matter before one of the committees requests that a member of the committee, other than the chair, recuse himself or herself, a final decision on the issue of recusal shall be made by the committee chair, subject to review as hereinafter provided. In the event a request is made that the chair recuse himself or herself, the decision shall be made by the President, subject to review as hereinafter provided.

E. Committee action shall be determined by majority vote.

F. When a committee member is unavailable to serve by resignation, disqualification, or other circumstance, the President of ATCB shall designate another registrant or certificant, or public member, if applicable, to serve as an interim member.

VII. DISCIPLINARY PROCEDURES

A. Submission of Allegations

1. Any person concerned with possible violation of ATCB Standards of Conduct, or other ATCB standard, policy or procedure, may initiate a complaint by identifying the persons alleged to be involved and the facts concerning the alleged conduct in as much detail and specificity as possible with available documentation in a written statement addressed to the Management Director. The statement should identify by name, address, and telephone number the person making the information known to ATCB, and others who may have knowledge of the facts and circumstances concerning the alleged conduct. ATCB may provide for the submission of complaints on forms to be supplied by the Management Director. After a complaint is received, the Management Director shall refer the matter to the Public Member of the ATCB Board of Directors (the "Public Member") for further action. The Public Member may initiate complaints, that shall be handled in the manner provided hereinafter for the review and determination of all complaints.

2. The Public Member shall review the allegations and supporting information and make a determination of the merits of the allegations, after such further inquiry as he or she considers appropriate, and after consultation with counsel as needed. The Public Member may direct the ATCB Management Director to assist with factual investigations or with administrative matters related to the initial review of allegations.

3. If the Public Member determines that the allegations are frivolous or fail to state a violation of the Standards of Conduct, or if ATCB lacks jurisdiction over the complaint or the person(s) complained about, he or she shall take no further action and shall notify the Board and the complainant, if any.

4. If the Public Member determines that probable cause may exist to deny eligibility or question compliance with the Standards of Conduct or any other ATCB policy or procedure, he or she shall transmit the allegations to the Ethics Officer.

5. The Ethics Officer shall review the allegations and supporting information provided and may make such further inquiry as he or she deems appropriate. The Ethics Officer also may research precedents in ATCB's files or in reported legal decisions, as he or she reasonably determines to be necessary in making a determination regarding probable cause of a violation of the ATCB Code of Professional Conduct or other misconduct. The Ethics Officer may direct the ATCB Management Director to assist with factual investigations or with administrative matters related to the review of allegations. If the Ethics Officer concurs that probable cause may exist to deny eligibility or question compliance with the Standards of Conduct or any other ATCB policy or procedure, he or she shall transmit the allegations and his or her findings to the full Disciplinary Hearing Committee, the complainant and the respondent. If the Ethics Officer determines that probable cause does not exist to deny eligibility or question compliance or that ATCB lacks jurisdiction over the complaint or the person(s) complained of he or she may take no further action and shall notify the Board, the respondent, and complainant, if any.

B. Procedures of the Disciplinary Hearing Committee

1. Upon receipt of notice from the Ethics Officer containing a statement of the complaint allegations and the finding(s) that probable cause may exist to deny eligibility or question compliance with the Standards of Conduct or any other ATCB policy or procedure, the respondent shall have fifteen (15) days after receipt of the to notice to notify the Ethics Officer in writing that the respondent disputes the allegations of the complaint and to request review by written submissions to the Disciplinary Hearing Committee, a telephone conference with the Disciplinary Hearing Committee, or an in-person hearing (held at a time and place to be determined by the committee), with the respondent bearing his or her own expenses for such hearing. If the respondent does not contest the allegations of the complaint, he or she may still request review by written submissions to the Disciplinary Hearing Committee, a telephone conference with the Disciplinary Hearing Committee, or an in-person hearing (held at a time and place to be determined by the committee), with the respondent bearing his or her own expenses for such hearing concerning the appropriate sanction(s) to be applied in the case. If the respondent does not submit a written contest to the allegations or notify the board of a request for review by written submission, telephone conference or in-person hearing as set forth in this paragraph, then the Disciplinary Hearing Committee shall render a decision and apply sanctions as it deems appropriate.

2. If the respondent requests a review, telephone conference, or hearing, the following procedures shall apply:

a. The Ethics Officer shall forward the allegations and response of the respondent to the Disciplinary Hearing Committee, and shall designate one of its members to present the allegations and any substantiating evidence, examine and cross-examine witnesses, and otherwise present the matter during any hearing of the Disciplinary Hearing Committee.

b. The Disciplinary Hearing Committee shall then schedule a written review, or telephone or in-person hearing as requested by the respondent, allowing for an adequate period of time for preparation, and shall send by certified mail, return receipt requested, a notice to the respondent. The notice shall include a statement of the standards allegedly violated, the procedures to be followed, and the date for submission of materials for written review, or the time and place of any hearing, as determined by the Disciplinary Hearing Committee. The respondent may request a change in the date of any hearing for good cause.

c. The Disciplinary Hearing Committee shall maintain a verbatim audio, video, or written transcript of any hearing.

d. During any proceeding before the Disciplinary Hearing Committee, all parties may consult with and be represented by counsel at their own expense. At any hearing, all parties or their counsel may make opening statements, present relevant documents or other evidence and relevant testimony, examine and cross-examine witnesses under oath, make closing statements, and present written briefs as scheduled by the Disciplinary Hearing Committee.

e. The Disciplinary Hearing Committee shall determine all evidentiary and procedural matters relating to any hearing or written review. Formal rules of evidence shall not apply. Relevant evidence may be admitted. Disputed questions regarding procedures or the admission of evidence shall be determined by the chair, subject to the majority vote of the full committee. All decisions shall be made on the record.

f. Proof shall be by preponderance of the evidence.

g. Whenever mental or physical disability is alleged, the respondent may be required to undergo a physical or mental examination at his or her own expense. The report of such an examination shall become part of the evidence considered.

h. The Disciplinary Hearing Committee shall issue a written decision following any hearing or written review and any submission of briefs. The decision shall contain findings of fact, a finding as to the truth of the allegations, conclusions of law and any sanctions applied. It shall be mailed promptly by certified mail, return receipt requested, to the respondent.

i. If the Disciplinary Hearing Committee finds that the allegations have not been proven by a preponderance of the evidence, no further action shall be taken, and the respondent, and the complainant, if any, shall be notified.

C. Appeal Procedures

1. If the decision rendered by the Disciplinary Hearing Committee is not favorable to the respondent, he or she may appeal the decision to the ATCB Board of Directors by submitting to the Management Director a written appeals statement within 30 days following receipt of the decision of the Disciplinary Hearing Committee. The Disciplinary Hearing Committee shall, in its sole discretion, consider requests for extensions based on the nature of the case and the public interest. The written appeals statement shall be accompanied by the appeal fee then required by ATCB as stated in the written decision. The Disciplinary Hearing Committee may file a written response with the Management Director. The Management Director shall immediately forward any appeals documents to the ATCB Board of Directors.

2. The ATCB Board of Directors by majority vote shall render a decision on the record without further hearing, although written briefs may be submitted on a schedule determined by the Board of Directors.

3. The decision of the ATCB Board of Directors shall be rendered in writing following receipt and review of briefs. The decision shall contain findings of fact, a finding as to the truth of the allegations, conclusions of law and any sanctions applied and shall be final. The decision shall be communicated to the respondent by certified mail, return receipt requested. The complainant, if any, shall be notified of the Board of Director's final decision.

VIII. SANCTIONS

Sanctions for violation of the Standards of Conduct, or any other ATCB standard, policy or procedure to which reference is made herein, may include one or more of the following:

a. Denial or suspension of eligibility for credentials for a stated period of time;
b. Forfeiture or revocation of registration or certification;
c. Suspension of registration or certification;
d. Non-renewal of certification;
e. Reprimand;
f. Publication of the complaint and its disposition; or
g. Other corrective action.

IX. RELEASE OF INFORMATION

Each applicant, registrant, and certificant agrees to cooperate promptly and fully in any review of eligibility or credential status, including submitting such documents and information deemed necessary to confirm the information in an application. The individual applicant, registrant, or certificant agrees that ATCB and its officers, directors, committee members, employees, Ethics Officer, agents, and others may communicate any and all information relating to an ATCB application, registration or certification, and review thereof, including, but not limited to, existence of or outcome of disciplinary proceedings, to state and federal authorities, licensing boards, employers, other registrants or certificants, and to the public.

X. WAIVER

An applicant, registrant, or certificant releases, discharges, exonerates, indemnifies, and holds harmless ATCB, its officers, directors, employees, committee members, panel members, Ethics Officer, and agents, and any other persons from and against all claims, damages, losses, and expenses, including reasonable attorneys' fees, for actions of ATCB arising out of applicant's application for or participation in the ATCB registration and/or certification programs and use of ATCB trademarks or other references to the ATCB registration and/or certification programs, including but not limited to the furnishing or inspection of documents, records, and other information and any investigation and review of applications or credentials by ATCB.

XI. RECONSIDERATION OF ELIGIBILITY AND REINSTATEMENT OF CREDENTIALS

A. If eligibility or credentials are denied, revoked, or suspended for a violation of the Standards of Conduct, eligibility for credentials may be reconsidered by the Board of Directors, upon application, on the following basis:

1. In the event of a felony conviction, no earlier than five years from and after the exhaustion of appeals, completion of sentence by final release from confinement (if any), or satisfaction of fine imposed, whichever is later;

2. In any other event, at any time following imposition of sanctions, at the discretion of the Board of Directors.

B. In addition to other facts required by ATCB, such an applicant must fully set forth the circumstances of the decision denying, revoking, or suspending eligibility or credentials as well as all relevant facts and circumstances since the decision. The applicant bears the burden of demonstrating by clear and convincing evidence that he or she has been rehabilitated and does not pose a danger to others.

XII. DEADLINES

ATCB expects its registrants and certificants to meet all deadlines imposed by ATCB, especially in regard to submission of fees, renewal or recertification applications, required evidence of continuing education, and sitting for its examinations. On rare occasions, circumstances beyond the control of the applicant, registrant or certificant, or other extraordinary conditions may render it difficult, if not impossible, to meet ATCB deadlines. Should an applicant, registrant, or certificant wish to appeal a missed deadline, he or she should transmit a written explanation and make a request for a reasonable extension of the missed deadline, with full relevant supporting documentation, to the ATCB Management Director, to the attention of the ATCB Board of Directors. The Board of Directors shall determine at the next meeting of the Board, in its sole discretion and on a case-by-case basis, what, if any, recourse should be afforded based on the circumstances described and the overall impact on the profession of art therapy. No other procedures shall be afforded for failure to meet ATCB deadlines.

XIII. BIAS, PREJUDICE, IMPARTIALITY

At all times during ATCB's handling of any matter, ATCB shall extend impartial review. If at any time during ATCB's review of a matter an applicant, registrant, certificant, or any other person identifies a situation where the judgment of a reviewer may be biased or prejudiced or impartiality may be compromised (including employment with a competing organization), such person shall immediately report such matter to the Management Director or President of ATCB.

REFERENCES

Agell, G., Goodman, R., & Williams, K. (1995). The professional relationship: Ethics. *American Journal of Art Therapy, 33*, 99-109.

Ahia, C.E., & Martin, D. (1993). *The danger-to-self-or-others exception to confidentiality.* Alexandria, VA: American Counseling Association.

Allen, P. (1995). *Art is a way of knowing.* Boston: Shambhala.

Allen, P. (1992). Guidelines for getting started in research. In H. Wadeson (Ed.), *A guide to conducting art therapy research.* Mundelein, IL: The American Art Therapy Association, Inc.

American Art Therapy Association. (2003). *Ethical principles for art therapists.* Mundelein, IL: American Art Therapy Association, Inc.

American Counseling Association. (1995). *Code of ethics and standards of practice.* Alexandria, VA: Author.

American Association for Marriage and Family Therapy. (1991). *AAMFT code of ethics.* Washington, DC: Author.

American Music Therapy Association. (1998). *American Music Therapy Association code of ethics.* Silver Spring, MD: Author.

American Psychological Association. (1995). *Ethical principles of psychologists and code of conduct.* Washington, DC: Author.

American Psychological Association. (1994). *Publication manual of the American Psychological Association,* Fourth Edition. Washington, DC: Author.

Anderson, F.E. (1983). A critical analysis of a review of the published research in literature in *Arts for the Handicapped*: 1971-1981, with special attention to the visual arts. *Art Therapy: Journal of the American Art Therapy Association, 1*, 26-39.

Art Therapy Credentials Board. (2005) *Code of professional practice.* Greensboro, NC: Author.

Austin, V. (1976). Let's bring art back into art therapy. In R.H. Shoemaker & S. Gonick-Barris (Eds.), Creativity and the art therapist's identity. *Proceedings of the seventh annual conference of the American Art Therapy Association*, 28-29.

Bennett, B.E., Bryant, B.K., VandenBos, G.R., & Greenwood, A. (1990). *Professional liability and risk management.* Washington, DC: American Psychological Association.

Bonhoeffer, D. (1961). *Church dogmatics,* Vol III, Bk 4. Edinburgh: T. & T. Clark.

Borum, J. (1993, Winter). Term warfare. *Raw Vision.* New York: Raw Vision Magazine.

Braverman, J. (1995). Retention of treatment records under the new AATA ethical standards. *American Art Therapy Association Newsletter XXVII* (1) 15.

Broszormenyi-Nagy, I., & Krasner, B. (1986). *Between give and take: A clinical guide to contextual therapy.* New York: Brunner Mazel.

Campbell, J. (1968). *Creative mythology: The masks of God.* New York: Penguin.

Carrigan, J. (1993). Ethical considerations in a supervisory relationship. *Art Therapy: Journal of the American Art Therapy Association, 10,* 130 -135.

Casado, M. (1980). *In search of the meaning and duty of modern art.* Unpublished manuscript. University of Kansas, Department of History, Lawrence, KS.

Cattaneo, M. (1994). Addressing culture and values in the training of art therapists. *Art Therapy: Journal of the American Art Therapy Association, 11,* 184-186.

Champernowne, H. (1971). Art and therapy: An uneasy partnership. *Art Therapy: Journal of the American Art Therapy Association, 10,* 142.

Cohen-Liebman, M.S. (1994). The art therapist as expert witness in child sexual abuse litigation. *Art Therapy: Journal of the American Art Therapy Association, 11,* 260 - 265.

Cohen, F., Ault, R., Jones, D., Levick, M., & Ulman, E. (1980). The founding of the American Art Therapy Association: Living history of the original ad hoc committee members. In L. Gannt & S. Whitman (Eds.), The fine art of therapy. *Proceedings of the eleventh annual conference of the American Art Therapy Association,* 115-118.

Cohen, B., Hammer, J., & Singer, S. (1988). The diagnostic drawing series: A systematic approach to art therapy evaluation and research. *The Arts in Psychotherapy, 15,* 11-21.

Cohen, B., Mills, A., & Kijak, A. (1994). An introduction to the DDS: A standardized tool for diagnostic and clinical use. *Art Therapy: The Journal of the American Art Therapy Association, 11,* 105-110.

Corey, G., Corey, M., & Callanan, P. (1998) *Issues and ethics in the helping professions.* Pacific Grove, CA: Brooks/Cole.

Cox, C. (1995). Letter to the Editor. *Art Therapy: Journal of the American Art Therapy Association, 12,* 157.

Dissanayake, E. (1988). *What is art for?* Seattle, WA: University of Washington Press.

Drachnik, C. (1994). The tongue as a graphic symbol of sexual abuse. *American Journal of Art Therapy. 11,* 58-61.

Das, A. K. (1995). Rethinking multicultural counseling: Implications for counselor education. *Journal of Counseling and Development, 74,* 45-52.

Farber, B. (1983). *Stress and burnout in the human service professions.* New York: Pergamon Press.

Feen-Calligan, H., & Sands-Goldstein, M. (1996). A picture of our beginnings: The artwork of art therapy pioneers. *American Journal of Art Therapy. 35,* 43-53.

Fletcher, J. (1966). Situation ethics. Philadelphia: Westminster Press.

Frankena, W. (1983) *Ethics.* New York: Prentice Hall.

Franklin, M., & Politsky, R. (1992). The problem of interpretation: Implications and strategies for the field of art therapy. *The Arts in Psychotherapy, 19,* 163-175.

Fromm, E. (1955). *The sane society.* New York: Fawcett Premier Book.

Frostig, K.E. (1997). A review: Organizing exhibitions of art by people with mental illness: A step-by step manual. *Art Therapy: Journal of the American Art Therapy Association, 14*, 131-132.

Gablik, S. (1984). *Has modernism failed?* New York: Thames and Hudson.

Gantt, L. (1986). Systematic investigation of art works: Some research models Drawn from neighboring fields. *American Journal of Art Therapy, 24*, 111-118.

Gardner, H. (1994). *The arts and human development: A psychological study of the artistic process.* New York: Harper & Row.

Gardner, H. (1983). *Frames of mind: The theory of multiple intelligences.* New York: Basic Books.

Good, D. (1999). Letter from the president. *American Art Therapy Association Newsletter*, Vol. XXXII, (1) 3.

Gorelick, K. (1989). Rapprochement between the arts and psychotherapies: Metaphor the mediator. *The Arts in Psychotherapy, 16*, 149-55.

Guthiel, T., & Gabbard, G. (1993). The concept of boundaries in clinical practice:Theoretical and risk-management dimensions. *American Journal of Psychiatry, 150*, 188-196.

Gussow, A. (1971). *A sense of place.* San Francisco: Friends of the Earth.

Haeseler, M. (1989). Should art therapists create artwork alongside their clients? *The American Journal of Art Therapy, 27*, 70-79.

Hall, L. (1996). Bartering: A payment methodology whose time has come again or an unethical practice? *Family Therapy News, 27*, 7, 19.

Henley, D. (1997). Expressive arts therapy as alternative education: Devising a therapeutic curriculum. *Art Therapy: The Journal of the American Art Therapy Association, 14*, 15-22.

Henley, D. (1999). *Art Therapy: The Journal of the American Art Therapy Association, 16*, (3).

Henley, D. (1987) Art assessment with the handicapped: Clinical, aesthetic, and ethical considerations. *Art Therapy: The Journal of the American Art Therapy Association, 4*, 65.

Hiscox, A., & Calish, A. (Eds.). (1998). *Tapestry of cultural issues in art therapy.* Bristol, PA.: Jessica Kingsley.

Horovitz, E. (1987). Diagnosis and assessment: Impact on art therapy. *Art Therapy: The Journal of the American Art Therapy Association. 4*, 127- 137.

Hutcheon, L. (1988). *A poetics of postmodernism.* New York: Routledge.

Ivey, A.E. (1990). *Developmental strategies for helpers: Individual, family, and network interventions.* Pacific Grove, CA: Brooks/Cole.

Jones, D. (1999). Exploring the dynamics of why art therapists must make art. *Proceedings of the 1999 Annual AATA Conference: Frameworks: A sense of place.* (p. 164). Orlando, Fl.: AATA.

Jones, D. (1999). *Personal communication.*

Jones, D. (1973). *Personal communication.*

Jourard, S. (1964). *The transparent self.* Princeton, NJ: Van Nostrand.

Junge, M. (1989). The heart of the matter. *The Arts in Psychotherapy, 16*, 77-78.

Kelly, W. (1982). *The best of Pogo.* New York: Simon & Schuster.

Knapp. N. (1992a). Historical overview of art therapy research. In H. Wadeson (Ed.), *A guide to conducting art therapy research.* Mundelein, IL: The American Art Therapy Association, Inc.

Knapp, N. (1992b). Ethics in research with human subjects. In H. Wadeson (Ed.), *A guide to conducting art therapy research.* Mundelein, IL: The American Art Therapy Association, Inc.

Kopp, S. (1972). *If you meet the buddha on the road, kill him.* New York: Bantam Books.

Kramer, S.A. (1990). *Positive endings in psychotherapy: Bringing meaningful closure to therapeutic relationships.* San Francisco: Jossey-Bass

Lachman-Chapin, M. (1983). The artist as clinician: An interactive technique in art therapy. *American Journal of Art Therapy, 23,* 13-25.

Levick, M., Safran, & Levine. (1990). Art therapists as expert witness. *The Arts in Psychotherapy, 18,* 277-283.

Lindberg, B. (1999). Report from the legislative consultant. *AATA Newsletter, Vol. XXXII,* (1).

Linesch, D. (1992). Research approaches within master's level art therapy training programs. *Art Therapy: The Journal of the American Art Therapy Association, 9.*

Linesch, D. (1988). *Adolescent art therapy.* New York: Brunner Mazel.

MacGregor, J. (1989). *The discovery of the art of the insane.* Princeton, NJ: Princeton University Press.

Malchiodi, C.A. (2000). *Art Therapy and Computer Technology: The Virtual Studio of Possibilities.* London: Jessica Kingsley.

Malchiodi, C., & Riley, S. (1996). *Supervision and related issues: A handbook for professionals.* Chicago: Magnolia Street.

Malchiodi, C.A. (1996). Addressing ethical and legal issues in art therapy training and supervision. In C. Malchiodi & S. Riley, *Supervision and related issues: A handbook for professionals.* Chicago: Magnolia Street.

Malchiodi, C. (1995a). Does a lack of research hold us back? *Art Therapy: Journal of the American Art Therapy Association, 12,* 218-219.

Malchiodi, C. (1995b). Editorial. *Art Therapy: Journal of the American Art Therapy Association, 12,* 2.

Malchiodi, C. (1994). Introduction to special issue on ethics and professional issues: Professional courtesy. *Art Therapy: The Journal of the American Art Therapy Association, 11,* 242-243.

Malchiodi, C. (1992). Writing about art therapy professional publications. *Art Therapy: The Journal of the American Art Therapy Association, 9.*

McCarthy, C. (1994). *The crossing.* New York: Alfred Knopf.

McCathy, P., Sugden, S., Koker, M., Lamendola, F., Mauer, S., & Renninger, S. (1995). A practical guide to informed consent in clinical supervision. *Counselor Education and Supervision, 35,* 130-138.

McNiff, S. (1998). *Art-based research.* London: Jessica Kingsley.

McNiff, S. (1998). *Trust the process.* Boston: Shambhala.

McNiff, S. (1992). *Art as medicine: Creating a therapy of the imagination.* Boston: Shambhala.

McNiff, S. (1991). Ethics and the autonomy of images. *The Arts in Psychotherapy,* 18.

McNiff, S. (1989). *Depth psychology of art.* Springfield, IL: Charles C Thomas.

McNiff, S. (1987). Research and scholarship in the creative arts therapies. *The Arts in Psychotherapy, 14,* 285-292.

McNiff, S. (1986). Freedom of research and artistic inquiry. *The Arts in Psychotherapy, 13,* 279-284.

McNiff, S. (1984). Cross-cultural psychotherapy and art. *Art Therapy: Journal of the American Art Therapy Association, 1,* 125-130.

McNiff, S. (1982). Working with everything we have. *American Journal of Art Therapy, 21,* 122-123.

Mills, A., Humber, N., Rhyne, J., & Vernon, W. (1993). A continuing dialogue on non-art therapists doing art therapy. *Proceedings of the American Art Therapy Association, 24th Annual Conference.* Mundelein, IL: The American Art Therapy Association, Inc.

Mills, A., Dougherty, M., Humber, N., Rubin, J., & Schoenholtz, R. (1992). A compassionate discourse: On non-art therapists doing art therapy. *Proceedings of the American Art Therapy Association, 23rd Annual Conference.* Mundelein, IL: The American Art Therapy Association, Inc.

Moon, B. (2003). *Essentials of art therapy education and practice.* (2nd ed.). Springfield, IL: Charles C Thomas.

Moon, B. (1999). Deconstructing rage: A day in the life of an art studio. *Proceedings of the 30th Annual Conference of the American Art Therapy Association: Frameworks: A sense of place. (p.153)* Orlando, FL: The American Art Therapy Association, Inc.

Moon, B. (1998). *The dynamics of art as therapy with adolescents.* Springfield, IL: Charles C Thomas.

Moon, B. (1997a). The gate is not burning. *Proceedings of the 28th Annual Conference of the American Art Therapy Association.* Milwaukee: The American Art Therapy Association, Inc.

Moon, B. (1997b). *Art and soul: Reflections on an artistic psychology.* Springfield, IL: Charles C Thomas.

Moon, B. (1997c). *Welcome to the studio: The role of responsive art making in art therapy.* Unpublished Dissertation. Cincinnatti: The Union Institute.

Moon, B. (1996). *Reimagining the ethics of assessment.* Unpublished Paper.

Moon, B. (1995). *Existential art therapy: The canvas mirror.* Springfield, IL: Charles C Thomas.

Moon, B. (1994). *Introduction to art therapy: Faith in the product.* Springfield, IL: Charles C Thomas.

Moon, B. (1992). *Essentials of art therapy training and practice.* Springfield, IL: Charles C Thomas.

Moon, C. (2002). *Studio art therapy: Cultivating the artist identity in art therapy.* London: Jessica Kingsley.

Moon, C. (1994). What's left behind: The place of the art product in art therapy. *Proceedings of the 25th Annual Conference of the American Art Therapy Association.* Mundelein, IL: Author.

Moreno, H.P., & Wadeson, H. (1986). Art therapy for acculturation problems of Hispanic clients. *Art Therapy, 3*(3).

Moustakas, C. (1995). *Being-in, being-for, being with.* New York: Jason Aronson.

Nash, R. (1975). *The rainmaker.* p. 99. New York: Bantam Books.

National Association of Social Workers (1996). *Code of ethics.* Washington, DC: Author.

National Organization for Human Service Education (1995). *National Organization for Human Service Education.* Author.

Nelson, C. (1998). Confidentiality: Sacred trust and ethical quagmire. *The Journal of Pastoral Care, Vol. 52.*

Neufeldt, V. (Ed.). (1988). *Webster's new world dictionary* (3rd ed.). New York: Simon & Schuster.

Neustadt, L. (1995). Letter to the Editor. *Art Therapy: Journal of the American Art Therapy Association, 12.*

Pedersen, P. (1991). Multiculturalism as a generic approach to counseling. *Journal of Counseling and Development, 70,* 6-12.

Peck, M. S. (1978). *The road less traveled.* New York: Simon and Schuster.

Pope, K.S., & Vasquez, M.J.T. (1991). *Ethics in psychotherapy and counseling: A practical guide for psychologists.* San Francisco: Jossey-Bass.

Prinzhorn, H. (1922). *Artistry of the mentally ill* (revised). New York: Springer-Verlag.

Richards, M.C. (1962). *Centering in pottery, poetry, and the person.* Middletown, CT: Weselyan University Press.

Riley-Hiscox, A. (1999). Critical multiculturalism: A response to "questioning multi-culturalism." *Art Therapy: Journal of the American Art Therapy Association, 16,* 145-149.

Rinsley, D. (1983). *Treatment of the severely disturbed adolescent.* New York: Jason Aronson.

Robbins, A. (1988). A psychoaesthetic perspective on creative arts therapy and training. *The Arts in Psychotherapy, 15,* 95-100.

Robbins, A. (1982). Integrating the art therapist identity. *The Arts in Psychotherapy, 9,* 1-9.

Rogers, C. (1965). *Client-centered therapy.* Boston: Houghton Mifflin.

Rosal, M. (1998). Research thoughts: Learning from the literature and from experience. *Art Therapy: Journal of the American Art Therapy Association, 15,* 47-50.

Rosal, M. (1989). Master's papers in art therapy: Narrative or research case Studies? *The Arts in Psychotherapy, 16.*

Rosenburg, H., Ault, R., Free, K., Gilbert, J., Joseph, C., Landgarten, H., & McNiff, S. (1983). Visual dialogues: The artist as art therapist, the art therapist as artist. *Proceedings of the 1982 Annual AATA Conference. Art Therapy: Still Growing.* (pp. 124-125). Baltimore, MD: The American Art Therapy Association, Inc.

Rubin, J. (1998). *Art therapy: An introduction.* New York: Brunner/Mazel.

Rubin, J. (1986). From psychopathology to psychotherapy through art expression: A focus on Hanz Prinzhorn and others. *Art Therapy, 3,* 27-33.

Rubin, J. (1984). *The art of art therapy.* New York: Brunner/Mazel.

Schaverien, J. (1995). *Desire and the female therapist: Engendered gazes in art therapy and psychotherapy.* London: Routledge.

Spaniol, S., & Cattaneo, M. (1994). The powerful use of language in art therapy art therapy relationships. *Art Therapy: The Journal of the American Art Therapy Association, 11,* 266-270.

Spaniol, S. (1994). Confidentiality reexamined: Negotiating use of art by clients. *American Journal of Art Therapy, 32,* 69-74.

Spaniol, S. (1990a). Exhibition art by people with mental illness, process and principles. *Art Therapy: Journal of the American Art Therapy Association, July,* 70-78.

Spaniol, S. (1990b). *Organizing exhibitions of art by people with mental illness: A step-by-
step manual.* Boston: Center for Psychiatric Rehabilitation, Boston University.

Sartre, J.P. (1947). *Existentialism.* Translation by B. Frechtman. New York:
Philosophical Library, Inc.

Tibbetts, T.J. (1995). Art therapy at the crossroads: Art and science. *Art Therapy:
Journal of the American Art Therapy Association, 12.*

Tyler, J. M., & Tyler, C. L. (1997). Ethics in supervision: Managing supervisee rights
and supervisor responsibilities. In *Hatherleigh guide to ethics in therapy* (pp.75-95).
New York: Hatherleigh Press.

Vick, R. (1999). Utilizing prestructured art elements in brief group art therapy with
adolescents. *Art Therapy: Journal of the American Art Therapy Association, 16,* 68-77.

Vonnegut, K. (1987). *Bluebeard.* New York: Dell.

Wadeson, Junge, Kapitan, & Vick. (1999). Why do you make art? *Proceedings of the
1999 Annual AATA Conference: Frameworks: A sense of place.* (p. 157). Orlando, Fl.:
The American Art Therapy Association, Inc.

Wadeson, H. (1995). Invited response. *Art Therapy: Journal of the American Art Therapy
Association, 12,* 258-259.

Wadeson, H. (Ed.)(1992). *A guide to conducting art therapy research.* Mundelein, IL: The
American Art Therapy Association, Inc.

Wadeson, H. (1986). The influence of art-making on the transference relationship.
Art Therapy: The Journal of the American Art Therapy Association, 3, 81-88.

Wadeson, H. (1980). *Art psychotherapy.* New York: John Wiley & Sons.

Wadeson, H. (1978). Some uses of art therapy data in research. *American Journal of Art
Therapy, 18,* 11-18.

Wadeson, H., Landgarten, H., McNiff, S., Free, K., & Levy, B. (1977). The identity
of the art therapist: Professional self-concept and public image. *Proceedings of the
1976 Annual AATA Conference: Creativity and the Art Therapists Identity* (pp. 38 - 42).
Baltimore, MD: The American Art Therapy Association, Inc.

Waller, D. (1989). Musing cross culturally. In A. Gilroy, & T. Dalley (Eds.), *Pictures
at an exhibition.* London: Tavistock/Routledge.

Webster, M. (1994). Legal and ethical issues impacting unlisenced art therapists and
their clients. *Art Therapy: Journal of the American Art Therapy Association, 11,* 278 -
281.

Author. (1988). *Webster's new world dictionary: Third college edition.* New York: Simon
& Schuster.

Wheeler, N., & Bertram, B. (1994). Legal aspects of counseling: Avoiding lawsuits
and legal problems. (Workshop material and video seminar.) Alexandria, VA:
American Counseling Association.

Wilson, L. (1987). Confidentiality in art therapy. *American Journal of Art Therapy 25,*
75-80.

Winnicott, D.W. (1960). *The maturational processes and the facilitating environment:
Studies in the theory of emotional development.* New York: International Universitites
Press.

Wirtz, G. (1994). Essential legal issues for art therapists in private practice. *Art Therapy: Journal of the American Art Therapy Association, 11*, 293 - 296.

Wirtz, G., Sidun, N., Carrigan, J., Wadeson, H., Kennedy, S., & Marano-Geiser, R. (1994). *Legal issues: Can art therapists stand alone?* Denver, CO: National Audio Video tape # 58-149.

Wolf, R. (1995). Invited response. *Art Therapy: The Journal of the American Art Therapy Association, 12*, 259.

Wolf, R. (1990). Visceral learning: The integration of aesthetic and creative process in education and psychotherapy. *Art Therapy: The Journal of the American Art Therapy Association, 7*, 60-69.

Yalom, I. (1995). *The theory and practice of group psychotherpy.* New York: Basic Books.

INDEX